REFORMING
THE
UNITED NATIONS

REFORMING
THE
UNITED NATIONS

The Challenge of Relevance

K.P. SAKSENA

Sage Publications
New Delhi/Newbury Park/London

In memory of my uncle **Bhagwan S. Hajeley,** *M.A., LL.B., C.P.A. (London) (14 October 1907 – 15 April 1990) artist, architect, author-litterateur, educationist, film director and producer, philanthropist, and above all a true practitioner of universal brotherhood and an exemplary human being*

Copyright © *K.P. Saksena, 1993*

First published in 1993 by

Sage Publications India Pvt Ltd
M–32, Greater Kailash Market – I
New Delhi 110 048

Sage Publications Inc
2455 Teller Road
Newbury Park, California 91320

Sage Publications Ltd
6 Bonhill Street
London EC2A 4PU

Published by Tejeshwar Singh for Sage Publications India Pvt Ltd, phototypeset by Mudra Typesetters, Pondicherry, and printed at Chaman Enterprises.

This volume is published on behalf of the Indian Council for Research on International Economic Relations (ICRIER), New Delhi, and emanates from one of its research projects.

Library of Congress Cataloging-in-Publication Data

Saksena, K. P., 1929–
    Reforming the United Nations: the challenge of relevance / K.P. Saksena
        p.   cm.
    Includes bibliographical references and index.
    1. United Nations—Finance.   I. Title.
JX1977.8.F5S25   1993   341.23—dc20   92–559

ISBN: 81–7036–303–9 (India)
        0–8039–9445–1 (US)

Contents

Foreword

The United Nations has been confronted with an unprecedented crisis, since the mid-1980s, threatening its very viability and solvency. Protracted negotiations and debate that followed for reform and restructuring the world body have failed to yield substantive results, although a few institutional changes and some procedural reforms have been incepted in pursuance of General Assembly resolution 41/213 of December 1986.

The Indian Council for Research on International Economic Relations (ICRIER) deemed it essential to make its own contribution to the ongoing debate with a view to promoting a wider understanding of the issues involved in the effort to enhance the effectiveness of the international system. Early in 1987 initial steps were taken in consultation with experienced practitioners and noted scholars to design a research study. We were fortunate that a scholar of the standing of Prof. K.P. Saksena agreed to undertake it. His practical experience as a member of the Indian Delegation and as an official in the UN Secretariat provided valuable insights. A grant-in-aid from the Ministry of External Affairs, to ICRIER, enabled us to meet its cost.

The UN structures and their functioning especially in the economic and social sectors are highly complex. It requires great patience and sustained efforts to delve into them and to attempt an evaluation of the efforts made at reform and reorganization during the last five years. It goes to the credit of the author to have undertaken this difficult exercise and do a commendable job.

The study presented here is comprehensive in its scope and deals with its multiple facets concisely and with clarity. It is based not only on UN documents and secondary sources but also on personal interactions and interviews with scores of UN Diplomats, both retired and serving, as well as senior UN secretariat officials.

This is perhaps the first comprehensive study attempted by a distinguished scholar from a developing country uniquely committed to the United Nations. It therefore represents a point of view different from what is found in the existing literature on the subject, largely contributed by Western scholars. The author's attempt has been not so much to suggest innovative institutional changes as to bring together in a single compass the results of penetrating analysis of the developments in the economic and social framework of the United Nations over the last four decades and plus. The objective has been not to advance preconceived notions but to provide information and insights for comprehending the difficulties that confront the system, for appreciating the contrary pulls in its direction and for exercising the options available to policy makers for building the United Nations of tomorrow.

I hope this study will prove useful to laymen as well as scholars who can not afford to go through the myriad of UN documents, studies and reports on the subject and more particularly to those whose views and participation in the ongoing exercise for reform and reorganisation would help to bring about a consensus in consonance with the emerging requirements of the International Community over the Nineties.

The Cold War is behind us but a peace dividend has still to be earned. The new spirit which most member-states have demonstrated in recent years generates confidence in the future of the United Nations as an effective instrument for debating and resolving global issues.

Chairman   K.B. Lall
Indian Council for Research
on International Economic Relations

Preface

In recent years, there has been a sudden and new-found euphoria about the United Nations. In an increasing number of cases, its role has been looked upon as pivotal to the settlement of problems that not long ago appeared intractable. The awarding of the Nobel Peace Prize in the autumn of 1988 to the United Nations was symbolic of the growing recognition of its distinct role. The new-found relationship between the superpowers, their disarmament agreements and the progressive resolution of major conflicts (such as, the Iran–Iraq war, Afghanistan, Namibia and Western Sahara) have been both the sustenance and the outcome of the new context. The United Nations' prompt response to Iraq's occupation of Kuwait (August 1990) is widely regarded, as UN Secretary-General Javier Perez de Cuellar put it, as 'revitalizing' the UN peace and security system.

These developments and enthusiasm for the United Nations have, however camouflaged the basic issue confronting the world body since the early 1980s and more so since 1985–86; namely, reform and reorganization. For the last five years or so, the United Nations has been lingering on the brink of financial bankruptcy. Its programmes in the economic and social fields are in a paralytic state. Protracted negotiations spread over four years on the question of restructuring the inter-governmental machinery in the economic and social fields have reached an impasse. What is more disturbing is a widely held apprehension that, given the current financial and political pressures, the United Nations might lose the character it has evolved since its establishment, as a non-partisan global forum to harmonize contending interests for common goals. Thus, the unresolved basic issues and the changing international environment have placed the United Nations in perhaps the most critical phase of its existence. It is not just experiencing another crisis like the ones it weathered in the past, but is in the

throes of a far more powerful and profound transformation that
transcends anything it has experienced so far. Whether the United
Nations will survive this crisis is not the question; just how and in what
form it will survive is of great significance to the future and larger
interests of mankind.

This study analyzes the United Nations system as it has evolved,
especially in the economic and social fields. It examines the complex
interplay of factors behind the demands for and efforts at reform and
reorganization, the continuing crisis and the ramifications involved.
The framework of this study is elaborated in the introduction. The
task of encompassing more than four decades of the United Nations'
functioning, especially in the complex economic and social sectors, has
been a formidable and challenging one. At the same time it has been
an exciting and rewarding experience as it provided a perspective
which would have been lacking, had it been confined to a limited
period or area of activity or just to the current exercise of reform and
reorganization. The purpose here is not so much to suggest any
innovative institutional changes in the UN system, but to provide the
basis for understanding the present crisis situation and to indicate the
options available. As such, the study is addressed to scholars and more
particularly to those whose views and participation in the on-going
exercise for reform and reorganization could help lead the United
Nations in the desired direction.

This study has been prepared under the auspices of the Indian
Council for Research in International Economic Relations (ICRIER),
New Delhi. I have had the privilege of the guidance and advice of such
a versatile scholar and veteran diplomat as the Chairman of the
Council, Dr. K.B. Lall. No words are adequate enough to express my
gratitude to him.

The study is based largely on documented research and on interviews
and personal interactions, during the summer of 1988 and winter
1989–90, with UN Secretariat officials, members of various permanent
missions to the United Nations in New York and Geneva and officials
of the Ministry of External Affairs, Government of India, New Delhi. I
am grateful to all of them for sparing the time to share their views.
Special thanks are due to Dr. Abdel Halim Badawi, Chairman, Special
Commission on the Indepth Study of the United Nations Inter-
Governmental Structure, who was kind enough to find time during
the concluding session of the Commission, in May 1988, to share his
candid thoughts with me. Personal interaction with Chairman Badawi

and with the delegates to the Commission was a very rewarding experience and provided me with an insight into the contending issues involved in the crisis. I also wish to express my gratitude to Mr. Rikhi Jaipal and Mr. N. Krishnan, both former Permanent Representatives of India to the United Nations. Mr. Krishnan also served as an expert member of the Group of 18 and his critical comments and views on the text have been of immense help in giving final shape to this study.

In addition, I have had the benefit of the exchange of views and interactions with a number of scholars in India and abroad. Mention in particular should be made of an international conference organized by a consortium of international academic associations on 'The United Nations System and its Future' held in Ottawa, Canada, 3–7 January 1990. This conference brought together scholars from eighteen countries (including the five permanent members of the Security Council and various regional groups). Other participants included diplomats and senior officials of the UN Secretariat. It was a unique congregation of highly knowledgeable persons from different parts of the world representing varied viewpoints and experiences. The exchange of views and personal interactions with them have been stimulating and revealing. I am grateful to the organizers of the Ottawa conference and to the participants.

I am obliged to several of my colleagues in the School of International Studies, Jawaharlal Nehru University, New Delhi, who have helped me in various ways in the preparation of this study. I particularly made mention of Professor Sumitra Chisti, Dr. C.S.R. Murthy and Dr. Kanan Gahrana. Thanks are also due to Dr. R.S. Saini who painstakingly assisted me in collecting the material, and to Mr. Udaibhanu Singh and Mr. P.K. Mishra for research assistance. I would like to express my appreciation and thanks to various officials of the United Nations Information Centre, New Delhi, especially Mr. D.K. Bose. I also wish to record my appreciation and thanks to Sri S. Raju Aiyer for painstakingly typing several drafts of the study and assisting me in putting the text into final shape. The publishers have been both supportive and helpful.

While acknowledging the assistance received and expressing gratitude to those whose views, comments and criticism helped me in the preparation of this study, it should be noted that I alone am responsible for the contents and views expressed here and for any ommissions or errors.

Introduction

Reform and reorganization of its structure and operational system have been more or less a continuous process from the very inception of the United Nations. Its inter-governmental machinery, especially in the economic and social fields, has evolved and expanded in response to the growing needs of the international community and its obligations under the Charter. Additional programmes, emphasising new areas of concerns, have been instituted. By the early 1980s, the United Nations, together with its specialized agencies, had put into operation an array of institutional arrangements with a programme of activities that covered practically all the problems being dealt with by the governments of the member-States and which affect the day-to-day life of the common people throughout the world.

As the inter-governmental structure grew and its activities widened, the UN has had to grapple with endemic institutional problems relating to effectiveness and efficiency. These problems have been addressed, for the most part, in an ad hoc and incremental manner. There have been junctures, however, at which member-States have felt it necessary to look at the functioning of the inter-governmental structure as a whole and make more systematic changes leading to the overall or partial restructuring of the existing institutional arrangements. For example, a major effort to restructure the economic and social sectors of the United Nations took place in 1977. Despite this, its capacity, resources and overall performance still leave much to be desired. Many of the shortcomings have been due to its inherent character, namely, an association of sovereign states, largely dependent on member-States for the implementation of its decisions and recommendations. Efforts to overhaul its administrative machinery, which had grown too complex and unwieldy, were already underway when a new and unprecedented challenge loomed large, threatening the very viability and solvency of the organization.

Since the early 80s the United Nations has been under severe attack from irate critics, including its chief architect, the United States of America, who did not want the body involved in certain activities. Such critics, who are also major contributors to the regular UN budget, began to withhold or delay their financial apportionments. The situation reached crisis proportions in 1985 when the US Congress, asserting that funds were being wasted on undesirable programmes and activities, demanded that the UN reduce its budget and Secretariat staff and introduce a voting system which would provide more influence in budget decisions to major contributors. The United States further threatened to withhold its financial support unless reforms were carried out by 1986.

As the United States' contribution amounts to 25 per cent of the budget, its 'default', more than that of any other member-State, posed a grave threat to the day-to-day functioning of the United Nations. To meet the exigency, the General Assembly appointed a Committee of eighteen High Level Inter-governmental Experts (Group of 18) in 1985 to review the efficiency and administrative and financial functioning of the United Nations. The Group submitted its report in August 1986. Subsequently, the General Assembly adopted a set of recommendations, with far-reaching ramifications, contained in the UN General Assembly Resolution 41/213 of 10 December 1986. The Secretary-General, the Economic and Social Council (ECOSOC) and the General Assembly, along with its subsidiary inter-governmental bodies, engaged in protracted discussions and negotiations over these recommendations. Thereafter, a series of procedural reforms and some restructuring of the Secretariat were carried out. However, the question of restructuring the inter-governmental machinery in the economic and social fields and overall UN operational programmes for development, led to sharp differences between the industrialized and the developing countries and remain unresolved.

While other major contributors, such as France, Germany, Japan, UK and the USSR (Russia*) paid their arrears beginning 1986–87 and

---

* USSR (succeeded by the Russian Federation on 28 December 1991) cleared all its arrears as well as annual apportionments from 1987 to 1990. However, because of domestic economic and political upheavals it owed the United Nations part of its arrears in 1991. As of February 1992 it owed $46 million as arrears and $92 million as its contribution payable for 1992, part of which is likely to be paid by the other former constituent republics of the USSR who have joined the United Nations as independent states. See table and notes on p. 144.

have been more or less regular in paying their apportionments to the regular budget, the United States continues to withhold a major part of its arrears as well as its annual contribution. As of February 1992, member-States owed more than one billion dollars to the regular budget, of which some 565 million was due from the United States. This amounts to nearly two-thirds of what the United Nations spends in meeting its responsibilities in one whole year. Consequently, UN programmes in the economic and social fields are in a paralytic state. And the United Nations continues to face a severe crisis challenging its solvency and viability, indeed its relevance in an inter-dependent world. The major contributors to the budget have not been the only ones unhappy with the UN system. The developing countries, representing two-thirds of the world's population, have also been critical because they believe that the United Nations was not doing what it ought to do, especially with regard to North–South issues, the debt burden, development assistance and related areas, all of which are of vital concern to them.

The growing disenchantment with the United Nations, the factors responsible for the US holding back its contribution and the real issues which have led to the impasse between the developing and the developed countries are discussed in this study. Among the other issues taken up are: the extent to which the reforms, carried out in pursuance of General Assembly Resolution 41/213 of December 1986, have brought about any significant changes; whether recent developments, characterized by the end of the Cold War, add to the strengthening of the United Nations; and what these developments augur for the organization as it has evolved over the last forty years—a true townhall of the world, the first ever in the history of mankind. The ongoing crisis appears to be a financial one only on the surface. The issues are actually political. The basic controversy is over what the United Nations should or should not do and not on what it should spend in doing it. Intriguingly, however, the major thrust of the attack has been on the administrative and financial functioning of the United Nations in the economic and social fields. The recommendations of the Group of 18 and consequently that of Resolution 41/213 of December 1986 are largely confined to those specific areas.

This study, therefore, concentrates on the question of the reform and reorganization of the economic and social sectors of the UN

Organization.* Its aim *inter alia* is: (*a*) to review the organizational set-up in these sectors as they have evolved over the years; (*b*) to identify areas of overlapping activities and duplication of programmes; (*c*) to analyze details of various programmes with a view to examining their continuing relevance and usefulness; and (*d*) to propose changes in jurisdiction, procedures and processes, with a view to assisting UN operational activities in the economic and social fields to become more effective. While this study focuses on the economic and social sectors of the United Nations, political environments, which often condition the performance of the UN system as a whole, have also been taken into account. There is more to the situation: the interface of politics and economics in inter-state relations is so obvious that one cannot analyze one in isolation of the other. On the other hand, improvement in the functioning and efficiency of the economic and social fields of the UN is a more likely prospect than improvement in the field of peace and security and is one practical way to create a better climate for international peaceful cooperation. As such, the concluding chapter deals with the entire gamut of reforms and reorganization of the system and covers both the economic and political dimensions of the United Nations' role in an interdependent world.

The study is divided into five chapters. Chapter 1 reviews the UN economic and social framework as it has evolved over four decades. To critically evaluate the present and to plan for the future, it is essential to know the past. Hence this chapter discusses what the UN system was designed to be, traces developments from the inception of the organization in the early 1940s, and outlines the impact of the Cold War followed by the North–South conflict.

Chapter 2 studies the question of financial resources, their management and accountability and how apportionments of the contributions of member-States to the UN budget, are determined. Decisions with regard to the allocation of these resources in terms of programme planning and budgeting and how they are arrived at are also examined. One of the issues addressed is whether it is true, as is widely alleged, that some ten member-States bear the main financial burden (75 per cent

* The United Nations Organization represents more than twenty-five inter-governmental agencies of varying degrees of independence from the United Nations. The subject of this study is the so-called United Nations proper, and relates to those programmes in the economic and social fields which are covered by the regular UN budget and also those which, while funded through voluntary contributions, are subject to budgeting and programming by the UN General Assembly.

of the UN budget) but individually have only one vote in determining budget allocations for UN activities in the social and economic fields. The existing machinery to determine programme planning, monitor implementation and evaluation and related subjects are also discussed in this Chapter.

Chapter 3 scrutinizes how UN resources are distributed among major programmes and sub-programmes relating to economic and social activities, and the amount of resources available both in terms of budgetary provisions and human resources (i.e., professionals assigned to the UN Secretariat). It also evaluates the cost-effectiveness of these programmes and the extent to which they have promoted the goals of international economic and social cooperation enshrined in the UN Charter in general and Article 55 in particular. This chapter also examines the fundamental question of the extent to which the existing financial resources and UN apparatus are adequate to meet the responsibilities of a world of growing inter-dependence and mutual vulnerability.

While this study was in progress, significant procedural and institutional changes, in the wake of mounting financial pressure and the adoption of General Assembly Resolution 41/213 of December 1986, were instituted or are underway. Hence, to keep the subject in perspective, the first three chapters (which review the situation as it existed prior to the demand for reform and reorganization) are followed by a chapter which outlines the developments that ensued after the US Congress resolution demanding reform and reorganization of the financial and administrative system of the UN organization, the recommendations of the Group of 18 and its consequences. Chapter 4 covers developments up to April 1992.

Chapter 5 constitutes the concluding part of the study. It analyzes the factors which led to the demand for reform and reorganization, the directions these efforts have taken and the ramifications involved. It presents an overall assessment of the multilateral system of the UN especially in the context of the recent radical changes in the international environment. The analysis, bearing derivative evaluation, also indicates various options available for a more effective and viable world body.

1

Reviewing the Evolving Framework

On the fortieth anniversary of the United Nations, an array of heads of governments, including US President Ronald Reagan, attended the commemorative session and pledged anew their commitment to the ideals of the UN Charter and, with notable unanimity, acknowledged the need to strengthen the United Nations so that it might better meet the needs of the future. However, what followed a couple of weeks later was much to the chagrin of the UN Secretary-General, Javier Perez de Cuellar:

> ... in marked contrast to sentiments expressed during the fortieth anniversary [the period that immediately followed] has witnessed the United Nations subjected to a severe crisis challenging its solvency and viability. Precisely at the time when renewed efforts have been called for to strengthen the Organization, its work has been shadowed by financial difficulties resulting primarily from the failure of member-States to meet obligations flowing from the Charter.[1]

What the Secretary-General said was by way of drawing attention to the growing practice among member-States of paying lip service to the principles of the Charter and acting differently, or exhorting others to do what they would not do themselves. Indeed, what the

[1] Introduction to the Report of the Secretary-General on the Work of the Organization, 1986, *General Assembly Official Record (GAOR)*, Forty-first Session, Supplement No: 1A/41, para 2.

United Nations has been confronted with over the last couple of years has not come as a bolt from the blue, but at a culmination of the hostile atmosphere which had long been building up against the world body. Some member-States have been on the war-path because they do not want the United Nations involved in certain activities which, according to them, amounts to wasting precious resources. At the same time, the United Nations has been subjected to criticism by those constituting the majority, who feel frustrated because the body has not been doing what they believe it ought to do.

What really is wrong with the world body that provokes so much disenchantment with its performance? A widely, or perhaps 'wildly' expressed view is that the organizational set-up is faulty and that Secretariat officials are not doing their jobs right. A concretizing of such a view is reflected in the report of the Group of High Level Inter-governmental Experts to Review the Efficiency of the Administrative and Financial Functioning. It refers to the growth in the number of conferences, their frequency and duration and the increase in the volume of documentation, none of which yield results commensurate to the activity, time, money and personnel involved, and that 'the considerable resources allocated to conferences and meetings are not put to maximum productive use'.[2] It seems that the report blames the Secretariat and its 'management capacity, especially with regard to the need to maintain overall administrative efficiency, productivity and cost effectiveness'. It insists that the 'quality of the work performed needs to be improved upon. The qualification of staff, in particular in the higher categories are inadequate and the working methods are not efficient' and finds its structure 'too complex, fragmented and top heavy'.[3] That such observations, though partly true, are largely misplaced, are obvious to any keen observer of UN affairs.[4] This issue is taken up in detail later.

Another aspect relating to the organizational framework has also been subjected to criticism on the grounds that there is fragmentation of effort, and duplication or overlapping of responsibilities and that

---

[2] *GAOR*, Forty-first Session, 1986, Supplement no. 49 (A/41/49), para 3.

[3] Ibid., para 4.

[4] Reacting to these observations, the Administrative Committee on Coordination (ACC) succinctly notes: '*While the underlying causes of the growing budgetary problems are political* the structural and administrative efficiency of the organization are also being questioned'. Emphasis added. *Comment of the Administrative Committee on Coordination on the Report of the Group of High Level Inter-governmental Experts ...* Doc. A/41/763, 24 October 1986, para 1.

the same problem is being tackled by different departments and inter-governmental agencies without yielding results commensurate to the activity.[5]

Why this regrettable state of affairs? Is it because of inadequate or inefficient machinery, the lack of resources or the necessary political will among its members? To find an answer to these and related questions and to attempt remedial measures, developments from the very inception of the United Nations have to be examined.

THE BEGINNING: A EURO-CENTRIC WORLD

When the United Nations was conceived in the mid-1940s, the world was still Euro-centric. European[6] experiences of the inter-war years and the League of Nations' experiments in coordinating international economic relations, especially the recommendations of its Bruce Committee Report,[7] considerably influenced the making of the economic and social sectors of the UN system. By far the most influential factor in the making of the post-war international organiza-tion was the role of the United States. Well aware of its growing ascendency in the world economy, the United States envisaged a framework so that its ascendency would be enabled to persist.[8] At the San Francisco conference of April–June 1945, which gave final shape

[5] See, 'Some Reflections on Reform of the United Nations', Maurice Bertrand *Joint Inspection Unit Report*, UN Doc. JIU/REP/85/9 (A/40/988, 6 December 1985), paras 10-43.

[6] The term European is used here in the civilizational sense and includes the United States, Canada, Australia and New Zealand.

[7] Reference here is to the League Committee chaired by Stanley Bruce (Australia) which submitted its report for restructuring the economic and social framework of the League at the fag end of the League's life (August 1939). Its one major recommendation for the improvement of the League's machinery in the economic and social fields was for instituting an Economic and Social Council. For details, see F.P. Walters, *A History of the League of Nations* New York: Oxford University Press, 1952, vol. II, pp. 752–62.

[8] To achieve its objective, US efforts were first directed at forcing the United Kingdom to give up its Empire Tariff Preferences and in general to seek the overall reductions of trade barriers and elimination of discriminatory practices in international trade. It partly succeeded in its objective when it obliged the United Kingdom to sign the Lend-Lease Agreement in February 1942. For details, see in particular Ruth Russell, *A History of the United Nations Charter* Washington DC: Brookings Institution, 1958, pp.f. 27.

to the UN Charter, there were two contending interests—one represented by the United States and the other by the rest of the Europeans
led by the British Commonwealth of Nations. The Soviet Union, with
the East Europeans under its influence, as it turned out, opted to work
out their own arrangements independently of the United Nations. At
the time, there was hardly any Afro-Asian country free from European
colonial rule or any other kind of domination. The Latin American
countries were still in the shadow of their mighty neighbour in the
North. The point here is that while designing the UN framework for
economic and social cooperation, the problems and difficulties that
were to confront the developing countries or the so-called Third
World were not envisaged or provided for in the Charter.

In planning the bases of post-war economic relations, the United
States sought to assert its emerging position of dominance. One
objective was to seek a non-discriminatory free trade system, knowing
well that in such a system, the war-ravaged countries of Europe could
not compete with the United States. This would help build up the
United States as a global economic power. Thus, at the San Francisco
conference, as in earlier meetings at Dumbarton Oaks (1944), the
United States presented a draft of the relevant provision of the Charter
with a view to justifying the principles of non-discriminatory free trade
and a competitive market economy. The European countries were not
in a position to challenge the text proposed by the United States.
However, the British Commonwealth countries, led by Australia,
loaded the text with stronger objectives such as 'full employment',
higher standards of living and conditions of economic and social
development.[9] The reasoning behind the Australian move and its
support by the European countries, was that, since promises like 'full
employment' were not to be fulfilled, the Commonwealth and other
European countries, could in turn, justifiably undertake 'defensive'
discriminatory measures.

Charter: Premise and Promises

As a result of the contending interests at San Francisco, the Charter
was loaded with laudable ideals and high principles of international
economic and social cooperation particularly in Article 55. The

[9] For a summary of the debate at San Francisco on this question, see *Ibid.*,
pp. 781–88.

Economic and Social Council (ECOSOC) was given a higher status and wider responsibility than envisaged in the Dumbarton Oaks proposals and the United Nations was placed in the central position in international economic relations, albeit in principle only. It is true that the system that emerged from the San Francisco conference did not envisage the problems and needs for international development assistance that were to confront the newly emerging nations during the post-war period. However, the ECOSOC was given an overall mandate to undertake activities in the light of future developments and to handle matters not within the province of any specialized agency. As an analyst has aptly noted:

> Essentially, [ECOSOC] was expected to have a triple task: (*a*) to act as chief inter-agency and inter-unit coordinator of activities of the UN proper and of the specialized agencies; (*b*) to be an innovator in relation to the establishment of new programmes and to be their supervisor once these programmes were established; (*c*) to serve as a general forum for the discussion of economic and social issues.[10]

Bretton Woods Institutions

Initially the United States planned to institute three other major organizations, one dealing with trade and the other two with monetary and fiscal problems. While the two institutional arrangements, namely the International Monetary Fund (IMF) and the International Bank for Reconstruction and Development (IBRD) were established by the United Nations Monetary and Financial Conference which met at Bretton Woods (USA) in July 1944, the International Trade Organization (ITO) was still-born. In its place, the United States found it more expedient to institute what is known as the General Agreement on Tariffs and Trade (GATT).[11] The IMF and IBRD, with their regulative

[10] Johan Kaufmann, 'The Economic and Social Council and the New International Economic Order', in David P. Forsythe, ed. *The United Nations in the World Political Economy* (London: Macmillan, 1989), p. 55; also see Russell, n. 8, pp. 797.

[11] The ITO was to have come into existence when the Havana Charter, adopted by the UN Conference on Trade and Employment convened in Havana, Cuba, 21 November 1947–24 March 1948, was ratified by fifty-four states. However, it could

and supervisory roles in the fiscal and monetary fields and weighted voting system, were primarily designed to promote a market economy and to allow the United States a considerable grip on the national economies of the participating states. The erstwhile Soviet Union, of course, did not join the Bretton Woods institutions.

UN IN OPERATION: THE INITIAL PHASE

It is common knowledge that the ink on the Charter had hardly dried when politics took over the implementation of its provisions. The Cold War that ensued between the two European groups of power, one led by the erstwhile USSR and the other by the United States, undermined the functioning of the United Nations. The USSR kept out of the Bretton Woods institutions and from the GATT. The United States directed its efforts towards the reconstruction of western Europe and, to support its allies, initiated European Recovery Programmes and the Marshall Plan. What is significant is that these programmes were launched ignoring, and independently of, the United Nations. Furthermore, as by the Gentleman's Agreement of 1946,[12] the Soviet Union along with the other four permanent members was assured of a permanent seat in the eighteen-member Economic and Social Council, the tendency to keep major economic issues out of ECOSOC grew. In the process, the Council lost its central role in economic and social matters and Article 58 remained merely on paper.

This was not all. The United States and the western powers instituted

---

not be set up as a result of US refusal to ratify the Charter. The reason was that at Havana, the countries of Latin America had obtained considerable concessions in their favour, which were not to the liking of the United States. Indeed, the United States, anticipating these unfavourable developments, had already worked out the General Agreement on Tariffs and Trade (GATT) negotiated in Geneva (April-October 1947), which was ratified by the United States as an Executive Agreement and which became effective from 1 January 1948. GATT gave some concessions to the European partners of the United States but safeguarded the US' basic trade interests.

[12] By this informal agreement the five permanent members were not to put up their nationals for the office of the President of the General Assembly or that of the Secretary-General but were assured membership of all the organs and subsidiary bodies of the United Nations.

programmes and institutions independently of the United Nations. For instance, the US sponsored a network of institutions under what became known as the Organization for European Economic Cooperation in 1949 which later became known as the Organization for Economic Cooperation and Development (OECD) in 1961. The Soviet Union and the East Europeans instituted the Council for Mutual Economic Assistance (CMEA). Thus, the United Nations was increasingly reduced to the position of a non-factor in international economic relations among the developed market economy countries of the West as well as the centrally-planned economies of the East. The remaining non-European world, the so-called South, remained peripheral to the centre of economic power held by the industrially advanced countries.

Specialized Agencies

Much of the work towards achieving the UN objective of improved economic and social conditions for the people of the world was envisaged to be carried out by the specialized inter-governmental agencies. The UN Charter provided that these agencies, with their wide international responsibilities in economic, social, cultural, educational, health and related fields, were to be brought into a relationship with the United Nations. The ECOSOC was envisaged to provide coordination and overall direction. Accordingly, agreements which the UN signed with the ILO, FAO, UNESCO, ICAO, and the WHO respectively, contained provisions by which these specialized agencies recognized the desirability of establishing close budgetary financial relationships with the United Nations.[13]

The agencies agreed to hold consultations with the United Nations in the preparation of their budget, which included their programme of activities, and to transmit their proposals to the United Nations annually for examination and recommendation by the General

---

[13] See, *Agreements Between the United Nations and the Specialized Agencies ...* (UN Publication, Sales No. 61, x. 1).

Among the existing inter-governmental organizations prior to the formation of the United Nations only the ILO constituted (1919) an autonomous part of the League of Nations. Its expenditures were covered by the League of Nations budget.

Assembly. The terms of agreement with UPU and ITU (old established institutions) were less specific, stating only that the 'annual budget of the agency shall be transmitted to the United Nations and the General Assem ly may make recommendations thereon'. The agreements with the Bank and the Fund were clearly restrictive stating that the two organizations would furnish to the UN, copies of their annual report and quarterly financial statements, but specifying that the appropriate authorities of the two agencies would enjoy full autonomy in deciding the form and content of their budget. In practice they were recognized as completely independent organizations.

Over the years, other specialized agencies also built up their 'independence' of the United Nations. They did continue to furnish their annual reports but gradually the ECOSOC's coordinating role declined. The reports submitted to the Council were merely 'taken note of' and no detailed discussion took place. During the 1970s, the specialized agencies stopped sending even their annual reports. Thus, for all practical purposes, the agencies function independently and coordination through the ACC exists only in name. One of the main reasons for this lies in the fact that national delegations to each of the specialized agencies are drawn from different ministries within national governments and there is a lack of coordination at national levels.

Technical Assistance

From its very inception the United Nations, following the pattern set by the League of Nations and the United Nations Relief and Rehabilitation Administration (UNRRA),[14] initiated various programmes to assist member-States in the reconstruction of war-devastated areas, evacuation and rehabilitation of refugees and an emergency fund for the welfare of children and mothers. To begin with, all such activities were concen rated in Europe. Nonetheless, they raised hopes among the non-Europeans also.

[14] UNRRA was established in November 1943 to assist the devastated countries as the war came to an end. It closed its operations in 1947–48. Much of its staff was moved to UNICEF and the International Refuge Organization (later the UN High Commissioner for Refugees, UNHCR) both of which were established to continue UNRRA's functions in those fields, other functions having been transferred to relevant specialised agencies.

The post-war period was characterized inter alia by two sets of developments: the escalation of the de-colonization process and the expansion of the foreign aid concept for underdeveloped countries. On 20 January 1949, US President Harry S. Truman proposed the Point Four Programme of technical assistance, which was to be implemented partly through UN channels. Other industrially advanced countries also initiated foreign aid programmes. The United States Act for International Development which established the Point Four Programme in 1950, defined its motives as 'charitable, economic and strategic'. Other countries adopted one or more of these as their leitmotif. Some saw it as a means of exerting strategic, political, economic or cultural influence or of finding new markets for their expanding economies. In some countries, usually former colonial powers, the paternalistic note was apparent. In others, economic and social miseries were seen as the root cause of disorder and war to be eradicated and aid for development was seen as a desirable end in itself. In some cases the concept of aid was formalised at one per cent of the national income, the target which the developed countries were to keep in mind while earmarking resources for the developing countries of the non-European or Third World.[15] This target however, was scarcely met. Most of the so-called foreign-aid really meant, 'Buy now and pay later' or the outright grant of surplus goods. No bilateral aid was given without some strings attached. Furthermore, foreign aid did not mean the availability of capital to be used by the governments concerned on projects of their own choice. At the same time, the Third World countries were obliged to seek international aid for development as they needed capital and technical knowhow from the industrially advanced countries. With the pre-war flow of capital in those countries declining severely and wartime destruction eliminating Europe, although temporarily, as a capital exporter, potential investors in the US found opportunities for profitable investment. Again, the terms of trade, as they emerged after the war, were most unfavourable. The prices of raw material, the main foreign exchange earner of the underdeveloped countries declined sharply, while the prices of the manufactured goods they imported, went up.

Reports and studies indicated urgent and growing needs for

[15] Sir Robert Jackson suggests that the idea of one per cent grew at a discussion between Lord Keynes and Harry D. White in September 1943 and was applied in the UNRRA operations. *A Study of the Capacity of the United Nations Development System* Geneva: United Nations, 1969, vol. II, p. 4.

development in the underdeveloped countries where more than two-thirds of the world lived in illiteracy, poverty, hunger and disease. In a rapidly changing and de-colonizing world, the UN system of organizations could not remain indifferent to the developmental needs of the newly emerging nations. The Charter itself contains a clarion call to all nations of the world to unite in solving their economic and social problems. The United Nations had an added advantage to commend that role. It could provide access to the resources of all member-States on a virtually world-wide basis and a multilateral channel as a forum for mutual cooperation in which both the developed and developing countries could take part on equal and mutually agreed terms. It had a special interest in the welfare of the newly independent countries, some of which it had helped into the world and which desperately needed assistance in finding their feet. And, given its responsibility for ensuring world peace and security, it was appropriate that it should help alleviate the conditions of hunger, poverty, sickness and homelessness, which many regarded as the basic cause of conflict and war.

The concept of UN assistance for developmental purposes began early with General Assembly Resolutions 32(1) and 58(1) of 1946 and ECOSOC Resolution 51(V) of 1947 instructing the Secretary-General to establish the machinery for providing expert assistance to member governments. The most significant step was taken in 1948 when the General Assembly, through Resolution 200(III), authorized technical assistance (TA) to be carried out by the UN Secretary-General, in addition to the programme already undertaken by some of the specialized agencies. Approximately one per cent, amounting to $288,000 of the regular budget, was earmarked for technical assistance. In 1949 on the basis of a 328-page report, Technical Assistance for Economic Development (prepared in response to General Assembly Resolution 200(III) of 1948), the ECOSOC adopted, on 15 August, Resolution 222(IX) which established the Expanded Programme of Technical Assistance for Economic Development of Under developed Countries. The EPTA, as it came to be known, was to be financed by voluntary contributions. To begin with, it was envisaged that the amount available would be $2 million.[16] The EPTA began operating in 1951.

[16] According to Sir Robert Jackson, the amounts envisioned for this technical assistance towards the development of two-thirds of humankind were approximately 1/500th of the aid provided under the US Marshall Plan for European economic recovery from the Second World War. *Generation: Portrait of the United Nations Development Programme, 1950–1985* (Sales No. 85. III B. 2), p. 12.

Initially these programmes were welcomed by the developing countries but they soon realised that the budget reserved for Technical Assistance was too small to be of any real assistance and that the EPTA merely amounted to TA with a slightly increased quantum. Both programmes restricted their activities to providing expert advice, training programmes of personnel/technicians of underdeveloped countries both abroad and in the countries concerned and the allocation of equipment for 'administrative purposes' which in practice was very small and there the 'assistance' ended. In other words, a recipient country seeking Technical Assistance, for example for the construction of roads, bridges or family planning centres, could receive advice and a blueprint prepared by experts sent by the UN. Their fee was to be paid out of the fund alloted to TA (from the UN budget) or the EPTA (voluntary contribution). Their local expenses, however were met by the recipient country and once the blueprint was prepared by the UN experts, the recipient countries were left to their own resources to seek equipment, technology and the necessary capital in foreign exchange. At this point, the so-called multi-nationals and international commercial banks came in and the 'beneficiary' countries concerned were to find themselves trapped in a vicious circle.

DEMAND OF DEVELOPING COUNTRIES

It soon became clear that assistance, as provided by TA and the EPTA, was highly inadequate. It was also clear that what the underdeveloped countries needed was not just trained personnel or technical advice but also foreign exchange resources which they were finding difficult to obtain to finance economic development. What further aggravated the foreign exchange problem was that while the prices of the primary.commodities that the developing countries exported were going down, the prices of the manufactured and industrial goods and machinery they were obliged to import from the industrially advanced countries were going up.

By the early 1950s, UN study reports also indicated that while the per capita income in the developed countries had increased sharply, ranging from 25 to 45 per cent, the increase in per capita income in the developing countries had varied merely from zero to 5 per cent.[17] The Measures for Economic Development of Underdeveloped Countries[18] report calculated that, on the basis of a per capita national income increase of 2 per cent annually (a minimum considered desirable), the underdeveloped areas would need a capital of more than $19 billion, of which they could generate from their own savings only $5.2 billion. The shortfall of $13.8 billion had to be met by other resources. These estimates related only to capital needed for the development of industry and agriculture, excluding expenditure on, for example, social services. The report further indicated that increases in the rate of the savings would decrease the deficit, but the annual capital needs would continue to run well above $10 billion. However, not even a fraction of this capital was available from bilateral sources. The developing countries were also learning the hard way that the IMF and IBRD were not the institutions to help finance plans for economic development, which because of foreign exchange problems, could not be financed from their country's own resources. Hence the demand for a UN mechanism, which could assist the developing countries in obtaining capital as well as technical knowhow for their economic development, gained momentum. Several such proposals were made by one developing nation or the other which, at the time, were not very many.

Rao's Proposal

One such comprehensive plan was initiated by V.K.R.V. Rao[19] of India in 1949. The proposal envisaged the establishment of an overall United Nations Economic Development Administration (UNEDA) covering five fields of activity: (a) technical assistance to the under-developed countries, (b) coordination of technical assistance as

---

[17] World Economic Survey 1955. New York: United Nations, 1956, p. 5; also see Paul G. Hoffmann, 'Operations Breakthrough', *Foreign Affairs*, October 1959, p. 33.

[18] UN Document E/1986-ST/ECA/10, 3 May 1951 (UN Sales No: 1951.II. B.2).

[19] V.K.R.V. Rao submitted India's proposal during the session of the Sub-Commission on Economic Development (of which he was the Chairman). For details, see, Report of the Third Session of the Sub-Commission ..., *ECOSOC Official Records* Ninth session, Supplement No. 11B (E/CN.I/63&Annex); See also UN Secretariat Study, *Methods of Finalising Economic Development in Underdeveloped Countries* (Sales No. 1949 II.B.4).

extended by the UN and the specialized agencies, (*c*) assistance to the underdeveloped countries in obtaining materials, equipment, personnel etc., for economic development, (*d*) financing or helping to finance schemes of economic development which could not be financed by the country's own resources and for which loans could not be asked for on strict business principles and (*e*) the promotion, and, if necessary, the direction and financing of regional development projects. Similar proposals were made by Iran, Argentina, Mexico and other Latin American countries. Nothing came of them.

SUNFED and Growing Frustration

By the early 1950s, however, a number of more or less nebulous proposals shaped into a concrete one: the establishment of a Special UN Fund for Economic Development (SUNFED). The debate, expert reports, studies, interactions and negotiations that followed, were perhaps most significant developments. They proved to be highly educative to the new states, helping identify the basic issues and the existence of not one, but three economic worlds.[20] The real nature of such UN institutions as the IBRD, IMF and the GATT were exposed in that they were neither intended to, nor capable of, meeting the problems concerning the developing countries of Africa, Asia and Latin America. These exercises further helped identify and promote an awareness of the commonality of interests among the countries of Africa, Asia and Latin America.

The debate over the establishment of the Fund was also an educative experience in multilateral diplomacy for the developing countries. From 1952–57, SUNFED remained on the agenda of the General Assembly, the ECOSOC and related UN bodies concerned with economic matters. Scores of studies, and expert reports were called for. However, at the twenty-fourth session of the ECOSOC in 1957, when all was set for the final recommendations for the establishment

[20] See, in particular, Susan Strange, 'The United Nations and International Economic Relations', in Kenneth Twitchett, ed., *The Evolving United Nations* (London: Europa Publications, 1971), pp. 100–19. She argues convincingly that there is not one but three economic worlds and a vast area of international economic relations where the United Nations plays no role.

of the SUNFED, the US, followed by the UK and Canada, put their thumbs down.[21] A few weeks later, when the General Assembly was to take up the recommendations of the ECOSOC (which had obtained fifteen votes in favour and three against), the United States discretly introduced a new proposal calling for the establishment of a Special Fund. The name was not very different from SUNFED but its premises, contents and objectives were. The US, making good use of corridor and parliamentary diplomacy, obtained priority considerations of its proposal and had it adopted before few could grasp what it was all about. The new Special Fund thus established was merely an expansion of the existing UN programmes of technical assistance including TA and the EPTA and the basic objectives[22] sought through SUNFED were quietly scuttled.

The Weak and the Strong

Nonetheless, the studies and reports prepared in the context of the SUNFED proposals and the statistical data and periodical studies such as the World Economic Situation[23] which began publication, in 1948–49, were quite revealing of the position of the developing countries in the post-war world economic system-that of, as the title of a book succinctly indicates, *The Weak in the World of the Strong*.[24] As in the case of international trade, the international monetary system too is controlled by the industrialized countries of the North. The developing

[21] For a summary of these developments, spread over seven years, see in particular, John Hadwen and Johan Kaufmann, *How United Nations Decisions are Made* New York: Oceana, 1961, pp. 85–108.

[22] SUNFED called for the setting up of a fund with an initial capital of $250 million to provide grants-in-aid and long-term, low interest loans for the financing of the economic and social infrastructures for development.

[23] Reference here, in particular, is to such UN publications as: *Salient Features of the World Economic Situation; World Economic Report; Restrictive Business Practices in International Trade: and Review of International Commodity Problems*. Published during the 1950s they partly helped in exposing the lopsidedness of the post-war economic system which worked to the advantage of the industrially advanced countries at the cost of the developing countries.

[24] Robert L. Rothstein, *The Weak in the World of the Strong: The Developing Countries in the International System*, New York, Praeger, 1974.

countries have little or no say; their role, as Pierre-Paul Schweitzer aptly notes, has been that of 'innocent bystanders and victims'.[25] They were learning the hard way that, although politically independent and legally sovereign, they continued to be in economic serfdom to an international system which generates neither cooperation nor even co-existence, but sheer exploitation. In their frustration and helplessness they could not but turn to the United Nations to seek redress of their grievances, which had given them the status of 'sovereign equality', and a Charter which enshrined the principles of international economic cooperation with a view to providing a 'higher standard of living ... conditions of economic and social progress and development'. From then onwards, the forum of the United Nations became their refuge for seeking a fair deal in the existing international economic [dis]order.

NORTH VERSUS SOUTH

That was the beginning of the protracted and continuing struggle between those who wanted the UN involved in a meaningful, regu-lative role and those who sought to keep it out of that role in international economic relations. That was also the beginning of the recognition of the most fundamental conflict of our time—the conflict between the haves of the North[26] and the have-nots of the South. From then on, the lines were increasingly and realistically drawn on a North–South rather than on an East–West basis.[27] The developing

[25] Cited in *UN Chronicle*, October 1982, p. 43. The former managing director of the International Monetary Fund made the observation in 1971, when the Bretton Woods system broke down.

[26] The North includes all the twenty-four members of the OECD (the countries of Western Europe, Canada, the United States, Australia, New Zealand and Japan) and the European component of the CMEA (East Europeans including the erstwhile Soviet Union). See in particular, K.P. Saksena, 'The United Nations and the North-South Conflict', in M.S. Rajan and S. Ganguly, eds., *Great Power Relations, World Order and the Third World* (New Delhi: Vikas, 1981), pp. 65–83; also, the Brandt Commission Report of the International Commission on International Development Issues: *North-South: A Programme for Survival* Cambridge, Mass: The MIT Press, 1980, pp. 31–32.

[27] In an article published in 1981, the author of this study argued that despite differences in ideology and economic systems etc., both the so-called East and West had more in common than either of them had, especially in terms of economic factors, with the Third World. The Cold War between the East and the West was, in fact, a conflict

countries, wiser by experience and deliberations at the UN, now put forth their demands from various forums for a three-pronged institutional arrangement—the availability of capital funds, transfer of technology, and equitable trade relations.

By the early 1960s, the influx of newly emerging nations had swelled their ranks and encouraged them to acquire a warring posture. The egalitarian principle of one state one vote and the all-comprehensive functions assigned to the General Assembly by the UN Charter provided the necessary tools and their demands sprouted into three specific proposals: (a) the establishment of a UN capital development fund; (b) a UN industrial development organization; and (c) a body dealing with international trade and with that objective, the convening of a UN conference on trade and development.

New Institutions: Bereft of Authority

In the changed scenario, the industrially advanced countries of the West changed their tactics. They allowed the new institutions sought by the developing countries, now constituting nearly a two-third majority, to be established and at the same time added their own. But in each case, the new institutions were deprived of their basic objectives and have existed either in name only or with their operational capacity camouflaged to conceal their being bereft of the authority and funds needed to meet their responsibilities. In the process, the UN institutions, inter-governmental committees and therefore the Secretariat departments proliferated, adding to the paper work. Although this included valuable studies and technical assistance to the developing countries, it effected no substantial or qualitative dent in the existing order of international economic relations.

---

for world domination between the two groups of states both belonging to Europe or a European-derived political culture. For one thing the conflict was referred to as of East and West. East and West of what? Europe, of course. Ibid., Saksena, pp. 70–82.

The developments that unfolded, beginning 1989, bear the point: One side of the Cold War has thrown in the towel and the other side is offering (to its cousins) the 'warmth' of surplus capital earned from its exploitative relationship with the countries of the poor South.

UNCTAD

The UN Conference on Trade and Development (UNCTAD) established in 1964 for instance, ran into a deadlock on the question of its decision-making process. As a compromise, the UNCTAD was established as an organ of the General Assembly but reduced to the status of functioning as a lobby for the developing countries to meet the other two groups of states periodically, to discuss trade and development matters. It was not even to be a pressure group of the majority. The limitations of the UNCTAD were demonstrated by the adoption of conciliation procedures regarding voting on all important issues. No wonder, therefore, that negotiations during and in between the eight sessions of the UNCTAD, to evolve a consensus have yielded little or practically no progress in obtaining any worthwhile equitable trade preferences for the Third World.

Capital Development Fund

The UN Capital Development Fund, after protracted discussions, negotiations and expert reports spread over nearly a decade, was eventually established in 1966 by sheer voting strength despite the opposition of both the western countries and the socialist countries of eastern Europe. It remained capital-less until 1974, because the only contributions which it could attract were from the developing countries whose currencies have no 'respectability' or convertability status in the international market. Eventually, the Scandinavian countries put in some hard currency and the fund became operative in 1975. In the process, however, its basic purposes remained unfulfilled. It was primarily set up to provide capital assistance by means of grants and particularly long-term loans, free of interest or at low interest. However, its limited funds (which for example, in 1983 amounted to $25 million), have restricted its operations to concentrating mainly on community development projects that directly benefit the lowest income groups in the least developed countries.[28]

---

[28] Since 1983, the amount of total pledges have declined. The major industrialized countries have kept out of the pledging conference. Japan made a token contribution of $5,00,000 in 1983. The other major donors are the Netherlands, Norway, Sweden, Switzerland and Italy.

UNIDO

The United Nations Industrial Development Organization (UNIDO) instituted in 1965, has also fallen short of its objectives as the necessary financial support from the industrially advanced countries has not been forthcoming. Until 1986, its administration continued to be financed by the regular UN budget and its operational activities were confined to being an executive agency of the TA and UNDP projects.[29]

Science and Technology

The various programmes instituted at the demand of the developing countries for development through the application of science and technology have met a similar fate. Following the UN Conference on the Application of Science and Technology for the Benefit of the Less Developed Countries (February 1963), an Advisory Committee, ACASTD came into being. Composed of experts and not government representatives, its work and recommendations failed to be effective. After protracted debate and demand, the developing countries succeeded in getting the appropriate UN structure, as recommended by the Vienna Conference of August 1979[30], instituted, but it has not been able to meet its objectives fully for lack of funds and support from the industrialized countries.[31]

[29] In January 1986, the UNIDO, after a long delay, became a specialized agency with a loan from the regular UN budget to meet the expenses of its initial operations. In its new form, the UNIDO has not fared better either. As usual, there are financial and political pressures to keep it away from its basic objectives. 'There are resolute and concerted efforts ... by major developed market economy countries, to impose on organizations' such as the UNIDO and UNCTAD, 'roles based on preferred strategy of development without regard to the interest and concerns of the majority of the nations of the world'. Muchkund Dubey, 'A New Dynamic Multilateralism', *Development* Journal of the Society for International Development, no. 4, 1989, p. 74.

[30] See, *Report of the UN Conference of Science and Technology for Development*, Vienna, 20–31 August 1979, UN Doc. A/CONF.81/71 New York: United Nations, 1979.

[31] For instance, the UN Financing System for Science and Technology for Development (UNFSSTD), instituted to finance the implementation of the Vienna Programme of Action (1979) and designed to strengthen science and technology capacities in the Third World countries, failed to attract the necessary funds. In 1987, it was terminated, and instead a Trust Fund in the UNDP was established.

QUEST FOR NEW ECONOMIC ORDER

Ever since the North–South conflict dominated UN proceedings, there was one occasion when it appeared as though the world body would acquire a meaningful role in international economic relations after all—in the aftermath of the crisis generated by the oil price hike in 1973–74. Hitherto the western countries had attempted to reduce the United Nations to a non-factor in international economic relations. For the first time, and only when they experienced a serious threat to their own economic welfare, they sought the forum of the United Nations for resolving the energy crisis. The immediate development that followed again demonstrated that the United Nations still remains the best hope for resolving differences and for harmonizing the actions of states towards mutual welfare, including economic questions. France called for a special session of the General Assembly to discuss the energy crisis, the objective being to put pressure on the oil-producing countries. In this effort, they needed (indeed, much expected) support of the non-oil producing countries of the Third World who were more severely hit by the flaring hike in oil prices. The Third World countries widened the scope of the special session by the inclusion of overall discussions on 'raw material and development'. The special General Assembly Session convened in May 1974, led to the adoption of the Declaration and Programme of Action on the establishment of a New International Economic Order. The programme was further streamlined at the twenty-ninth session (1974) and the seventh special session (September 1975) of the General Assembly. It included the equitable sharing of world trade in manufactured goods, international shipping, reforms in the international monetary system and the restructuring of the economic and social sectors of the UN system.[32] Within a year however, the western powers realized that petro-dollars were being recycled after all to the western world and the developments arising from the oil price hike posed no serious threat to their hegemony. Once again they went back to the old tactic of agreeing in principle but not conceding any change in the power structure of the existing international economic system.[33]

[32] For a perceptive analysis of the Declaration and the Programme, see M. Dubey, 'Problems of Establishing a New International Economic Order', *India Quarterly* New Delhi, vol. 32, no. 4, July-September 1976, pp. 269–89.

[33] The story has been a familiar one for those seasoned in UN diplomacy, but thanks to Daniel P. Moynihan we have it, perhaps for the first time, from the horse's mouth and in print too. In his memoirs relating to his stint as the chief US representative to the

Dead End?

What followed the seventh special session, was the same old story of the adoption of resolutions, the setting up of expert committees and some new institutions, again largely on paper. A little patchwork here and there was effected but no substantial change took place. For instance, after years of protracted negotiations, the proposal for the creation of a Common Fund to finance multi-commodity buffer stock as a safeguard against price fluctuation in day-to-day market rates at a given time, was agreed upon in 1983. It remained on paper for five years.[34]

In brief, the last one decade has seen a lot of activity but the result has been neither commensurate with the amount of activity nor with the gravity of the situation. In that context, the Cancun Summit held in October 1981, was perhaps the most significant event. For the first time, twenty-two heads of states/governments, representing both the rich North and the poor South met to discuss the problems facing the world economy. What actually happened was that the North looked at the poverty of the South and stared it down. Although the leaders of the industrialized powers agreed that the world economy was in shambles, they believed that they themselves would try to find ways and means of resurrecting it, by planning and coordinating their policies through the 'Summitry of Seven'[35] and the institutions they

---

United Nations, he candidly puts on record the inside story. He talks about what was a familiar pattern followed in the 1950s and 1960s of arm twisting, pursuasion, threats and at the same time, identification with the aspirations of the Third World leaders 'in form but not in substance'. He further tells of Henry Kissinger's (the then US Secretary of State) draft plan for his famous Milwaukee speech (14 July 1975) to be made a couple of weeks before the inception of the seventh special session of the General Assembly. Ir that speech, he confides, was to be a hard punch, but in a velvet glove, to the Third World countries. The speech was to provide the background to the two-fold objectives which the United States sought: 'First, to keep the industrialized nations together; second, to split the Third World'. *A Dangerous Place*, Indian Ed. New Delhi: Allied Publishers, 1979, pp. 113–39.

[34] In June 1989, the Common Fund become operative. However, the United States and some of the other major industrialized did not, as of January 1992, ratify the Agreement.

[35] In the wake of the oil crisis, the seven heads of governments of the major industrialized countries of the West—Canada, France, West Germany, Italy, Japan, the United Kingdom and the USA, first met in 1974, to work out a common strategy. Since then these summit meetings of the seven have become a bi-annual feature.

controlled, and not through the United Nations. Since then the so-called North–South dialogue has reached, it seems, a dead end.

Restructuring: The 1970s

A restructuring of the economic and social sectors of the United Nations was effected in the latter part of the 1970s, a result of the protracted negotiations, expert reports and consensus reaching that began with the report of the twenty-five inter-governmental experts.[36] What followed represents perhaps the most glaring example of how institutions and offices are created to scuttle the just demands made by the vast majority of UN members and agreed upon by a 'consensus' of the entire membership. The Report recommended a meaningful re-organizing of the UN system which included changes in the central structure for global policy planning and development, programming and in the structures of the sectoral activities of trade, monetary reforms, food, agriculture and industrialization. The developed countries, including both the market economies of the West and the centralized economies of the East, did not like the report. At the seventh special session of the General Assembly, acclaimed as a historical 'consensus' session, they saw to it that the report was referred to an ad hoc Committee of the Whole to prepare action proposals. After protracted debates and negotiations, spread over two years, one recommendation, relating to the restructuring of the economic and social sectors of the UN system that materialized, was the institution of a new office, the Director-General for Economic Development and International Economic Cooperation.

However, some important aspects of the proposal relating to the coordination and monitoring, by the office of the Director-General, of the various activities of the UN bodies and specialized agencies including the IMF and IBRD were obliterated. One of the main recommendations of the Group of 25, was an overall authority for the economic and social sectors.[37] A related proposal was that the Director-General should be a national of a developing country, as the

---

[36] *A United Nations Structure for Global Economic Cooperation*, Report of the Group of Experts on the Structure of the United Nations System (E/AC.62/9) New York: United Nations, 1975.

[37] Ibid., paras 27–32.

Secretary-General (Kurt Waldheim at the time) was from a developed country. The western countries conceded the demand, but who received the appointment turned out to be the million dollar question.[38]

With this appointment other important matters relating to the role of the office were worked out in ambiguous terms. It goes without saying that the powers and functions of an office, to a certain extent, depend on the personality of the incumbent of that office. From the crucial initial stage, the office of the Director-General remained a high-sounding decorative functionary. The other recommendations that emerged from the Committee of the Whole were largely directed towards the restructuring of the Secretariat with a view to meet the growing developmental needs of the Third World. It is to be noted that the present structure of the UN Secretariat which, of late, has been under severe attack, is the one worked out in the late 1970s as per the recommendations of the Group of 25, and the consensus reached at the seventh special session and the Committee of the Whole (1975–77).

---

[38] The appointment went to an international civil servant-cum-diplomat of a developing country. He happened to be a Cambridge graduate who had served in the UN Secretariat intermittently from 1963 to 1975 rising from P-4 level to D-2 level. In May 1975, he resigned his Secretariat job, joined the services of his government in the national capital and within a month, returned as his country's Permanent Representative to the United Nations Office in Geneva where the ad hoc Committee of the Whole was to begin its first session, in June 1975. (For a resume of his career, see *UN Chronicle*, April 1978, p. 62). The negotiations that followed among the members of the Group of 77 on one side and the industrialized countries of the West on the other, resulted in getting him named Chairman of the Committee. For the next two years he guided the proceedings of the Committee. It was not surprising that the same Chairman was appointed to what was regarded as the most important office in the restructuring of the economic and social functioning of the United Nations—Director-General for Development and International Economic Cooperation.

When his first term expired in 1983, his successor as per the earlier understanding was chosen from among the nationals of the industrialized countries of the North (Jean L. Ripert of France). The outgoing Director-General was made the Secretary-General of the UNCTAD. It should be noted that all such high level appointments are made by the General Assembly, on the recommendation of the Secretary-General who, in turn, does so after consultations with the major interest groups.

Question of Coordination

The importance of coordination within any organized system as a means of control and in the interest of efficient management is obvious. However, a review of four decades of the functioning of the United Nations finds that the salient feature has been the disproportionate balance between the time and effort spent on this exercise and that which is allocated to the elaboration and execution of programmes or even the implementation of the coordination agreed upon. The intriguing part is that, notwithstanding all the exercises, there is no coordination worth the name in the area in which it is most essential.

The ECOSOC was assigned by the Charter the major role of coordinating not only the economic and social activities undertaken by the UN proper but also those operated by the system as a whole, including its specialized agencies and related bodies. From the very inception of the UN operational system, however, the ECOSOC and for that matter the General Assembly or any other UN body, has been denied that role, largely because of Cold War politics and the pursuit of vested interests by the industrially advanced countries. From the initial stage, the agreements signed with the specialized agencies under Article 63 of the Charter made an exception under US pressure, with regard to the IMF and IBRD, relieving the Bretton Woods institutions of the responsibility of coordination with the UN and of any obligation to accept its recommendations. Over the years the exception became the rule as other specialized agencies took to the same course. The net result is that in their relations with the specialized agencies, the General Assembly and the Economic and Social Council cannot enforce their recommendations or issue binding guidelines. Even within the UN system, the new inter-governmental bodies (the Governing Council of Special Funds established in 1959 followed by the UNCTAD, UNDP and the UNIDO etc.) took to the same pattern.[39] Thus, as of now, notwithstanding such bodies as the Administrative

[39] At the initial stage, the western powers undermined the role of the General Assembly and the ECOSOC by setting up programmes independently of the UN. Between 1961 and 1966, the developing member-states disregarded the ECOSOC in view of its 'unrepresentivity' and tended to rely more on the General Assembly in the programme and coordination areas, thereby encouraging programmes and activities directly responsible to the General Assembly. Although the ECOSOC membership expanded (in 1966) to twenty-seven and again to fifty-four, it failed to regain ground.

Committee on Coordination (ACC), the Advisory Committee on Administrative and Budgetary Questions (ACABQ), the Joint Inspection Unit (JIU), the Committee for Programme and Coordination (CPC) and the Committee for Development Planning (CDP), there is no effective overall coordination or consultation on economic and social programmes.

Still, over the decades and especially since the 1960s, coordination has been an almost obsessive preoccupation of the United Nations. Indeed, as and when the developing countries sought new operational activities, there were counter-proposals for better coordination of existing programmes. This led to innumerable resolutions calling for studies and management surveys as well as for the creation of a sizeable number of inter-governmental advisory organs and ad hoc committees, not to mention the committees of experts and teams of consultants, in addition to the numerous inter-Secretariat bodies. The net result is that the quest for coordination has not only resulted in the proliferation of institutions but has seriously overstrained limited UN resources, as it extends priority to procedures and mechanics over substantive matters. This has also made the system inward looking to a point where coordination tends to become an end in itself rather than the means for reaching the objectives enshrined in the UN Charter. This point is reiterated by time itself. From the inception of the Group of High Level Inter-governmental Experts to review the efficiency of the administrative and financial functioning of the United Nations, to the last couple of years, senior officials of the Secretariat have spent more time studying reports and answering questions, than exercising effective control of the system and execution of the tasks at hand.

SUMMARY

The United Nations, despite being the only global organization in existence, has not acquired any regulative role in international economic relations. It was given a responsibility by its Charter without endowing it with the authority commensurate with the task. Over the decades, its economic and social framework has expanded both in size and complexity, partly as a by-product of the North-South conflict. One side, by virtue of its voting strength, has had new programmes instituted and the other side by the power of its purse has denied the new programmes adequate resources. To counter further demands, the North has succeeded in establishing new bodies to seek coordination and cost effectiveness of the existing programmes. Indeed, as noted earlier, there have been more inter-governmental, as well as expert, committees on coordination and cost-effectiveness than on any other subject.

These developments apart, the most important factor responsible for the expansion of the framework has been the escalating phenomena of interdependence. Programmes relating to energy, environment, human settlement, development and disarmament, water resources, ocean resource technology, transnational corporations and narcotics among others, have added to the growth and complexity of the UN structure. These programmes and related institutions have come up in response to the new challenges facing the international community—challenges which one member-State, however mighty cannot meet on its own. It has to be a collective, indeed global response. Another aspect of the analysis presented in the preceding pages, is that far from being a decision-making centre for international economic relations or even a significant partner, the United Nations has been actually reduced to a non-factor. The IMF, controlled by the western market economy countries, is minding the money and credit problems and taking care of the national economic policies of its member-States. The IBRD and its affiliates are concerned with financing development and lay down their own terms and conditions to developing countries. The Development Assistance Committee (DAC) in the OECD regulates and coordinates aid to the developing countries, but the aid, which has come to mean 'buy now and pay later', has resulted in the mounting debt burden which is now touching the more than one trillion dollar mark. The Transnational Corporations largely control global trade in the primary commodities[40]—main foreign exchange earner of the developing countries. The powerful regional organizations, such as the OECD, the European Community and the erstwhile Council for Mutual Economic Assistance (CMEA) and related institutions dealing

[40] For instance, a study by the UN Centre on Transnational Corporations (CTC) indicates that in the year 1980, about 80 to 90 per cent of global primary commodities worth $900 billion were accounted for by three to six multi-commodity transnational corporations. Frederick F. Clairmonte, 'Reflections on Power: TNCs in the Global Economy', *CTC Report*, no. 15, Spring 1983, New York: United Nations, 1983, pp. 37–39.

with cooperation at the inter-continental and regional levels, which until recently promoted the interests of the two respective economic worlds—then market economies led by the US and the centrally planned socialist economies led by the erstwhile USSR.

In brief, in the economic and social fields the role of the United Nations proper has been mostly confined to debate and discussion of the world economy, debates on North–South relations, the channelling of a very small portion of official development assistance through the UNDP and some specific negotiations (through the UNCTAD) on commodities.

Nonetheless, the UN does carry out some meaningful activities, particularly those relating to disaster relief, refugee and human rights, the collection and distribution of world statistics, research and advisory services in such fields as population and environment, development and disarmament, human settlement, transnational corporations, and the application of science and technology for development. Thus, almost all human endeavour with international dimensions has been of UN concern. Indeed, the United Nations today represents the largest reservoir of data-information and depository of experience and expert services in all aspects of international relations. What is perhaps more significant is that the United Nations continues to be important, primarily and exclusively, as the vehicle of symbolic action, expressing ideas of collective concern at a global level which cut across economic and ideological differences. Whether this collective concern, representing the governments and people of the world, can be translated into collective action remains a moot point.

2

Finance, Management and Accountability

While reviewing the finances and management of the United Nations, one has to examine some relevant issues. Is it true, as is widely alleged by the critics, that over the years the UN budget has grown excessively? Is it true that a handful of industrialized countries bear the main burden (75 per cent) of the UN budget but have little say in determining the appropriation of funds and pattern of activities? Is it true, as is implied by the allegations of 'wastage of precious resources', that there is no effective machinery to monitor the programming, budgeting, and evaluation of activities in the economic and social sectors? What are the reasons for the so-called crisis?

CURRENT CRISIS

Since 1976, the General Assembly has had on its agenda every year an item entitled 'Financial Emergency of the United Nations'. The reason behind this item has been the non-payment of assessed contributions to the budget. The withholding of funds has become an increasing threat to the UN's viability, indeed to its very existence. Article 17 of the Charter lays down a simple principle that the General Assembly shall consider and approve the budget and decide the apportionment or contribution of each member-State. There is also a penalty clause, in Article 19, which suggests that should the arrears of a member-State amount to more than two years apportionment to the budget, that member may be deprived of the right to vote. However, the bitter experience of what led to a different kind of financial crisis in 1964–65[1] showed that it is not politically advisable to invoke the punitive provisions of Article 19, especially when the defaulter happens to be a major power.

Charter obligations with regard to the regular budget apart, several members have withheld their contributions for various reasons. From the 1970s and till recently, six countries of East Europe, led by the erstwhile USSR, had objected to the inclusion in the regular budget of appropriation for Technical Assistance, insisting that such programmes be financed on a voluntary basis as is the case with the UNDP. Similarly, the US and Israel have over the years withheld apportionments from their contributions for programmes related to the Palestine question. The United States has also withheld funds for the Law of the Sea activities connected with deep seabed mining. In addition it has withheld funds for activities related to the South West Africa Peoples Organization (SWAPO) and, for the so-called 'first and second decades', to combat racism and racial discrimination. Indeed, it has become quite a practice among member-States to deduct those amounts from their contributions which relate to programmes they oppose. The amounts involved, however, have been small and as such the impact has not been that severe on the financial functioning of the United Nations.

[1] Some members including France and the USSR questioned the validity of arrangements, approved by the General Assembly, relating to the expenditure involved in such peace-keeping operations as the UNEF and the ONUC instituted in the wake of the Suez Crisis (1956) and the Congo crisis (1960) and refused to pay their respective apportionments. The United States threatened to invoke the provisions of Article 19, during the 1964 session of the General Assembly. The arrears of these members by then had accumulated to an amount which would subject them to punitive measures: the denial of the right to vote. The 'defaulting' members, including the USSR and France, threatened to walk out of the Organization if the General Assembly 'illegally' rescinded their vote.

In the face of the confrontational politics of the superpowers, the larger UN membership first sought the postponement of the General Assembly session from September to December 1964, with the hope that negotiations between the two sides would help ease the crisis. When this did not happen they resorted to the extraordinary device of taking decisions only on such matters which could not be postponed to the next session, by consensus and not by the usual voting procedure. On the eve of the Twentieth session of the General Assembly, the crisis was over when the United States announced in August 1965 that it would no longer insist on invoking Article 19. The outstanding arrears to the peace-keeping operations were met by voluntary contributions. For details see K.P. Saksena, *The United Nations and Collective Security* Delhi: D.K. Publishing House, 1974, pp. 276–80.

What added the critical dimension to the financial emergency was the United States' decision to withhold 50 per cent of its contribution, on the grounds that the UN budget was excessive and that funds were mismanaged. By January 1986, the unpaid assessments rose from $120 million in 1976 to an estimated $504 million. Of that amount, $242 million represented contributions due to the regular budget while the rest consisted of the deficit to the support accounts of the UN peace-keeping operations. It was the amount withheld from the regular budget that threatened the financial viability of the United Nations. And it is the United States' withholding of its assessed contribution—whice rose from a comparatively small amount in 1984 to $130 million in 1985 and more than $300 million by 1987—that posed the most serious threat to the viability and financial solvency of the United Nations.

While over the decades, the UN budget has increased, reaching more than $1600 million by 1984–85, and for the biennium 1992–93, more than $2 billion, its working capital (reserve) fund has been kept relatively low at $100 million. This has created increasingly serious cash flow problems. As such, the Secretary-General was obliged to suspend or cut down several programmes in 1986 and again in 1987. By December 1987, there were no funds left to even disburse the salaries of all UN employees in January 1988. The United States then doled out a sum of $90 million to enable the Secretary-General to do the needful. This kind of precarious situation has continued unabated.

FINANCIAL RESOURCES

The three main categories of the financial resources of the UN are:

1. The income from revenue-producing activities (visitors' pro-grammes, sale of UN documents, etc.) and staff assessment.[2]

---

[2] Staff assessment is not really income accruing to the United Nations. It is basically an 'income tax' levied on the base salaries (i.e., excluding post adjustment amounts) of UN employees. The money collected is then distributed to member-States according to their scale of assessment. For example, the United States collects 25 per cent of the staff assessment money which is adjusted in the income tax accounts of its nationals who are employees of the United Nations. Thus, staff assessment is one item which appears in both the income and expenditure categories.

During the years 1984–85 this amounted to $294.3 million, in 1986–87 to $327 million and for the biennium 1990–1991, to $400 million.

2. Voluntary contributions which are given either to trust funds such as the UNICEF or channelled to the UN through the UNDP. This category of resources does not form part of the regular budget.

3. The assessed contribution to the UN budget. The total final appropriations for 1984–85 amounted to $1,608 million, for 1986–87, $1,711 million and for 1990–91, to 2, 167 million. Deducting the income including staff assessment, the net budget for the three bienniums amounted to $1,366 million, $1,450 million and $1,767 million, respectively.

The scale of assessment is calculated by a format that takes into account the absolute level as well as the per capita national income of each member-State. In the case of the United States, however, where the national income now touches $5 trillion, there is a set limit of a maximum of 25 per cent of the United Nations' budget.[3] If this is calculated on the basis of the formula applied to other countries, it would be much higher. The contribution of each member-State is fixed by the General Assembly on the advice of an eighteen-member Committee on Contribution. The total budget and the factors determining the actual apportionment which each state must contribute are decided by the General Assembly after considering the two-year budget proposed by the Secretary-General along with the recommendations of the Advisory Committee (ACABQ) and the Committee for Programme and Coordination.[4]

[3] The assessment process is geared to the capacity to pay. This principle of fairness was laid down by the Preparatory Commission of the United Nations (1945–46) at its inception and has never been formally repudiated. The first scale of assessment was worked out in 1946. The Committee of Contributions proposed, going by the gross national income of the United States, that 49.89 per cent of the budget be paid by that country. This was vigorously opposed by the United States which eventually agreed to pay 39.89 per cent. In 1954, under the insistent prodding by the US delegation, the Assembly reluctantly limited the top contribution to 33.33 per cent. In 1972, the United States again succeeded in bargaining the maximum ceiling down to 25 per cent. That year the United States' contribution ought to have been 38.4 per cent had it been strictly based on the capacity to pay as determined by national income. Since 1972, while the maximum ceiling has stayed at 25 per cent, the minimum has come down from 0.04 per cent to 0.01 per cent.

[4] This Committee, which reconstituted in 1969, was composed of twenty-one members and had a proportionately larger share of representation of the major contri-

Table 1 provides a list of member-States who contribute more than one per cent to the regular UN budget. From the time the United Nations came into existence, there have been, with some exceptions, only slight variations in the apportionments, of major contributors. The share of the United States has varied from more than 39 per cent to a maximum ceiling of 25 per cent set in 1972 which has remained unchanged since.

One exception has been China's apportionment which during the initial years was more than 5 per cent. It came down to around 4.5 per cent in the 1960s to 0.77 per cent currently. Another sharp variation, on the ascending side, has been that of Japan's contribution. In 1956, when Japan joined the United Nations, its apportionment was set at 2.9 per cent. This was raised to slightly more than 3 per cent in the 1960s and to 3.78 per cent in 1970. It went up to 7.8 per cent in 1973, to more than 10 per cent in the early 1980s and, as of now, amounts to 12.45 per cent. Thus, Japan has become the second largest contributor to the UN budget since 1985.

India's apportionment in 1946 was more than 3 per cent and remained so until the 1960s. Until then it was the seventh largest contributor, after the five permanent members of the Security Council and Canada. Its apportionment was reduced to a little more than 2 per cent in the 1960s and to less than one per cent in the 1970s. India's current share is 0.36 per cent, amounting to $2.5 million approximately.

Nearly 100 countries contribute what is set as the minimum or 0.01 per cent of the total budget. This is to emphasise the equality of all member-States and currently adds up to a little more than $70,000 per annum. This figure may appear 'peanuts' to many, but for countries like Gambia and Equatorial Guinea, it amounts to more than 0.5 per cent of their total national incomes. For Uganda, Guinea Bissau, Grenada, and the Maldives the set minimum amounts to around 0.3 per cent, but if this figure were applied to the United States it would amount to 0.029 per cent of its total national income.

---

butors to the UN budget. In 1976, the General Assembly decided that the CPC should be the main subsidiary organ of both the ECOSOC and the General Assembly for planning, programming, and coordination. As a major component of its work, the Committee alternates annually between reviewing the draft budget and the draft medium-term plan.

In the wake of the reforms that followed General Assembly Resolution 41/213 of December 1986, the membership of the CPC was expanded to thirty-four. This development is discussed in chapter 4.

Table 1
Major Contributors to the Regular UN Budget
(More than one per cent)

Member-State	Scale of Assessment (Per Cent)		
	1983–85	*1989–91*	*1992–94*
United States of America	25.00	25.00	25.00
USSR*	10.54	9.99	9.41
Japan†	10.32	11.38	12.45
Federal Republic of Germany*	8.54	8.08	8.93
France	6.51	6.21	6.00
United Kingdom	4.67	4.86	5.02
Italy	3.74	3.99	4.29
Canada	3.08	3.09	3.11
Spain	1.93	1.95	1.98
The Netherlands	1.78	1.65	1.50
Australia	1.57	1.57	1.51
Brazil	1.39	1.45	1.59
German Democratic Republic**	1.39	1.28	—
Ukrainian SSR	1.32	1.25	1.18
Sweden	1.32	1.21	1.11
Belgium	1.28	1.17	1.06
Total	**84.38**	**84.13**	**84.14**

* General Assembly Resolution 46/221 of 20 December 1991, while deciding the scale of assessments for the contribution of member-States for the triennium 1992, 1993 and 1994 indicates 9.41 per cent against the contribution of the USSR. But a week later the country was succeeded by the Russian Federation. As a result of the disintegration of the USSR, eleven constituent republics have gained UN membership as independent states. Their apportionment will be decided, on the recommendations of the Committee on Contributions, by the General Assembly at its Forty-seventh Session. Accordingly, the apportionment of the Russian Federation will be reduced further. Also see p. 237.

† Japan became the second largest contributor in 1985, when its apportionment was raised to 10.84 per cent. The further increase for Japan and deduction for the USSR, as the figures above indicate, have been effected for the next two trienniums.

** After the two Germanies united and became one member of the United Nations on October 3, 1990, their combined contribution is listed as Germany's contribution.

Budgetary Decision-Making

It is a widely held belief that all members, irrespective of their contributions, are treated on an equal footing where the budget is concerned.[5]

5 A study by the Heritage Foundation of the United States, for instance, complains that while the US contributes 25 per cent of the budget, it has only one vote, out of 159, on deciding UN programmes and budgeting. *Report on the US and the UN: A Balance Sheet* Washington DC, The Heritage Foundation, 1984, p. 9.

This is not true. For one, budget proposals prepared by the Secretary-General are first discussed by smaller bodies which are invariably represented by the United States in particular and other major contributors in general. For instance, since the very inception of the United Nations, the ACABQ[6] has always had a proportionately larger representation of the major contributors. This is also true of the eighteen-member Committee on Contribution and the Committee for Programme and Coordination.

Consensus System

There are two separate systems governing the way in which the UN appropriates funds. One is the formal voting system. The other is a series of informal practices and unwritten rules by which the 159 member-States of the UN seek a consensus which includes both the main contributors and the 144 other members. The fifteen main contributors obviously play a greater role in the second system. To bring about a working relationship between the two systems, the Secretary-General plays a crucial role in drawing up the successive budgets for the organization. He must calculate the costs involved in the carrying out of the many activities that the inter-governmental bodies have approved. At the same time, he has to ensure that the total budget does not exceed what the member-States, particularly the main contributors, are prepared to pay. In order to obtain such a balance, the Secretary-General must bear in mind the views of a wide cross-section of member-States. While he has to be sensitive to the desires of the developing countries in finding sufficient resources to ensure the adequate implementation of activities important to them, the concern of the larger contributors naturally occupy a special place in such discussions.

As the various bodies that approve new activities are numerous and

[6] The ACABQ was instituted in 1946 with six members of which five experts were nationals of the permanent members of the Security Council. In 1950 its membership was raised to nine and in 1971 to sixteen. In accordance with the Gentleman's Agreement of 1946, all five permanent members of the Security Council are included, if they so wish, in all the subsidiary bodies of the United Nations. Indeed, in 1971 when the Peoples Republic of China got its seat, the first thing it demanded was membership in ACABQ and it was included.

not directly in touch with financial constraints, the Secretary-General and the General Assembly have, over the years, evolved the mechanism and procedural steps to streamline financial procedures. One rule lays down that the financial implications and the report of the ACABQ thereon, are to be taken into account before voting on any proposal is considered by a main committee or subsidiary body of the General Assembly.

After protracted discussions and consultations with the ACABQ and the CPC, followed by the reports of the Committee of inter-governmental experts, the General Assembly adopted comprehensive guidelines on programmes and planning which are spelled out in General Assembly Resolution 37/34, dated 21 December 1982. One major recommendation approved, was a medium-term plan based on a UN legislative mandate. The six-year plan serves as the framework for the regular budget and constitutes the principal policy directive of the UN. To further streamline budgetary procedure, the Secretary-General formulated the Regulations and Rules Governing Programme Planning, the programme aspect of the budget and the Monitoring, Implementation and Methods of Evaluation (ST/SGB/204). These regulations and rules were endorsed by the General Assembly in 1984 and in 1985 and are being progressively implemented.

The Secretary-General continues to hold the responsibility of pre-paring the draft of the budget. Once the proposals for the biennium, prepared after wide consultations, are ready, they are submitted to the CPC and the ACABQ.[7] The two committees, after a thorough scrutiny, make recommendations invariably by consensus. Voting has rarely been resorted to. Thus, in evolving a consensus, the US and other major contributors do have a large say. It is, unfortunate, however, that having participated in the evolving of the consensus, the US conti-nues to cast negative votes when the budget is finally voted upon by the General Assembly.[8] Each biennium budget is voted through by the General Assembly on three occasions, normally during three successive

---

[7] This was the practice until 1986. The changes introduced by General Assembly Resolution 41/213 of 19 December of that year are discussed in Chapter 4.

[8] Since 1978, while the voting pattern of the major industrialized countries have varied from year to year and from issue to issue, the United States, up to recently the USSR and its East European allies consistently cast negative votes on all resolutions relating to budgetary and financial matters, leaving aside those resolutions which are adopted without vote. The situation changed from 1987 when resolutions relating to budgetary matters have been variably adopted without a vote.

Decembers. This includes the year it goes into effect, the end of its first year and again in its second year.[9] It is to be noted that the recommendations of the ACABQ, the Committee on Contribution and that of the CCP have never been turned down on substantial matters by the Fifth Committee of the General Assembly. On occasion, it has made minor changes on the recommendations of the ACABQ or the other committees concerned. Thus, it is clear that the one member one vote theory is not truly the case in decision-making on administrative and budgetary questions.

Unfair Burden?

A lot has been written of the unfair financial burden the US and the western countries supposedly carry in the United Nations. This is not true. For one, if the contribution, calculated at a percentage of the national income is taken into account, countries such as Gambia, Equatorial Guinea and Comoros contribute larger percentages of their national incomes to the UN budget.[10] It should also be noted that the developing countries pay their contributions in hard-earned foreign currency.

UN Budget: Too Heavy and Excessive

It is true that over the decades, the appropriation of the UN budget has multiplied manifold. From around $20 million in 1946, to $50 million in 1960 and $850 million in 1986, the revised appropriation for

---

[9] The second and third votes provide the revised appropriations of funds for the biennium concerned. The budgetary process analysed here relates to the practice as it prevailed until the introduction of Resolution 41/213, in 1986, when some modifications were introduced. The modifications and changes are discussed in Chapter 4.

[10] In 1984, for instance, Gambia made the largest contribution: 0.59 per cent of its total national income. The other member-States paying such large percentages were Equatorial Guinea at 0.437 per cent, Comoros, 0.371 per cent and Grenada, 0.312 per cent. The current percentages remain more or less the same.

the biennium 1990–91, as approved by General Assembly Resolution 46/184, dated 20 December 1991, amounted to $1,767 million. The increase does not necessarily call for explanation. For one, the impact of inflation alone is responsible for a 70 per cent increase over the last ten years. Second, and more importantly, the growing interdependence of the world has led to new challenges and for the UN, the need for more finances for programmes relating to disaster relief, energy, food, environment, HABITAT, outer space refugees, seabeds and ocean floors and transnational corporations among others. Despite these global interests, it is significant that the budget for a single year for the New York City Police Department is higher than that of a one-year UN budget. Again, the world community spends more money on armaments every hour of the day than the sum of the UN budget reserved for two years.

Return Benefits

A large portion of the UN budget is spent in countries which are major contributors. Thus a significant proportion of the money that some major donors contribute to the UN system returns to them in terms of the money the system spends in their countries on operating expenses, salaries and material purchased. In 1984, the UN spent about $372 million to operate its headquarters in New York, $117 million to run its office in Switzerland and $86 million on its office in Austria.

The 35,000 or so members of the diplomatic community representing member-States, spend their hard-earned foreign exchange in New York, Geneva and Vienna. In 1981, for instance, New York City's economy gained more than $690 million over the previous year from UN expenditure and that of its diplomatic community.[11] A similar study prepared by the New York City Commission for the United Nations and Consular Corps, released on 11 December 1989, indicated that the UN presence in Manhattan brings an estimated $830 million to the city each year. The total of some $860 million in UN-related revenue is offset by the $25 million or so that the city

[11] See, New York City Commission for the United Nations, *The Economic Impact of the Diplomatic Community on New York* New York: December 1981, p. 4.

spends annually on services for the United Nations and the Foreign Diplomatic Corps, in terms of lost revenue for real property tax exemptions and uncollected parking fines and towing charges.[12] *On this count alone, apart from the other financial benefits accruing to the host country, the United States gets back more than 300 per cent of what it contributes to the regular UN budget.* Voluntary contributions to such programmes as the UNDP and the UNICEF also bring substantial returns to the donor country. For example, it is estimated that the salaries paid to US experts and the purchase of US equipment and services by the UNDP, put back into the American economy 45 per cent more than it gets from its contribution. Similarly, the UNICEF reports indicate that its salaries for experts, purchase of supplies and freight costs, return more than 65 per cent of the annual contribution to it by the United States government and American citizens combined.

The Secretariat's professional jobs are supposedly determined by geographical distribution, but the quota for each country is fixed largely by each member-State's assessed share of the UN budget. For member-States assessed at the minimum rate, the General Assembly's quota range is from two to five. For the largest contributors, however, as for instance the United States, the range is 406–549.[13] The overall figures show that the nationals of the developing countries presently occupy 42 per cent of the posts subject to geographical distribution, while those of the developed countries hold 48 per cent. There are some 10,000 posts in the general services category, about 80–90 per cent of which are held by the nationals of those countries hosting UN headquarters or offices—New York, Geneva and Vienna, with the exception of Nairobi.[14]

MONITORING AND ACCOUNTING

Once the budget is approved, the UN concerns of monitoring, implementation and evaluation continue. The Secretary-General is given the

---

[12] *UN Chronicle*, March 1990, p. 13.

[13] As of January 1986, of the 3,046 professionals, 482 were US citizens.

[14] It is interesting to note that not only UN headquarters and offices but also those of the specialized agencies are located in the cities of industrially advanced countries.

responsibility of monitoring programme implementation internally through a central unit in the Secretariat, reporting to the General Assembly through the CPC. Once again, to determine as systematically and objectively as possible, the relevant efficiency and impact of the organizational activities, an overall evaluation is attempted periodically at an inter-governmental level. Other bodies, such as the Joint Inspection Unit undertake external evaluation and its reports are made available to the ACABQ, CPC, ECOSOC, the General Assembly and to other bodies within the larger UN system, including the specialized agencies.

Finally, the expenditure and accounts are fully audited. The Board of Auditors[15] transmits to the General Assembly the financial statements of accounts for the regular budget and for the various extra-budgetary accounts and other programmes of the UN system undertaken in the previous financial period. Under the provisions of Article XII of the Financial Regulations of the UN, the Board submits reports to the Assembly on the results of its audit. It also issues opinions as to whether the financial statements properly reflect the recorded transactions and whether these transaction are in accordance with the Financial Regulations and legislative authority and present fairly the financial position as at the end of the financial period of each of these activities. The reports of the Board of Auditors are commented upon by the ACABQ which then submits a report to the Assembly.

[15] The Board of Auditors, established by the General Assembly in 1946, is composed of members who are appointed Auditor General, or the official equivalent title of their countries and not as individuals. Members are elected for a period of three years, each member retiring by rotation every year. In 1990–91, the Board comprised the President of the Federal Court of Audit of Germany (until June 1992), the Auditor General and Chairman of the Commission of the Audit of the Philippines (until June 1993) and the Auditor General of Ghana (until June 1994). For details see UN Doc. A/46/100, 15 June 1991, pp. 68–69.

3

Programmes, Distribution of Resources and Structure

The economic and social programmes of the United Nations, notwithstanding the various declarations and plans for international development strategies,[1] are modest in scale and objectives as the larger international economic activities operate outside its framework. The programmes vary in type of activity and are unequal in terms of the resources assigned to them. Some, such as those relating to refugees and disaster relief, are financed largely by extra-budgetary resources, with the UN budget merely providing symbolic administrative assistance. Other programmes receive mixed sources, of funding and are handled by a variety of inter-governmental mechanisms including the five regional economic commissions. In general, the economic and social

---

[1] Reference here is to the broad programmes and policies outlined for the First Development Decade (the 1960s) by the General Assembly, to help increase economic growth in the developing countries by at least 5 per cent at the end of the decade. The target was not met largely because of unfavourable trade patterns and heavy debt burdens—the same trends and tendencies that increasingly acquired graver dimensions in the 1970s and 1980s. For the Second Development Decade (the 1970s), the General Assembly, after protracted preparatory work and negotiations, worked out the International Development Strategy (Resolution 2626 XXV) which also failed to meet its target. This was followed by strategy for the Third Development Decade (Resolution 35/56) which met the worst fate in the wake of the continuing financial crisis, when its strategy was relegated to oblivion. Nonetheless, the General Assembly is continuing the 'ritual' by emphasising the urgent need for the reactivation of the economic and social development process of the developing countries by launching the international strategy for the Fourth Development Decade (Resolution 42/193).

programmes seek to promote the establishment of common norms or standards, to facilitate the compatability of national policies that will contribute to the formulation of common principles and to assist the developing countries in the formulation of their development policies. The programmes provide assistance ranging from the technical, to surveys, studies and development planning for specific projects in individual fields such as energy, water resources, agriculture and industrial development.

The UN Secretariat's departments or units in charge of such programmes prepare studies, documents and reports in support of the work of the inter-governmental or expert bodies. These are published for distribution to national services, other users and sometimes for the public at large, as for example, the *World Economic Survey: Current Trends and Policies in the World Economy*, an annual publication. In addition, these units support some operational activities. It should be noted that not all of these programmes or activities are directly involved with any specifically planned assistance 'as a whole', or 'from the inception to the finish'. This holds true of operational activities also and for technical assistance provided to member-States, which could be in the form of technical advice, preparation of a blueprint for a particular project, the training of personnel or, in some cases, the supply of small amounts of necessary equipment.

The programmes acquired a new dimension as a result of the General Assembly's decision to initiate biennial programme budgeting in 1975. Beginning in 1976 with a medium-term plan for the period 1978–81 (Resolution 3392/XXX), at its Thirty-seventh Session in 1982, the General Assembly adopted a medium-term plan for a six-year period from 1984–89. The biennium budgets were expected to adhere to the medium-term plan, but the financial crisis, beginning in 1986, upset priorities. The major programmes and sub-programmes[2]

[2] The presentation and classification of the activities of the organization by major programmes, programmes, sub-programmes and programme element was incepted by the ACC in 1975. A major programme corresponds to a major purpose or function of the organization for which objectives may be set by for example; population, United Nations; Education, UNESCO; Environmental Health, WHO. The sub-programme is a coherent collection of several activities directed at the attainment of one objective (of a major programme) and which is capable of being evaluated in terms of output indicators. The programme is a grouping of related sub-programmes directed at the attainment of one or more objectives that contribute to the broader objectives of the major programmes (for example: Population in the ESCAP region, United Nations; Adult education, UNESCO). The programme element is either a project directed at a precise objective in

in the economic and social sectors, as set by the medium-term plan of 1984–89, financed by the regular UN budget and extra-budgetary resources and subject to budgeting and programming by the UN General Assembly are:

1. *Disaster and Relief*: One major programme; four sub-programmes, partly met by the regular UN budget and partly by voluntary contributions; twenty-four professionals.
2. *Energy*: Seven programmes; eighteen sub-programmes; fifty-seven professionals.
3. *Environment*: Six programmes; eighteen sub-programmes; seventy-four professionals.
4. *Food and Agriculture*: Six programmes; eighteen sub-programmes; seventy-six professionals.
5. *Human Rights*: One programme; four sub-programmes; forty-eight professionals.
6. *Human Settlement*: Six programmes; twenty-five sub-programmes; 124 professionals.
7. *Industrial Development*: (UNIDO, now a specialized agency with regional economic commissions): Eleven programmes; thirty-five sub-programmes; 394 professionals.
8. *International Trade*: (including the International Trade Centre, the UNCTAD and regional economic commissions): Nine programmes; nineteen sub-programmes; 244 professionals.
9. *Marine Affairs*: (Ocean, Economics and Technology): One programme; four sub-programmes; eleven professionals.
10. *Natural Resources*: seven programmes; nineteen sub-programmes; fifty-nine professionals.
11. *Population*: Six programmes; twenty-three sub-programmes; 123 professionals.
12. *Public Administration and Finance*: Three programmes; nine sub-programmes; thirty-five professionals.
13. *Refugees*: (2 per cent of UNRWA and 4 per cent of UNHCR's budgets come from UN assessed contributions): Two programmes; ten sub-programmes; 473 professionals.
14. *Science and Technology*: Seven programmes; twenty sub-programmes; fifty-four professionals.

---

terms of output over a prescribed period of time, the achievement of which can be verified, or it is a continuing activity with a measured output. For more details, see Joint Inspection Unit Report 78/1 on Programme and Evaluation in the United Nations.

15. *Social Development*: Five programmes, twenty sub-programmes; 104 professionals.
16. *Transnational Corporations*: One programme; three sub-programmes; fifty professionals.
17. *Transport*: Seven programmes; thirty-two sub-programmes; eighty-three professionals.

POLICY-MAKING ORGANS FOR ECONOMIC AND SOCIAL ACTIVITIES

The regular UN budget provides the expenditure for the convening and servicing of the Economic and Social Council (ECOSOC), its standing committees, functional commissions and other subsidiary bodies.[3] For the biennium 1984–85, the total expenditure of these policy-making organs amounted to $1.362 million and for 1986–87, the revised appropriation amounted to $2.66 million.[4] Part of the allocations are spent in meeting the travel costs and subsistence allowances of (*a*) members of such committees or commissions as are nominated either as experts (such as the members of the Committee for Development Planning) or those who serve in their individual capacity (such as members of the Committee on Contribution or the Investments Committee); and (*b*) Secretariat officials who travel from UN offices located away from the venue of the meeting.

Travel costs or subsistence allowances are not provided to members

[3] The terms of reference of the ECOSOC, its functional commissions and other subsidiary bodies, as revised over the decades, are set out in documents E/5435/Rev and E/1983/INF.4.

[4] The Budgetary figures and other details specifically relating to personnel employed in each department and the analyses of the various programmes and sub-programmes are based on the three volume document entitled Programme Budget for the Biennium 1986–1987, *GAOR*, Fortieth Session, Supplement No.6(A/40/6). This is so because it takes four to five years before the voluminous details are made officially available in print. More importantly, this chapter places developments in perspective, with regard to the structure and programmes as they evolved and existed before the demand for reform gained momentum in 1985–86. Since then the situation has been in a state of flux and almost every year there have been reductions and reshuffling of personnel. The comparative figures for the programmes and sub-programmes in the economic and social fields are not available.

The changes that followed in the wake of the demands for reform and restructuring and discussed in Chapter 4. Budgetary allocations for the biennium 1992–1993 under their existing heads are given in Appendix III, Programme Budget for the Biennium 1992–1993.

who constitute the various inter-governmental committees and subsidiary bodies and attend meetings as representatives of their respective governments. However, an exception has been made for members of the Committee for Programmes and Coordination (CPC), the budgetary provision for which is listed under a separate head relating to executive direction and management. The budget also makes provision for the policy-making organs in the economic and social sectors for the convening of their international conferences. In the biennium 1986–87, the budget bore the costs of the UN Conference for the Promotion of International Cooperation in Peaceful Uses of Nuclear Energy which was held in Geneva from 10–28 November 1986. The overall expenses of the conference were estimated at $1.24 million.

The inter-governmental and other subsidiary bodies whose conference-convening expenses are covered by the heading of policy-making organs, are:

The Economic and Social Council

The fifty-four-member Council meets thrice a year; once for a short duration to organize its work in the month of February and then for two regular sessions, one held in New York and the other in Geneva. The sessions generally last a month. The representatives of member-States travel at the expense of their governments and are not entitled to subsistence allowance. However, officials specifically attending the two regular sessions from the five regional commissions (one staff member only) are given both travel and subsistence allowances. Other committees or commissions of the ECOSOC normally meet for eight working days with the exception of the Committee for Programme and Coordination which holds a five-week session annually.

Committee on Natural Resources

The fifty-four members meet once in two years for a period of eight days. Both their travel and subsistence allowances are borne by their respective governments.

The questions of sovereignty, development and the utilization of the natural (non-agricultural) resources of the developing countries have been put before the General Assembly since the early 1950s. Conferences have been convened and several ad hoc committees constituted to discuss wide-ranging issues from conservation and the utilization of

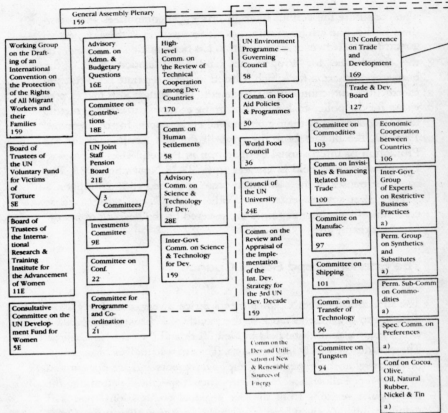

United Nations: Economic and Social Structure

Inter-governmental and Expert Bodies

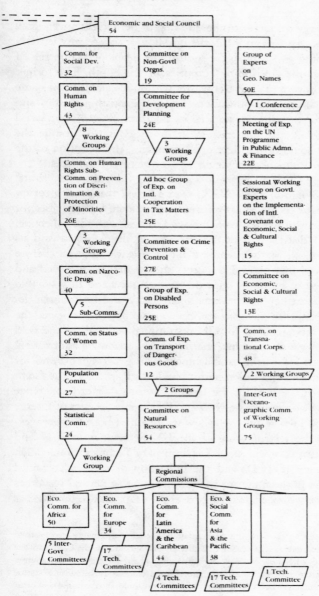

water and energy resources to the question of permanent sovereignty over resources. As early as 1952, the question of sovereignty left UN membership into two camps, the industrially developed countries of the North and the developing countries of the South. The former opposed the concept of sovereignty over natural resources in the name of international law and obligations under the existing treaties and agreements and the latter demanded its assertion through the United Nations. In 1962, the General Assembly pronounced, despite the opposition of some of the developed countries, the adoption of the Declaration of Permanent Sovereignty over Natural Resources.[5]

In 1970, the ECOSOC constituted a Standing Committee on Natural Resources (Resolution 1535/XLIX) with a broad mandate to review arrangements for technical assistance, to coordinate UN activities for the development of natural resources and to deal with the collecting, analyzing and distribution of information on development and its prospects. Working on the premise that planning was necessary before exploitation and that natural resources should first be surveyed and then developed in harmony with the environment and in ways that promote social justice and international equity, the Committee developed guidelines for advisory services to governments, reviewed the coordinating arrangements for UN operational activities in the field and discussed ways of collecting, analyzing and distributing information. The discussions led to the establishment of the Revolving Fund for Natural Resource Exploration within the UNDP in 1973. The Committee prepared the way for the United Nations' Water Conference (1977) and the Conference on New and Renewable Sources of Energy (1981) and was involved in the follow-up action of both conferences.

Ever since the restructuring of the UN Secretariat in 1977 and especially the establishment of the Department of Technical Cooperation for Development (DTCD) and the utilization of regular Technical Assistance, the programme for the development of natural resources has acquired new dimensions. Thus, over the years, the Committee has

---

[5] Over the last two decades the concept of permanent sovereignty over natural resources has been reiterated in several UN instruments. Specifically, the Charter of the Rights and Duties of States, of 1974, unequivocally upheld the right of the country concerned to exercise sovereignty over its natural resources, but the question of capital investment and technical know-how needed for the exploitation of natural resources remains a key issue. Should the United Nations provide assistance in this regard? This is one question indicative of the North–South divide at the United Nations and partly responsible for the ongoing controversy regarding reform and reorganization.

made valuable contribution to the development of natural resources and has more than justified its existence as a standing committee of the ECOSOC. Nonetheless, the old controversy has been revived and this time, the developed countries are arguing that the Committee of Natural Resources has not been functioning satisfactorily and, for the sake of economy and efficiency, should be terminated. Such a move could have far-reaching implications as the continuance of this international body is closely linked with the future of the DTCD and the regular programmes of Technical Assistance. It should be noted that the meeting of this Committee, held once in two years, incurs the least expenditure—less than $20,000.

The following four standing subsidiary bodies whose travel expenses only are met by the United Nations meet once in two years, unless decided otherwise, for eight working days. These subsidiary bodies were established in 1946–47, on a regular basis, as functional commissions[6] of the ECOSOC.

The Commission on Status of Women

The thirty-two-member Commission was instituted to prepare recommendations on measures for the promotion of women's rights in the political, economic, social and educational fields and to make recommendations on problems requiring immediate attention in this field. Ever since its inception it has performed commendably.

The Population Commission

Instituted with the objective of advising the ECOSOC on population trends, statistics, demographic surveys, and inter-relationship of demographic, economic and social factors, the Commission comprises twenty-seven members.[7] As the supply and quality of statistical data

[6] Following the pattern of the allocation of funds in the programme budget of 1986–87, the Commission of Human Rights and its subsidiary bodies are discussed separately, in this chapter, under the heading, Human Rights. Likewise, the inter-governmental, bodies concerned with the activities of the Transnational Corporations are taken up under that heading.

[7] For instance, to help overcome the difficulty arising from the lack of adequate data and research relating to the less developed countries, a pilot study was carried out jointly with the Government of India in Mysore State on the relationship between population changes and economic and social factors, the reports of which were submitted in 1956.

improved, it began to give more attention to analytical studies, the preparation of population estimates and projects and the publication of technical manuals on demographic methods. While the UN Fund for Population Activities (UNFPA) concentrates on population control and family planning, the Population Commission's task is to analyze the population problem in its totality. The commission cuts across the regional and specialized approaches taken by the various agencies concerned, which tend to view and analyze population from their respective points of view, making it desirable that the two functions and responsibilities be kept separate.

The Commission on Social Development

Earlier known as the Social Commission, it was instituted in 1946 with a broad mandate relating to all matters in the social field not covered by specialized agencies or other inter-governmental bodies, specifically to promote 'social progress and a better standard of life in larger freedom' as promised in the Charter. As early as 1949, the need to promote and finance social as well as economic development and the importance of coordinating both was recognized. The mandate of the Commission was accordingly expanded and today it is the principal body for the review of social and development issues. Under its direction, the Secretariat publishes the Report on the World Social Situation,[8] a comprehensive review of topics affecting all levels of society throughout the world. This comprehensive report, in turn, forms the basis of much of the Commission's work. The thirty-two members of the Commission meet once in two years for a session of eight working days.

The Statistical Commission

The Commission's twenty-four members provide expert advice on the development of the statistical services of the Secretariat and to the various bodies of the UN on general questions relating to the collection, interpretation and dissemination of statistical information.

Thus, these four functional commissions have been contributing, from their very inception, useful input to the economic and social programmes of the United Nations. In 1981, however, under financial

[8] The first issue of this study was brought out in 1952 and was published once in two years, but financial constraints led to its publication being reduced to once in four years. The first issue in the quadrennial series came out in 1974.

pressure, the ECOSOC was obliged to limit their biennial sessions to just eight working days, thus further reducing their financing to the possible minimum.

The two committees composed of experts, for which both travel and subsistence allowances of members are met out of the regular UN budget are:

The Committee of Experts on Crime Prevention and Control

Composed of twenty-seven members, one of its major tasks is preparing the agenda for the sessions of the international congresses on crime and the treatment of offenders. The Committee also reports on the progress made in implementing the resolutions of the previous congress.[9] The first UN congress on the subject was convened in 1955. The eighth congress met in Havana, Cuba, from 27 August to 7 September 1990, congregating hundreds of diplomats, representatives of intergovermental and non-governmental organizations, jail warders, police chiefs, criminologists, jurists, sociologists and others with the expertise relevant to this social problem. Its five-point substantive agenda dealt with international terrorism and organized crime, especially drug trafficking, juvenile justice, conditions of prisoners world-wide and community-based alternatives to traditional imprisonment.

Besides convening such congresses periodically, the functions of the Committee also include the promotion and cooperation among the concerned UN bodies and the discussion of major issues related to social defence, including juvenile delinquency and the prevention and detection of crimes and treatment of offenders. More importantly, it has provided input for the international development strategies for

---

[9] The Economic and Social Council in August 1948 adopted a Resolution to the effect that the United Nations should assume leadership in the promotion of work in this field, making the fullest use of the knowledge and experience of competent international organizations such as the International Penal and Penitentiary Commission (IPPC). Negotiations between the United Nations and the Commission which had been functioning since 1872, led to an agreement providing for its dissolution and for the transfer of its functions to the United Nations. Subsequently in 1951, the IPPC was dissolved and integrated into the United Nations. This agreement was approved by the General Assembly in 1950. One of the responsibilities which the United Nations assumed was the convening of periodical international congresses, a function which the IPPC performed from 1872 to 1950.

successive decades, from the 1960s to 1990s. The Committee meets once in two years for eight working days.

The Committee of Development Planning

Composed of twenty-four members, it was established in 1966 and is the only UN Committee dealing with development issues at the global level, representing various economic systems. It meets annually to consider policy analysis and the problems encountered in implementing development plans and monitors the progress (or lack of it) of international development strategies for the UN Development Decades. The Committee's contribution has been widely acknowledged as an effective mechanism involving outside experts to provide intellectual inputs to the economic and social sectors of the United Nations. Its reports and recommendations, however, have not had the desired impact as even the ECOSOC has little opportunity to discuss them in detail, much less seek their implementation. While it is desirable that the various UN bodies concerned with operational activities and development planning give serious consideration to its recommendations, the question of funds and lack of political will have hampered global planning and its implementation.

Other Subsidiary Bodies

Apart from the functional commissions and standing committees already mentioned the other subsidiary bodies whose meetings are serviced by the Secretariat are:

The Committee of Experts on the Transport of Dangerous Goods

This Committee was set up by the ECOSOC[10] in 1957 to list dangerous goods and make appropriate recommendations for their transport. Governments were requested to lend the services of their experts to

[10] Following a proposal of the Transport and Communication Commission of the ECOSOC in 1950, a committee of experts to discuss the various aspects of the transport of dangerous goods was appointed in 1954. It helped identify and classify dangerous goods and also made recommendations concerning the listing, ceiling and shipping of such goods.

the Committee. The travel costs as well as the fees for the experts are borne by the respective governments. Initially composed of experts from nine countries—Canada, France, Italy, Japan, Norway, Poland, the UK, USA and the USSR—the Federal Republic of Germany joined the Committee later. Membership was increased to fifteen in accordance with the 1975 Resolution of the ECOSOC to include the representation of the developing countries. As of now, however, there are only thirteen members, as only three developing countries—Iraq, Iran and Thailand—named their experts to the Committee. The permanent missions of Brazil and China have participated as observers of the Committee since 1985. In 1987, India also expressed an interest in participating as an observer. It is essential for India, as for the other developing countries, to develop the sufficient expertise to attend subsequent meetings as full members. The work of the Committee covers all modes of transport and has provided a useful base for follow-up action in the specific areas which fall under the classification of dangerous goods. As the developing countries are involved, either as exporters or importers of such goods, they have vital stakes in the discussions and recommendations and the formulation of regulations governing the transport of such goods.

The periodic meetings of the Committee, do not involve any expenditure for the United Nations other than the servicing of the meetings. In a sense the involvement of the Secretariat is minimal, as the basic documents and studies for the meetings are provided by the OECD.

The Ad hoc Group of Experts on International Cooperation in Tax Matters

This Group was established by the ECOSOC Resolution 1273/XLIII of 4 August 1967. It consists of twenty-five experts and administrators— ten from the developed and fifteen from the developing countries— appointed by the Secretary-General to serve in their individual capacities. The Group was instituted with a view to promoting the flow of investments useful to the economic development of the developing countries, by suggesting ways and means of facilitating the conclusions of tax treaties between the developed and developing countries. Initially it met biennially but lately its convening has been staggered and it meets, as and when indicated by the ECOSOC. The travel and subsistence allowances of its members are paid for by the United Nations. It is the only international body where tax experts from the developed and developing countries can exchange information pertaining to double taxation, national tax policies and other related issues.

Inadequate expertise, however, has been responsible for the lack of active participation by the developing countries. The Group's proceedings are dominated by the World Bank and the OECD, as documentation is largely provided by experts at their own cost. Of late, the practice has been that the agenda is prepared on the basis of documents available. It is desirable that the Group of 77 be better represented but the question of the availability of expertise has left, even today, one position for the developing countries lying vacant. The ECOSOC's heavy work load merely allows for the reports to be taken note of. One viable solution is for the plans to be reformulated, so that the agenda not only reflects the interest of experts (inevitably dominated by those from the OECD) but includes the priorities set by the ECOSOC and other UN bodies. It is also necessary to revise the Group's mandate, the frequency of its meetings and reporting procedure.

Inter-governmental Committee on the Development and Utilization of New and Renewable Sources of Energy

Membership is open to all members of the United Nations interested in participating in this programme. The Committee meets once in two years. While the travel costs and per diem of the members are met by their respective governments, the UN expenditure relates to the servicing of the Committee and the preparation of reports and research work. For the work, undertaken by the DIESA, the expenditure on this programme in 1986–87, amounted to $1.7 million. The personnel employed include nine professionals and five in the general service category. The Committee reports to the General Assembly through the ECOSOC.

The oil price hike in 1973 affected countries all over the world, but the plight of the oil-importing developing countries was acute. The need for substantial and rapid progress in the transition from an international economy primarily dependent on hydrocarbons to the development and introduction of new and renewable sources of energy in order to meet future requirements, particularly in the developing countries, was widely felt. To explore this possibility and to build up a viable programme, the General Assembly convened the Conference on New and Renewable Sources of Energy, in Nairobi in 1981. The Nairobi Conference, calling for a long-term solution to the energy problem, adopted a programme of action pointing to transition as one of its fundamental objectives for development of new and renewable sources to meet the future energy requirements, particularly in developing countries.

In 1982 the General Assembly established the inter-governmental Committee on the Development and Utilization of New and Renewable Sources of Energy. Its programme of action focused on the great hydro-electric potential that remains untapped in Africa and Asia and on the study of bio-gas development,improved charcoal burning and geo-thermal, solar, tidal and wind power. Despite the various programmes opening up new areas of development and the utilization of new and renewable sources of energy, the Committee has been under attack by the western powers in general, and the United States in particular. The argument advanced by its critics is that energy programmes should be discussed and negotiated outside the framework of the United Nations and could best be developed and implemented by private entrepreneurs.

High Level Committee on Technical Cooperation among Developing Countries

Composed of all member-States participating in the UNDP, the Committee owes its inception to the negotiations and efforts that began in 1970 in pursuance of the International Development Strategy for the Second UN Development Decade. The strategy outlined certain principles that dealt specifically with the development and strengthening of schemes aimed at fostering the expansion of production and trade and general economic cooperation among the developing countries. It was noted that the wide scope technical expertise and equipment available among the developing countries could be used to mutual benefit. In 1974, the General Assembly, under Resolution 3251/XXIX, requested the administrator of the UNDP to take all appropriate measures for the implementation of the programme coordinated by the working group on technical cooperation among the developing countries. Subsequently, the General Assembly convened a conference on Technical Cooperation among Developing Countries in 1978, which worked out what became known as the Buenos Aires Plan of Action for Promoting and Implementing Technical Cooperation among Developing Countries (TCDC) within the UN system. In 1979, a unit of the TCDC was opened within the UNDP. Some funds were made available from the UNDP but its staffing has been inadequate and funds scarce. Nonetheless, the programme has made commendable progress and, to a considerable extent, meets its own costs. The lack of support from the industrialized countries has slowed its progress but it is a viable programme which could yield immense benefits to the developing countries.

The High Level Committee meets once in two years, with the expenses of its members' travel and per diem being borne by their governments. In most cases, the personnel of the respective permanent missions participate in its working, a point that has been criticized by the western countries. The fact is that the smaller countries cannot afford travel allowances for participants coming from national capitals. The point emphasized is that the expenses of the Committee borne by the United Nations are nominal. At the same time its work has been praiseworthy.

ADMINISTRATION AND OPERATIONAL ACTIVITIES

The Office of the Director-General for Development and International Economic Cooperation

As noted earlier, one of the key recommendations of the Group of 25, in 1975, on the restructuring of the United Nations, was to create an overall agency which would represent a central structure for the implementation, coordination and monitoring of the various activities, not only of the UN proper, but also of the specialized agencies and related bodies including the IMF, IBRD and the GATT. The negotiations that followed eventually led to the establishment of the office of the Director-General. Given the fact that it performs without even a semblance of the authority or functions vested in it, this office and its establishment should be done away with. Its limited functions can easily be transferred to the DIESA and the Department of Technical Cooperation for Development. Another viable and constructive alternative demands that the office of the Director-General be endowed with more resources and complete responsibilities in the economic and social fields as recommended by the Group of 25.[11] What is important is that either the office be given the functions and responsibility intended for it or it be disbanded.

For the biennium 1986–87, the maintenance of this office cost $3.813 million, in the preceding two bienniums, 1984–85 and 1985–86, the figures were almost the same: 3.899 million. The expenditure largely covers the office establishment which, apart from the Director-

[11] *A New United Nations Structure for Global Economic Cooperation*, Report of the Group of Experts on the Structure of the United Nations System, Doc. E/AC.62/9, May 1975.

General consists of one Assistant Secretary–General, one D-II and three D-I and eight other professional category personnel.

The Centre for Science and Technology for Development

Over the decades, one of the demands of the developed countries has been that the UN undertake a programme of activities for the application of science and technology for the benefit of the developing nations. After protracted negotiations, a conference on the subject was convened in Geneva in February 1963, which led to the establishment of the Advisory Committee for the Application of Science and Technology for Development (ACASTD). The Committee was given a broad mandate, including the review of progress in the field and the proposal of practical measures for the benefit of the less developed countries. It made several meaningful recommendations but these failed to gain the support of the industrialized nations and therefore, the necessary funds to implement them. One argument advanced was that the body was composed of experts functioning in their individual capacities and that their recommendations were made without regard to governmental commitments.

In 1970, the Advisory Committee presented the World Plan of Action for the Application of Science and Technology to Development (on which it had been working since 1965), as an integral part of the International Development Strategy. The plan outlined the priorities for research and the application of existing knowledge and called for the enhancement of indigenous capabilities in the developing countries. Recognising the need for governmental involvement in the implementation of these recommendations, the ECOSOC, in 1971, established the Inter-governmental Committee on Science and Technology for Development. The Advisory Committee was maintained to furnish its expertise to the Inter-governmental Committee. A series of recommendations by the ECOSOC and the General Assembly, led to the establishment of a Preparatory Committee for convening the UN conference on Science, Technology and Development. The Conference, convened in Vienna, from 20–31 August 1979, adopted a series of recommendations and the Vienna Programme of Action. The main objectives were the strengthening of the scientific and technological capacities of the developing countries, the restructuring of international scientific and technological relations, and the enhancement of the role of the United Nations system in this field.[12]

[12] For details see, *Report of United Nations Conference of Science and Technology for Development*, Vienna, 20–31 August 1979. Doc.A/CONF.81/16, UN publication Sales no.E.79.i.21.

The recommendations were adopted by General Assembly Resolution 34/218 of 19 December 1979. The institutional arrangement that emerged were:

1. *The Inter-governmental Committee on Science and Technology for Development*, open to all member-States, normally meeting once a year. The travel costs and subsistence allowances of member-States are met by the respective governments. An overall policy-making organ, it submits its reports and recommendations to the General Assembly through the ECOSOC.

2. *The Advisory Committee on the Application of Science and Technology for Development (ACASTD)* composed of twenty-eight experts, provides advice to the Inter-governmental Committee and to the General Assembly, the ECOSOC and other inter-governmental bodies of the United Nations. It normally meets once a year for a period of two weeks.

3. *UN Centre for Science and Technology for Development (UNCSTD)*, instituted as a new organizationally distinct entity in the UN Secretariat, under the supervision of the Director-General for Development and International Economic Cooperation. It replaced the former Office of Science and Technology. The Centre's activities aim at the implementation of the Vienna Programme of Action, under the direction of the Inter-governmental Committee.

4. *The UN Financing System for Science and Technology for Development (UNFSSTD)*, instituted to finance a broad range of activities aimed at strengthening the endogenous scientific and technological capacities of developing countries. Over the years, however, it failed to receive the appropriate contributions from the developed countries with the result that the financing systems accumulated the meagre sum of $50 million as against the initial target of $250 million. In January 1987, the UNFSSTD was terminated and instead, a trust fund in the UNDP established.

For the biennium, 1986–87, the Centre's budget allocation was $4.22 million which included an expenditure of $3,60,000 approximately, covering the travel of members of the Advisory Committee and of the staff from five regional commissions (one member from each). The Centre engages the services of seventeen professionals and fifteen general service and other category personnel.

The Centre for Science and Technology for Development, together with its policy-making organs, has proved to have provided the most viable activity in this field in rendering valuable services to the developing world. It works in close cooperation with all relevant members of the UN system and in liaison with the governments established through a network of national focal points. The Centre also maintains links with other bodies within the UN system, particularly through the mechanism established by the ACC to act in this field, such as the joint inter-agency Task Force on Science and Technology for Development. Member-States as well as individuals have received considerable help from the Centre in setting up their own science and technology systems in their respective countries. By 1986, nearly 75 per cent of the developing countries had information systems relating to science and technology, some quite developed and sophisticated and capable of interacting with external information facilities. The Technology Information Pilot System (TIPS) sponsored by the Centre has linked several developing countries, including India, into an information network, sharing their knowledge. Likewise, the Advance Technology Alert System (ATAS) has been an important milestone in the field, in informing all member-States of the implications of new technologies and the assessment of their use for development. In sum, this is one major programme which needs to be strengthened further and where there is absolutely no scope for curtailing its activities in the field of development.[13] It is regrettable that the current financial squeeze has caused some of its programmes to be dropped, including the sub-programme for policy analysis and research relating to development, regional profiles on policies, institutional mechanisms and infrastructures.

India has played an important role in building up the existing UN framework in this field. Professor M.G.K. Menon, whose work from January 1977 to February 1979 prepared the grounds for the Vienna conference of August 1979 was elected chairman of the Preparatory Committee. Over the years, apart from the Indians serving on the Advisory Committee,[14] the Department of Science and Technology, Government of India, has maintained close links with the UN Centre for Science and Technology and made significant contributions to the various programmes and sub-programmes to mutual benefit. In 1977,

[13] It should be noted that science and technology is also a concern of UNCTAD. Committee composed of ninety-six members meets every two years and has a small UNCTAD Secretariat unit attached to it. This concern is confined to the question of the transfer of technology to the developing countries. Of late the UNCTAD Committee has been concerned with the preparatory work and negotiations on a strategy for the technological transformation of developing countries and the legal questions linked to new technology. Thus the two areas of activity differ and there is no duplication.

[14] Dr. M.S. Swaminathan served the Committee for two consecutive terms of three years (1980–86), followed by Professor Yashpal (1986–89).

the ESCAP established the Regional Centre for Technology Transfer at Bangalore. The Centre receives support from both the ESCAP and the UNDP. In 1985, it was renamed the UNDP-ESCAP Asian and Pacific Centre for Transfer of Technology (APCTT). The programme emphasizes technology transfers among the developing countries and seeks to help upgrade national capabilities for undertaking information services and assists in promoting self-reliant management. UNDP assistance, amounting to $1.5 million, was extended to the third phase from 1987–90. The cash contributions of the participating governments amounted to $1,60,000 for the year 1986.

The Department of International Economic and Social Affairs (DIESA)

The DIESA was restructured in pursuance of General Assembly Resolution 32/197 of 20 December 1977. Its major functions include research, studies, statistical data and other services related to (*a*) Global development issues, planning and projection; (*b*) ocean economics and technology; (*c*) world population analysis; (*d*) world statistics in various fields such as shipping, infant mortality, economic growth, trade etc., and (*e*) surveys of the energy situation in its international context. It also provides support for programme planning and co-ordination.[15]

For the years 1984–85, appropriations from the regular budget amounted to $61.67 million. This was reduced in the revised appropriation for 1986–87, to the amount of $55.78 million. During this biennium, the services of 290 professionals and 234 personnel of general service and other categories were engaged. The professionals included consultants and *ad hoc* expert groups. The expenditure also covered the representation and travel allowances of staff. The various programmes of the Department have been also supported by extra-budgetary resources which amounted to $24.39 million in 1984–85 and $23.84 million for the biennium 1986–87.

[15] Functional arrangements and budgetary allocations discussed here are as set out in the manual of the organization ST/SBG/161 of 31 March 1978 and the budgetary programme for the biennium 1986–87. However, in the wake of the reform process mandated by General Assembly Resolution 41/213 of December 1986, several changes especially in DIESA have been effected. These changes are discussed in the next chapter.

Elaborating on some of the activities of the Departments, the studies on global development issues and their planning and projection include programme elements relating to international markets and policies affecting the pace of structural adaptation; international financial flows, their contributions to development and structural changes in the developing countries and the difference in the performances of the developing countries. Interrelations between social and economic factors in development and the fiscal and financial policies for the equitable distribution of income are also included in the studies on global development issues. Work relating to ocean economics and technology has programme elements on the marine dimensions of development, the analysis of trends, state problems and approaches to coastal area development, regional background studies and substantive support for technical cooperation, marine and coastal technology, an information service and a technology review. The world population analysis relates to policy and the international development strategy for the third UN development decade, the relationship between population, policies and human rights and the status of women, the factors affecting the acceptance of family planning programmes in surveys and, studies to enhance the effectiveness of such programmes.

The DIESA also provides substantive support and implementation services to the inter-governmental bodies dealing with the programmes mentioned such as the Committee for Programme and Coordination, the Population Commission, Statistical Commission and the Committee on Development Planning. In other words, being a successor of the old Department of Economic and Social Affairs, its activities cover all economic and social matters other than those transferred to new departments or centres as a result of the restructuring of the Secretariat, in accordance with General Assembly Resolution 32/197 of December 1977. Some of its activities are in the process of being transferred to other departments. These changes are discussed in the next chapter.

The Department of Technical Cooperation for Development (DTCD)

The Department of Technical Cooperation for Development, a successor of the UN Office of Technical Cooperation, was established in

March 1978 pursuant to General Assembly Resolution 32/197 of 20 December 1977. Regarded as one of the most progressive organizational entities in meeting the needs of the developing countries, which emerged as a result of the restructuring of the economic and social sectors of the UN system during 1978–80, it is both coordinator in the UN Secretariat for technical cooperation activities and the second largest executive agency for the UNDP, after the FAO. The Department administers and supports the technical cooperation carried out by the United Nations in the economic and social sectors, *not covered by other organs, programmes or specialized agencies*. Accordingly, it provides technical cooperation to governments in the fields of economic and social development, planning development administration and finance, population, natural resources and energy and statistics. The DTCD works in concert with other organizations including the specialized agencies, the UNDP and the UNIDO. The Department also undertakes research and analysis necessary for the support of its activities. Many of its projects aim at the building up of national institutions through planning, management, training activities and the promotion of investments. Its work is supported by a research programme which identifies the most viable solutions to common development problems. It collects information from countries and inter-governmental organizations of their experiences in dealing with specific development issues, and then prepares guidelines accordingly.

Its areas of activities are divided into five major fields: natural resource development including energy, water and minerals; population; public administration and finance; and cartography and statistics. Within its energy programme the DTCD has taken projects on the development of new and renewable sources of energy. Geo-thermal projects were carried out in China, Djibouti, Ethiopia, Kenya, Romania, Thailand, Yugoslavia and India. Solar, wind and bioenergy, energy conservation, and rural energy supply projects have also been implemented in several countries including India.

The Department's direct expenditure during the biennium 1984–85, within the regular budget, amounted to $17.59 million. The revised appropriation for 1986–87 amounted to $20.61 million. Its personnel, in 1986–87, included eighty-three from the professional services and 116 belonging to the general services category. Apart from them, a number of ad hoc consultants and expert groups numbering 102 professionals, with the support services of 116 personnel belonging to the general services and other categories, were financed by extra-budgetary resources, which for the biennium 1986–87, amounted $13.7 million.

The Department's activities relating to management and the substantial support of technical cooperation projects, are mainly financed by support cost reimbursements from funding sources which are directly related to project delivery. Activities dealing with the provision of technical advice or liaison services to the World Food Programme and the United Nations Fund for Natural Resource Exploration are financed by subventions from the Programme and the Fund (extra-budgetary resources). Over the last few years, the Department has experienced serious short-falls in project delivery. One major factor for this, is that while it is based in New York and its costs are incurred in US dollars, its level of reimbursements, which are earned on project deliveries overseas, are reduced in inverse proportion to the strength of the US dollar vis-a-vis the currencies of the countries where the technical cooperation projects are executed. Despite this the Department, since its inception in 1978, has more than justified its existence. It has been a major source of the development of technical cooperation among the developing countries. Its autonomy, distinct entity and present framework should be maintained.

The Office of Secretariat Services for Economic and Social Matters (OSSECS)

The Office of the Secretariat Services for Economic and Social Matters was established, pursuant to General Assembly Resolution 32/197 of 20 December 1977, with the structuring of the economic and social sectors of the United Nations, which provided, inter alia, that the technical servicing of inter-governmental and inter-Secretariat bodies be treated as distinct functions in separate organizational entities. The functions and responsibilities of the office were set out in Doc.ST/SGB/160 of 13 October 1977 and in ST/SGB/163 of March 1978.

The Office provided all technical and secretarial services for the various UN organs, subsidiary bodies and ad hoc committees dealing with economic and social matters, including their preparatory work, as well as an inter-Secretariatal coordination machinery. For instance, it was this office which provided a central point of reference for the ACC, its organizational committee and subsidiary bodies and monitored their programme implementation. It also provided technical services to the Committee on Coordination and Programming (CCP). The term 'technical services', as applied to this office, should be distinguished from 'conference services' which is the concern of the other units of the Secretariat. The principal activities of this office related to technical services for document planning, forecasting and monitoring and editorial control to ensure that the substantive inputs to inter-governmental and inter-Secretariat meetings were translated into effective, coherent and orderly proceedings.

Its personnel included a professional staff of twenty-one assisted by eighteen belonging to the general service category. For the biennium 1984–85, budget appropriations for this office amounted to $3.92 million and for the biennium 1986–87, to $4.38 million. This wing of the Secretariat was the first to receive the axe as a result of the economy measures recommended by the Group of 18. Most of the functions of OSSECS have been transferred to other departments.[16]

REGIONAL ECONOMIC COMMISSIONS

The Regional Economic Commissions are subsidiary bodies of the Economic and Social Council. It is interesting that the inception of what became the Regional Economic Commissions emanated from UN concern, beginning 1946, for the economic reconstruction of war-devastated areas. At the request of the General Assembly, the Economic and Social Council, on 21 June 1946, established a temporary sub-Commission on Economic Reconstruction of War-Devastated Areas, to examine the nature and scope of the problems of those countries which faced great and urgent tasks in this field. In the course of its work, the sub-Commission divided itself into two working groups—one for Europe and North Africa and the other for Asia and the Far East. Following the report of the groups, the General Assembly, in its Resolution 46(1) of 11 December 1946, recommended, inter alia that

---

[16] Whether such a move was in the right direction remains contentious and is discussed in the concluding section of this study.

in order to give effective aid to the countries devastated by war, the Economic and Social Council, at its next session, give favourable consideration to the establishment of an Economic Commission for Europe (ECE) and an Economic Commission for Asia and the Far East (ECAFE).[17] Consequently, the ECOSOC in its Resolutions 36(IV) and 37(IV) of 28 March 1947 established the two Commissions. The same year the Latin American countries also requested the creation of an economic commission for their region and the unanimous demand, through the Organization of American States (OAS), led to the establishment of the Economic Commission for Latin America and the Caribbean (ECLAC), in 1948. In the decades that followed, the Commissions were found to have done very useful work and similar Regional Commissions were established for Africa in 1958 and for West Asia in 1970.

In recognition of the fact that many of the economic and social problems are dealt with at regional levels, the General Assembly, in 1977, declared the Regional Commissions the main general economic and social development centres, within the UN system, for their respective regions. All actions taken by the Commissions are intended to fit into the framework of the overall economic and social policies of the United Nations. They work closely with other UN agencies, intergovernmental and non-governmental organizations and can make recommendations directly to the member governments and the specialized agencies. The basic functions of all the Commissions are almost identical in as much as their aim is to assist in raising the level of economic activity in their respective regions and to maintain and strengthen economic relations of the countries in each region, both among themselves and the countries of the world. Increasingly, the commissions have undertaken development programmes. After studies and research analysis, the issuance of statistics and in collaboration with the other UN bodies and specialized agencies, the Commissions undertake policy programmes of technical assistance.

The amounts appropriated from the regular budget during the bienniums 1984–85 and 1986–87 were: for the Regional Commission for Europe, $22.78 and $30.94; for Economic and Social Commission for Asia and the Pacific, $34.99 and $34.84; for the Economic Commission for Latin America and the Caribbean, $43.21 and $39.28; for

---

[17] ECAFE was renamed appropriately, in 1974, the Economic and Social Commission for Asia and the Pacific (ESCAP).

the Economic Commission for Africa, $46.35 and $46.06; for the Economic Commission for Western Asia, $27.30 and $32.72. In addition to the financial support from the regular budget for their activities, the Regional Commissions also have a share in the extra-budgetary resources available with the United Nations (for instance, with the UN offices for population activities, environment, energy, food etc.). In many cases, the relevant units of the Regional Commissions also act as executive agencies of the UNDP and coordinate their activities with the specialized agencies.

There are several areas in which there appear to the duplication of work in terms of programmes and nomenclatures of offices and departments in the UN Secretariats at New York, Geneva and Vienna and those of the five Regional Commissions. What appears so apparent to an educated ignoramus or a biased critic, however, can be disproved by an objective analysis. Thus such programmes as those relating to social development, environment, human settlement, statistical development and the transnational corporations are dealt with more effectively by the Regional Commissions in the regional context. Trade, shipping and food security are necessarily more global in scope but at regional levels too, there is a need to relationalise international trade procedures and remove trade obstacles. Again, the Commissions frequently organize preparatory meetings at the regional level for global conferences convened by bodies of the United Nations, such as the International Conference on Population (1984) and the World Conference to Review and Appraise the Achievements of the UN Decade for Women (1985).

DISASTER AND RELIEF

Ever since the very inception of the United Nations, the world body has provided, on an ad hoc basis, emergency relief to areas and peoples affected by disasters. In 1971, the General Assembly decided to establish a central office, within the UN, for the purpose of mobilizing relief more rapidly, coordinating it more systematically and reducing the risk of waste, duplication of efforts or the failure of timely supplies of essential items. Consequently, the UN Disaster Relief Office (UNDRO) began operating in March 1972, basing its headquarters in Geneva.

The Office has three broad functions of mobilisation, preparedness and prevention. The first is to ensure that in the case of disaster, emergency relief activities are mobilized and coordinated so as to supply the needs of the stricken area in a timely and effective manner. The second function is to raise the level of pre-disaster planning and preparedness, including disaster assessment and relief management capability in disaster-prone developing countries. The third function of prevention, is to promote the study, control and prediction, including the collection and dissemination of information, of technological developments. All three functions depend, for their adequate performance, upon the flow of information, both into and out of the UNDRO, and it was in recognition of this reality that a fourth sub-programme, disaster information, was included in the medium-term plan for the period 1984–89.

The Office has a staff of twenty-two professionals and fourteen personnel of the general services category. In addition, the ad hoc services of professionals and thirteen from the general services category are met by extra-budgetary resources. The contributions from the regular budget for the biennium 1984–85, as per the revised appropriation, amounted to $3.68 million and for the biennium 1986–87 to $3.99 million.

UN ENVIRONMENTAL PROGRAMME (UNEP)

Concern for the rapid deterioration of the environment through air and water pollution, erosion, noise, waste, biocides and other agents prompted the United Nations, in 1968, to give concerted attention to these problems by convening the UN Conference on Human Environment. The conference, convened at Stockholm in 1972, resulted in a Declaration on the Human Environment which was the first acknowledgement, by the international community, of the need to adhere to certain principles of behaviour and responsibility to safeguard the human environment. The participants of the conference also adopted a programme of action calling on governments, UN agencies and other organizations, both inter-governmental and non-governmental, to take specific steps to deal with the fast deteriorating situation. As a result of the Stockholm conference, the General Assembly established the United Nations Environmental Programme (UNEP) to monitor significant changes in environmental practices. The UNEP has its headquarters in Nairobi, the first agency to be based in a developing country.

The Programme comprises a Governing Council, composed of fifty-eight members who participate in meetings at the expense of their governments, a Secretariat, headed by an Executive Director and a Fund which provides financing for environmental programmes. The resources of the environment fund, to which governments donate on a voluntary basis, are used to support projects submitted by governments, United Nations agencies and non-governmental organizations or, as devised by the Programme's decision. Its programmes include Earthwatch, an international surveillance network with three main components; (a) Global Environmental Monitoring System (GEMS) which monitors, measures and interprets selected environmental variables to provide governments with the information necessary to understand and to anticipate and combat adverse environmental changes, whether man-made or natural; (b) the International Referral System for Environmental Information (INFOTERRA) which serves as a worldwide register of sources of environment information; and (c) the International Register of Potentially Toxic Chemicals (IRPTC), which works through a network of national correspondence to provide scientific and regulatory information on potentially toxic chemicals that may be dangerous to health and the environment.

Its policy-making organ is its Governing Council which meets annually. At its 1984 session, however, it decided to meet only once in two years. To facilitate work, the Governing Council has established an inter-governmental inter-sessional preparatory committee to assist it in carrying out its mandate on the environmental perspective up to the year 2000 and beyond.

For the bienniums 1984–85 and 1986–87, the appropriations from the regular budget amounted to $9.83 million and $11.37 million. The Extra-budgetary sources for the two bienniums were $78.57 million and approximately $84 million. The overall expenditure covers the cost of servicing the meetings of the Governing Council and its preparatory committee, including the travel allowances of some participants[18]

[18] As noted earlier, representatives of member governments meet their own travel and subsistence allowances. These, however, for representatives of national liberation movements recognised by the Organization of African Unity (OAU) and for officials of the Regional Commissions, are met by the United Nations.

and the operational costs of then various programmes. In 1986–87, the UNEP Secretariat had forty-six professionals, six general services category personnel and fifty-four local level employees. In addition, there are 102 professionals, eleven general services category personnel and approximately 200 local level employees holding ad hoc or temporary positions financed by extra-budgetary resources.

Human Settlement

The UN's concern for the problems of human settlement, particularly the deteriorating quality of living conditions and the need to link urban and regional development programmes with national plans, led to the convening of the first UN Conference on Human Settlement in Vancouver in May–June 1976. Consequently, in 1977, the General Assembly decided to replace the Centre for Housing Building and Planning and its Inter-governmental Committee[19] with a comprehensive programme of Human Settlement (Habitat). The Inter-governmental Committee was replaced by the Commission on Human Settlement comprising fifty-eight members. Because of its close links with the UNEP, Habitat headquarters were also established at Nairobi. The Centre moved to its new office in 1984. The Centre serves as a focal point for actions recommended in the Vancouver plan and to coordinate human settlement activities within the UN system. Its major areas of concern include the provision of technical assistance to government programmes, the organization of meetings of experts, workshops and training seminars, the publication of technical documents, and the dissemination of information through the establishment of a global network. The technical cooperation projects in the developing regions of the world cover such areas as national settlement policies and programmes, urban and regional planning, rural and urban housing and infrastructural developments, slum upgrading and site-and-service schemes, low cost building technology, technologies for urban and rural water supplies and sanitation systems, and the establishment or strengthening of national institutions concerned with human settlement

[19] The United Nations has been concerned with the problem of housing, building and planning since 1946. To provide a more concerted effort in that direction the Committee on Housing, Building and Planning was constituted by the ECOSOC in 1962.

programmes. In 1982, the General Assembly proclaimed 1987 the International Year of Shelter for the Homeless and decided that its objectives would be the improvement of the situation of the poor and disadvantaged at both individual and community levels.

As noted earlier, the Commission on Human Settlement in the policy-making body, composed of fifty-eight members elected by the Economic and Social Council who report to the General Assembly through the Council. Travel costs and subsistence allowances of members are met by their governments. For the biennium 1984–85, the appropriation from the regular budget amounted to $7.93 million and for 1986–87, it amounted to $8.36 million. The Secretariat staff, in 1987 consisted of fifty-one professionals and thirty-five personnel from the general services category and other levels, paid from the regular budget. Forty professionals and fifty-nine personnel from the categories served on an ad hoc basis and were paid out of extra-budgetary resources.

The basic mandate for the current programme of the Habitat Centre is contained in the International Development Strategy for the Third UN Development Decade, beginning 1981. It is unfortunate that the impact of the continuing, so-called financial crisis and the demand for overall reform and reorganization of United Nations, have disturbed priorities. In attempting the restructuring of the economic and social structures of the United Nations, there appears to be a strong case for placing Habitat (the UNCHS) and environment (the UNEP) under a combined working arrangement, both for the realization of the objectives of the two programmes and for cost-effectiveness. Indeed, the existing close relationship between the UNEP and Habitat, by way of sharing conference and printing services, favours this point of view. The point is taken up in the concluding chapter of this study.

HUMAN RIGHTS

The programme of work in the field of human rights is derived from the implementation of the mandates envisaged under Article 1, paragraph 3, Article 13, paragraph 1(*b*) and Articles 55 and 56 of the Charter of the United Nations. Its objectives are to achieve international cooperation in solving problems of a humanitarian character, assisting in the realization of human rights and fundamental freedoms, and the promotion of universal respect for, and observance of, human rights and fundamental freedoms for all without distinctions of race, sex, language or religion. The programme includes the inquiry and investigation of gross violations of human rights, advisory service, the holding of seminars and the dissemination of information.

The UN Centre for Human Rights in Geneva is the focal point of the activities of the organization and the primary unit within the Secretariat that assists in carrying out the programme of work. It is responsible for executive direction and management, the implementation of policies and programmes established by the various policy-making organs and their subsidiaries, for assistance in the carrying out of good office in other diplomatic or consultant exercises and for the functions relating to programme support. The major policy-making organs of the programme are the General Assembly, the Economic and Social Council and the Commission on Human Rights. Apart from these, sub-Commission on Prevention of Discrimination and Protection of Minorities, the Human Rights Committee, the Committee on Economic and Social Rights and the Committee on Elimination of Racial Discrimination also participate in the policy-making process.[20] In addition, there are several ad hoc committees and working groups which assist the policy-making organs.

As of 1987, the UN Centre for Human Rights had on its staff forty-eight professionals and thirty-three personnel from other categories. For the biennium 1984–85, budget appropriations amounted to $10.43 million and $14.07 million for the biennium 1986–87. Extra-budgetary resources are utilised for operational activities. The estimates for 1986–87 included $28,300 for the Trust Fund Programme of the Decade for Action to Combat Racism and Racial Discrimination; $600,000 from Voluntary Funds for Victims of Torture; and $428,000 for

---

[20] The Human Rights Committee of eighteen experts which came into being in 1976, monitors the implementation of the International Covenant on Civil and Political Rights. The Committee on Economic and Social Rights (eighteen experts) established by the ECOSOC, in 1985, as its subsidiary body, advises the Council on its work towards the realization and observance of the rights enshrined in the International Covenant on Economic, Social and Cultural Rights. The Committee on Elimination of Racial Discrimination (CERD), which came into being in 1969, monitors the implementation of the International Convention on Elimination of Racial Discrimination. The travel and subsistence allowances of all three committees as well as that of the sub-Commission are met out of the regular budget. Members of the UN Commission on Human Rights, however, participate at their own expense.

the Committee of Elimination of Racial Discrimination. The total estimate in 1986–87, of extra-budgetary resources assisting the programme, amounted to $1.15 million.

INTERNATIONAL DRUG CONTROL

The control of narcotic drugs has been a world concern ever since the first international conference on the subject was held in Shanghai in 1909. A series of treaties adopted under the auspices of the UN, exercise control over the production and distribution of narcotic drugs and psychotropic substances, combat illicit traffic, maintain the necessary administrative machinery and report to international organs on their actions. The two policy-making organs of the UN concerned with international drug control are the Commission on Narcotic Drugs and the International Narcotic Control Board (INCB). Reporting to the General Assembly and the ECOSOC, the forty-member Commission holds regular biennial sessions at Vienna. The INCB, consisting of a president, two vice-presidents and ten members, is mandated to meet twice a year but may meet more often at its discretion. In recent years, it has not held more than the stipulated sessions. For the biennium 1984–85, the appropriation from the regular budget was $6.47 million and for the biennium 1986–87, the revised appropriation amounted to $7.15 million. As noted earlier, the UN's budgetary provisions are largely indicative of the collective concern of the international community. A major part of the programme is financed by extra-budgetary resources which, for the biennium 1986–87 amounted to about $45 million. The International Narcotic Control Board Secretariat consists of thirteen professionals and eleven personnel of other categories including locals. The UN Fund for Drug Abuse Control (UNFDAC) which is financed entirely by voluntary contributions was established in 1970. The Secretariat attached to it has seven professionals and six of other categories. Expenses are met through extra-budgetary sources.

This is one programme of UN activity which reflects recognition of the ever growing interdependence of the world and of the fact that no nation or state, however powerful, can tackle the problem unilaterally. International action, at the global level alone, is the way to meet the

menace of illicit trafficking and its horrific consequences. It is grati-
fying to note that there is no controversy of substance on this UN
programme among member-States whether belonging to the East,
West, North or South.[21]

INTERNATIONAL TRADE AND DEVELOPMENT

The key organization for trade and development, envisaged at the
inception of the United Nations died at birth when its Charter, which
was ratified by fifty-four governments, failed to obtain the ratification
of the US government. As an ad hoc arrangement to what would have
emerged as the International Trade Organisation, the General Agreement on Tariffs and Trade (GATT) was instituted in January 1948. *It
should, however, be noted that the GATT is not directly linked with
the United Nations.* Over the decades, the Agreement has brought
about significant movement towards the liberalization and expansion
of international trade particularly among the developed countries. The
benefits to the developing countries arising out of the GATT negotiations, however, have been merely a by-product of the items of
interest to the major developed nations on which the talks have been
concentrated. In the early 1970s, the concepts of nonreciprocal, preferential and differential treatment for the developing countries were
entered into part IV of the GATT, but these principles have been
severely eroded by the subsequent trade policies and practices of the
industrialized countries. In brief, the existing structure of the GATT
cannot meet the needs of the developing countries.

[21] As noted in the introduction, this chapter analyses the UN structure and programmes as evolved, before the ongoing efforts for restructuring and revitalisation in the
economic and social fields were initiated in 1987. In several important areas, there have
been no meaningful breakthroughs because of the lack of agreement among member-
States. Nonetheless, in the area relating to drug abuse control, constructive changes are
being implemented. The General Assembly Resolution 45/179 of 21 December 1990
adopted the Secretary-General's recommendation (A/45/652, and Add.1, Annex.) to
institute a single integrated UN structure for Drug Abuse Control.

The United Nations Conference on Trade and Development (UNCTAD)

International trade plays a key role in economic development, not only through manufacturing and commodities, but involving related issues such as shipping, insurance, freight, traffic barriers, preferential and differential trade practices and the transfer of technology among others. As such, these issues have been the subject of discussion, not only of the Economic and Social Council, the General Assembly, and related bodies, but also of the Regional Economic Commissions.[22] Nonetheless, the UNCTAD remains the main body directly concerned with the whole gamut of international trade problems. Its major activities include money, finance, manufacture, commodities, economic cooperation among the developing countries, trade between countries with differing economic and social system, technology transfers, trade promotion and export development.

Right from its inception, the UNCTAD has not been looked upon with favour by the industrialized countries,[23] which have attempted to undermine the process of consensus-building and of reaching formal agreements. According to the consensus procedure agreed upon in 1964, if a limited number of countries or a group felt that its vital national interest was going to be adversely affected by a decision to be taken by the UNCTAD or its committees, it could ask for the suspension of voting and the initiation of a conciliation procedure. Only after the conciliation procedure was exhausted, could there be resorting to a majority vote. It is intriguing to note that the industrialized countries have never resorted to the conciliation procedure. After hard bargaining they would agree to a compromise or the so-called consensus, but the decisions thus reached have rarely been implemented.

---

[22] The United Nations Conference on Trade and Development was established in 1964 as an organ of the General Assembly. It was soon reduced to functioning as a tabloy for the developing countries to meet the two power groups in, without even appearing as a pressure group of the majority.

[23] For a critical appreciation of the UNCTAD's role, see in particular, Stanley J. Michalak, 'UNCTAD as an Agent of Change' in David P. Forsythe, *The United Nations in the World Political Economy*, London: Macmillan, 1989, pp. 69–85; also P.K. Dave, *et al.*, 'The United Nations Conference on Trade and Development and General Agreement on Tariffs and Trade and India' in Malcolm S. Adiseshaiah, ed., *Forty Years of Economic Development: UN Agencies and India*, New Delhi: Lancers International, 1987, pp. 157–76.

One glaring example was the integrated programme for commodities and the agreement establishing the Common Fund for Commodities which was adopted by the UNCTAD negotiating Conference in 1980. It became operative only in June 1989, having obtained the necessary number of ratifications, but without the support of some of the major developed countries including the United States of America. It is too early to say how this relatively new fund will to fare.

Currently, apart from the Trade and Development Board which meets biannually and the Conference which meets once in four years, the UNCTAD has several committees. These are the Committee on Commodities, the Committee on Manufactures, the Special Committee on Preferences, the Committee on Invisible Financing related to Trade, the Committee on Shipping, the Committee on the Transfer of Technology and the Committee on Economic Cooperation among Developing Countries. Also involved with the UNCTAD are the Inter-governmental Group of Experts on Restrictive Business Practices, the Permanent sub-Committee on Commodities (cocoa, olive oil, natural rubber, nickel and tin) and the Permanent Group on Synthetic and Substitutes (see the organizational chart of the UNCTAD). The Conference remains the most significant forum for harmonizing trade policies, resolving differences and promoting economic development. Its studies and reports contribute vastly to the understanding of the issues involved and provide the grounds for negotiations. Over the years, major segments of the international strategies for the UN development decades and the new international economic order, as well as a large number and variety of specific proposals for international actions in the field of trade and development, have originated and evolved either directly or indirectly, from the UNCTAD studies and deliberations.

From its inception, the UNCTAD Secretariat has provided conference service facilities to all three major groupings, and technical and substantive advice to the developing countries at their request. It has, perhaps, been the only Secretariat within the UN proper which has initiated proposals for the consideration of government representatives—a feature usually within the scope of the secretariats of specialized agencies. It should be noted that while the industrialized countries have built up their own organizations (e.g., the OECD) the developing countries have neither an organization nor the resources to equip themselves with the necessary data and technical information needed for negotiating with the other two groups. As such, they rely largely on the UNCTAD's technical services, another bone of contention with the developed countries, who have argued that the assistance, to one group of member governments, is incompatible with the international character of the UNCTAD Secretariat. Nonetheless, member governments of all groups have tended to accept the practice not only as unavoidable but useful. Of late, however, some of the developed countries have became more critical and seem determined to take a firmer line against the traditional role of the UNCTAD Secretariat.[24]

Over the years the UNCTAD has succeeded, in fair measure, in evolving the procedures and modalities for negotiations aimed at consensus-building among the member-States and groups thereof. The Technical Cooperation Service, which is responsible for the programme management of the operational activities of the UNCTAD, implemented approximately 110 technical assistance projects, eighty financed by the UNDP and thirty through bilateral donations. Its functions involve coordination between the substantive divisions and programmes of the UNCTAD and liaison with the UNDP and other executive agencies. The responsibilities of the services include the development and delivery of technical cooperation projects in cooperation with the divisions and programmes, and guidance and assistance to them in the formulation of project documents. With the exception of the post of the chief, which is financed by the regular budget, the staff of the services is financed from support cost reimbursements. Over the last few years, however, the volume of technical cooperation projects implemented by the UNCTAD has declined much, largely because of the funding constraints of the UNDP. Needless to say, its operations need to be strengthened.

The overall appropriations for the UNCTAD from the regular budget in the biennium 1984–85, amounted to $49 million and in 1986–87, to $51.94 million. Part of its expenditure is met by extrabudgetary sources. This includes the cost of services in support of programmes for technical cooperation reimbursement resources and operational costs for UNDP projects. The estimates for extra-budgetary resources for the biennium 1986–87 amounted to $19.49 million. The UNCTAD Secretariat staff, as of 1987, consisted of twenty-eight professionals and 196 personnel from the general services category whose expenses were met by the regular budget. In addition, eleven professionals and twenty-nine from other categories holding ad hoc appointments were paid from extra-budgetary sources.

---

[24] Thanks to financial and political pressures, changes are fast taking place in the Secretariat to the satisfaction of the developed countries. This is discussed in the concluding chapter.

The International Trade Centre (ITC): The Centre, instituted in 1964 by the GATT, became a joint enterprise of the UNCTAD and GATT, effective 1 January 1968, on a continuing basis and in equal partnership. Concerned mainly with trade promotion and export development within the existing regulations and mechanism governing it, the Centre promotes exports of the developing countries and improves their import operations and management, thus increasing their foreign exchange earnings. Substantial research and development on trade promotion and export development techniques, undertaken at its headquarters in Geneva, has made the Centre the leading institution in the UN system.

Under the overall management-responsibility exercised by the Executive Director, the Centre operates through five divisions.

1. The *Division of Technical Cooperation* dealing with the preparation, substantive management and supervision of the Centre's field projects is composed of four officers (one each for Africa, Asia and the Pacific, Latin America and the Carribean, and Europe, the Mediterranean and the Middle East). The Division is mainly responsible for the planning and development of programmes relating to the institutional infrastructure for trade promotion at the national level and for the implementation of integrated international projects that incorporate activities related to other programmes as well.

2. The *Division of Specialized Services* provides a comprehensive range of consultancy, research, technical support and related services in trade promotion functions and techniques.

3. The *Division of Product and Market Development* provides technical support to the entire programme in the form of trade information, market intelligence and product and market development.

4. The *Division of Programme, Finance and External Relations* which is responsible for establishing the Centre's medium-term plan, coordinates the planning and monitoring of technical cooperation programmes including their presentation to trust fund donor countries, the preparation and control of the Centre's regular budget and the financial management of its resources, the provision of general services and the coordination of the Centre's external relations.

5. The *Division of Personnel Management* deals with matters pertaining to the Centre's employees, including prospection for and the recruitment of field staff and experts for the various projects.

India, as many other developing countries, has been both a contributor and beneficiary of the technical cooperation extended by the ITC to developing countries. It has some forty-five technical cooperation projects carried out annually through major export promotion councils and commodity boards. Through the ITC, the developing countries arrange export promotion and market-tours. The training of personnel and market research is also provided for countries seeking such assistance. The ITC assists Indian participation in various trade fairs and provides export marketing advisors as well as equipment and support services abroad.

The overall expenses of the Centre are financed by the regular UN budget; and extra-budgetary resources. The regular budget is evenly shared by the GATT and the United Nations. For the biennium 1984–85 it amounted to $15.174 million. The apportionment from the UN budget was $7.89 million, approximately. For the years 1986–87, budget estimates amounted to $17.23 million, of which the UN and the GATT contributed $8.1 million each, the balance of $1.029 million, being met from miscellaneous incomes. As of 1987, the Centre's staff comprised sixty-five professionals and seventy-eight personnel of the general services and other categories. An additional staff of seventy professionals and forty-three from the general services category held ad hod appointments. The expenditure was met by extra-budgetary resources which, for the biennium 1986–87, amounted to $60.17 million.

On 1 January 1984, the Centre was granted an executive-agency status in the UN Development Programme in respect of its trade promotion activities. Over the years, however, the Centre has experienced serious financial constraints. Unable to increase the resources made available by trust fund donors to the required level, the Centre has failed to respond fully to new requests from the developing countries for a number of technical cooperation activities. It is necessary to increase the Centre's limited resources which could then be devoted to programmes currently heavily dependent upon Trust Fund contributions. The contributions, subject to fluctuation, both in terms of donor country priorities set in most cases on a yearly basis, and in terms of currency fluctuations, the contributions being made in international currency, have hampered vital areas of the Centre's progress.

REFUGEES

The two major programmes concerning refugees are the office of the High Commissioner for Refugees which deals with human rights problems the world over and the UN Relief and Works Agency for Palestine (UNRWA) which deals exclusively with the Palestinian issue. Only 2 to 4 per cent of their respective overall costs are met by the regular UN budget; the major portions of their expenditure are financed through voluntary contributions from member-States and from private sources. Both programmes are essential and there has been little or no demand for curtailing the minimum expenditure incurred by the UN. Indeed, this token contribution should continue as it represents a global involvement and responsibility for the welfare of refugees. Although the relief work provided by the UNRWA to Palestinian refugees has its humanitarian aspect, the entire problem has political dimensions and therefore constitutes part of the political activities of the United Nations. Hence, it is not necessary, for the purpose of this study, to discuss the UNRWA in detail. The office of the United Nations High Commissioner for Refugees, established on 1 January 1951, is mainly concerned with the provision of humanitarian assistance. The office provides international protection and seeks durable solutions to related problems. At the same time, it attempts to safeguard the fundamental principles of asylum, provide material assistance and ensure that the basic rights of refugees are respected and that they are treated in a decent and humane manner.

The budget of the UNHCR amounts to approximately $950 million. For the biennium 1984–85, the contribution from the regular budget amounted to $28.4 million and for the biennium 1986–87, to $36.7 million. The staff strength is some 11,000 personnel including approximately 400 professionals, thirty national officers and 400 personnel belonging to the general services category. In 1986–87, the regular UN budget covered the expenses of 120 professionals, sixty-nine general services category personnel and 101 belonging to other categories (national officers at local level). For the same biennium the number of professionals covered by extra-budgetary sources amounted to 279 professionals, 166 personnel from the general services category, and 341 from other categories.

Its policy-making organ is the Executive Committee, consisting of the representatives of forty countries and a representative of the UN Council for Namibia.[25] The Committee normally meets every year in October, at Geneva and for special sessions and informal meetings as and when required. Since 1976, a sub-committee of the whole on the international protection of refugees meets prior to the sessions of the Executive Committee to study the more technical and legal aspects of the protection of refugees. A sub-committee on administrative and financial matters was also established in 1981 to assist the Executive Committee in its consideration of the managerial, financial and administrative aspects of its work. Representatives of the Executive Committee travel at their own expense, but the travel costs of representatives of national liberation movements to the Executive Committee are met by the UN budget. This amounts to $16,000 per year on an average.

Technical Assistance: Regular Programme

The Technical Assistance (TA) programme, to assist the developing countries and provide marginal technical assistance to them, was incepted in 1948. Over the decades, it has been the one programme symbolic of the common concern of the United Nations community, in meeting its responsibility as spelled out in the Charter in general and Article 55 in particular. It was more aptly named the Regular Programme of Technical Cooperation in the GA Resolution 2514 (XXIV) of 21 November 1969. The word regular was retained, to underline that its basic character (multilateral as against bilateral assistance) was maintained and *that the expenditure, under this head, was to be met by the regular UN budget.* The same Resolution also endorsed programming and budgetary procedures as recommended by the ECOSOC in its Resolution 1434 (XLVII) of 1969.

One major orientation of the revised Programme is to complement the assistance available to the developing countries under other programmes, largely financed by extra-budgetary resources, and to provide the resources by which the substantive recommendations of the UN

---

[25] The Council, established in 1967, 'to administer' the territory of Namibia was dissolved once the country gained independence and membership of the United Nations, in April 1990.

legislative bodies can be given operational content. The Programme which comprises activities such as development issues and policies, public administration and finance, energy, human rights, human settlement, industrial development and international trade, natural resources, communication and tourism, social development, statistics and transport, is divided into three components. The sectoral advisory services and training programme are executed as deemed appropriate and essential, by the Department of Technical Cooperation for Development (DTCD), the Department of International Economic and Social Affairs, the Centre for Human Rights, the Centre for Human Settlement (Habitat), the Secretariat of the UNCTAD and the Secretariat of the Economic Commission for Europe (ECE). The regional and sub-regional advisory services are executed by the Secretariat of the Regional Commissions—the ESCAP, ECLAC, ECA and the ECWA. The third component, industrial development, is executed by the UNIDO.

The appropriation for the Technical Assistance programme for the biennium 1984–85, amounted to $32.93 million, but was reduced to $28.32 million in 1986–87, against the Secretary-General's budget proposal of $36.63 million. It was around this time that the financing of the technical programme from the regular budget came under severe strain. The socialist countries opposed the continuance of appropriations to the programme out of the regular UN budget, insisting that its work be financed entirely on a voluntary basis through the UNDP. They stopped dollar payments of the related part of their contributions to the UN budget from 1980 onwards and instead offered their assessed apportionment for the Programme's activities in their own non-convertible currencies, which of course could not be made use of outside the then Soviet bloc. The western countries also grew unenthusiastic about retaining the Programme's character. It is important, however, that the programme in its conceptualized form be maintained, as it is symbol of the common concern of the international community and its commitment to technical assistance to the developing countries. It is this representation which is significant; whether the expenditure is increased as is desirable or reduced because of the continuing financial crisis is not that important, at this stage.

TRANSNATIONAL CORPORATIONS (TNCs)

The role of the so-called multi-nationals in the world economy, especially their impact on development and international economic relations, became a subject of increasing concern to the Economic and Social Council in the early 1970s. What followed led to the establishment of a 'Group of Eminent of Persons' intimately acquainted with international economic, trade and social problems, which met during 1973–74. The Group concluded that fundamentally new problems had arisen as a direct result of the growing internationalization of production carried out by the multi-nationals. It urged the international community, through the United Nations, to tackle the problems without delay in order to ease tension and fully realise the benefits to be derived from the capital and technical know-how of the corporations.

On that basis, the ECOSOC decided, in 1974, to establish an Inter-governmental Commission on Transnational Corporations as the multi-nationals were renamed to act as a forum within the UN system for a comprehensive and in-depth consideration of the related issues. The Council also established, within the Secretariat, the UN Centre on Transnational Corporations. Its working aims at formulating an effective code of conduct and other international arrangements and agreements, enhancing contributions to development and minimising their negative effects and strengthening the capabilities of the host countries dealing with matters related to the TNCs.

The Inter-governmental Commission on Transnational Corporations remains the policy-making organ of the body. A subsidiary of the ECOSOC, it is composed of forty-eight members elected by the Council. It holds its sessions annually in New York, to which members travel at the expense of their governments. The Commission is assisted by advisor-experts numbering sixteen during the biennium 1986–87 whose travel and subsistence allowances are borne by the United Nations. They function in a private consultant capacity. The Secretariat attached to the UN Centre on Transnational Corporations (UNCTC) in 1986–87 comprised thirty-five professionals and thirty personnel belonging to the general services category. The main task of the Secretariat is the servicing of the Commission on Transnational Corporations and the annual session of the inter-governmental working group of experts on international standards of accounting and reporting. It also produces reports and studies, many of which are issued as sales publications. The Centre's joint units with the five Regional Commissions essentially perform liaison and support functions. The regional units also collect data and undertake research on the operations of the Transnational Corporations in their respective regions, provide technical assistance and advisory services to governments on request and provide the input for the UN Centre in New York on related matters and on the code of conduct at the national and regional levels. The budget estimate for the TNC's appropriation in 1984–85 was $9.78 million, which, in 1986–87, was revised to $10.17 million. In addition, its operational activities and advisory services are supported by extra-budgetary sources which, in 1986–87, were estimated to amount to $4.12 million.

The Centre, as part of the UN Secretariat in New York, and its joint units in the Secretariat of the five Regional Commissions, has more than justified its existence. It has brought out invaluable studies on the role and impact of Transnational Corporations in several sectors, notably banking, commodity trading, the food and pharmaceutical industries, insurance and tourism. The Centre organizes training workshops for officials, responds to inquiries for specific information and makes advisors available to the governments of developing countries with a view to strengthening their negotiating capacity when dealing with Transnational Corporations. Particular mention should be made of the Centre's voluminous study entitled: *License Agreements in Developing Countries: An Analysis of Key Provisions*, which was released in November 1987. The study, based on consultations with public and private ˌector organizations and the licensing situations of a large number of countries, provides a practical guide to negotiation. The study also provides overviews and sample clauses with separate analyses for major topics to be considered within the four corners of a licensing agreement.

While the Centre's valuable services to the developing countries and the UN concern with the TNCs are welcome developments, the process of achieving one of its main objectives—an agreed code of conduct for the TNCs—highlighted the need for UN action in two related areas. Therefore, to combat the corrupt practices of the TNCs and to meet the need for international standards of accounting and reporting, two intergovernmental bodies were established, on an ad hoc basis, by the ECOSOC. They are the Ad hoc Inter-governmental Working Group on the Problem of Corrupt Practices and the Inter-governmental Working Group on International Standards of Accounting and Reporting.

The Ad hoc Intergovernmental Working Group on the Problems of Corrupt Practices was instituted by ECOSOC in 1981. Members of the Group are not paid by the United Nations. Their travel and subsistence allowances are met by their respective governments, leaving UN expenses, in terms of servicing meetings at a minimum. The Group's work has aroused much criticism from the industrialized countries of the West, especially the United States, although it is widely recognised that the exposure of the corrupt practices of the TNCs will help both the developed and the developing countries.

The Inter-governmental Working Group of Experts on International Standards of Accounting and Reporting is composed of thirty-four experts, elected by and reporting to the ECOSOC through the Commission on Transnational Corporations. Established in 1982, the Group has underlined the fact, as studied by the UNCTC, that the variations and complexities of the accounting and reporting procedures of the TNCs, had concealed much of their corrupt practices. The group is working towards the achievement of greater comparability with regard to the disclosures of the TNCs. Travel costs and per diem expenses of the members of the group are met by the governments concerned. The UN expenses involved air travel and per diem to one staff member of each of the five regional commissions and the servicing of the meetings, which are convened once in two years.

SUMMARY

While an overall assessment of the framework for the economic and social activities, in terms of economy and efficacy, is made in the concluding part of this study, some relevant observations on the distribution of resources and the inter-governmental structure are mentioned here. Each of the programmes, their related inter-governmental bodies and support structures in the Secretariat, discussed in the preceding pages, cover wide-ranging activities complementary to the overall objectives of the Charter. They also cover new areas of activity, which emerged from the changing conditions and needs for international economic and social cooperation, in response to the challenges posited by the growing phenomena of global inter-dependence.

That the role of the United Nations has been reduced to that of a non-factor in international economic relations, is not for lack of commitment. It was due to the constant pressure of the developing countries for a meaningful and regulatory role, that structural changes were effected during the 1970s, especially in the wake of the recom-mendations of the Group of 25 in 1975. As a result, both in terms of inter-governmental machinery and support structures in the Secretariat, the UN activities acquired priority programmes responsive to the pressing needs of the international community. What is noteworthy is that these programmes introduced multilateralism in such areas as natural resources, energy (including its new and renewable sources), the application of science and technology for development and trans-national corporations, which were hitherto treated by the industrially advanced countries largely as the exclusive domain of bilateralism and the Transnational Corporations.

While it is true that the overall performance in these areas has not fully met expectations, it is not due to the lack of coordination or organizational inadequacy as to financial constraints and the failure of the powers that be to keep to their commitments. For instance, the programme relating to the development of science and technology has not attained its desired objectives, largely because the funding from the developed countries has not been forthcoming. The obvious pre-ference of the industrialized nations for bilateral arrangements rather than multilateralism, as represented by the United Nations, has hampered the programme's progress. Most of the inter-governmental bodies have been asked to limit their sessions to eight working days. Moreover, representatives of member governments are not paid travel and subsistence allowances, with the result that the governments, instead of sending experts from national capitals, depute officials of permanent missions to handle the work. For example, the inter-governmental working group of Experts on International Standards of Accounting and Reporting, established in 1983 after painstaking pre-paratory work by an ad hoc group of experts, has a clearly defined mandate and is the only universal body to deal with accounting and reporting. It is supposed to be a committee of inter-governmental experts, but as participation is at the expense of member governments, the meetings are variably attended by diplomats of the permanent missions. Hence, its performance has left much to be desired. Criticism has also been levelled at areas of UN activity, inter-governmental bodies and support structures of the UN Secretariat, in the name of efficiency and cost effectiveness. However, a careful scrutiny of such programmes as for the development of natural resources, energy, science and technology and, transnational corporations and technical cooperation among the developing countries, which though have not fully met their objectives, have added new dimensions to UN activities and are responsive to the needs of the developing countries. Efforts should be directed to strengthen, rather than dismantle, them.

The oft-repeated criticism of parallel growth in the inter-governmental machinery, the overlapping of agenda and duplication of work,[26] is based on superficial study, incorrect information (frequently of the more newsworthy type) or on partial evidence and analysis. Over the years the Joint Inspection Unit[27] and other relevant bodies have examined the mandates and activities of the various inter-governmental bodies, and the departments and units of the Secretariat. None of the reports of the Joint Inspection Unit or the evaluation studies carried out by the Secretary-General have given any indication of duplication of work. What is more revealing is the work of the Special Commission which undertook an in-depth study of the inter-governmental bodies. Never before was such an exhaustive study

---

[26] It is unfortunate that such criticism has also been reiterated by the Group of 18 and the Group did so without any intensive study of UN functioning. This point is discussed in the concluding part of the study.

[27] The Joint Inspection Unit (JIU), following the recommendations of the Ad hoc Committee of Experts to Examine the Finances of the United Nations and the Specialized Agencies, was established on an experimental basis by General Assembly Resolution 2150/XX of 4 November 1966. Its term was extended by General Assembly Resolution 2735/XXV, of 17 December 1970 and 2924B/XXVII of 24 November 1972. In 1976, the Unit was instituted as a subsidiary organ of the Assembly by General Assembly Resolution 31/192 of 22 December 1976, the annexe of which contains the statute of the Unit.

The JIU is composed of eleven members who have the status of Officials of the United Nations but are not members of the Secretariat staff. The Inspectors have wide powers of investigation in all matters bearing on the efficiency of the services and the proper use of funds. They make on the spot enquiries and investigations in any services of the organizations of the United Nations system. They may propose reforms and make recommendations they deem appropriate. Such reports are given due consideration by their executive head or heads concerned, who are required to submit them with or without their comments to the member-States of the organizations and inter-governmental bodies concerned. Such reports have led to the adoption of precise rules and regulations and measures for economy and efficiency. Thus this kind of periodical exercise leaves little scope for duplication of work.

undertaken as was done by the Commission. All the inter-governmental bodies, their subsidiaries and respective mandates were subjected to full scrutiny. The Commission reported no duplication or work.[28]

Of course, the overlapping of agenda and discussion is inevitable. If the Trade and Development Board, for instance, is discussing matters within its purview, it cannot ignore the problems emanating from the debt burden or fiscal and monetary policies. Similarly, while discussing the problems of development, the issues cannot be raised in isolation of the related problems of the Transnational Corporations or international shipping. The weakness that has crept in to the United Nations programmes and activities in the economic and social field, is certainly not duplication but fragmentation, which for obvious reasons is inevitable. This is so because each inter-governmental body and Secretariat unit examines the question and deals with the problem within its respective sphere of competence. For instance, there are some eighteen organizations, including the Regional Economic Commissions, involved in water-related activities. The FAO is concerned with projects relating to land and water development for agricultural purposes. The WHO and the UNICEF deal with the problems of water-borne diseases, water supply and sanitation schemes. The UNESCO provides training, research and education programmes relating to the assessment of water resources. The World Meteorological Organization is concerned with hydrological surveys. The UN Environment Programme is concerned with the environmental impact of water-related activities and the UNIDO, with industrial water resources, needs and pollution control.

What was experienced in certain cases, was that a member-State was left without assistance for part of water-related problems. It was in 1978 that the DIESA and the DTCD in the UN Secretariat attempted to step in to fill such gaps. The DIESA took up the coordination of water-related activities within the United Nations' family of organizations and the DTCD focused on the technical assistance not provided by any other UN organization. It also took up the execution of projects entailing the management of ground and surface water resources in the developing countries, including the strengthening of national water legislation and administration. While what the DIESA and DTCD have attempted to do by way of improvisation leaves much

---

[28] Report of the Special Commission of the Economic and Social Council on the Indepth Study of the United Nations Inter-governmental Structure and Functions in the Economic and Social Fields (Doc.E/1988/75 of 1 June 1988).

to be desired, it is also true that the components of the various programmes need to be dealt with by agencies with the necessary competence and that the implementation of the entire programme cannot be subjected to centralism. Some degree of autonomy to the various specialized agencies and regional bodies is essential. What is needed, however, is a central mechanism to oversee the entire process, formulate policies, coordinate activities and monitor progress in the overall field of economic, social cooperation and development.

Perhaps the most significant factor responsible for the lack of success in achieving targets set by the United Nations in the economic and social fields has been its lack of influence. The body may set the pattern and guidelines for development and make recommendations on global economic issues, but it has no role in influencing the factors that dominate the existing international economic [dis]order—factors which have directly impeded the implementation of strategies and priorities for development. The powers that be, in the existing international economic system, adopt policies either unilaterally or through the collectivity of the Summit of 7 or the OECD of the twenty-four industrialized countries. Keeping their own short-term economic interests in mind and with utter disregard for their commitments to the United Nations, they have opted for policies adversely affecting the interests of the developing countries which represent two-thirds of the world's population. The point emphasized here is that what is required to make the activity in the economic and social fields more effective and viable is not so much the question of institutional or procedural reform in the UN system, as changes in the attitude and policies of member-States, especially those of the developed countries.

4

Demand for Reform :
Subsequent Developments

The preceding pages provide a detailed analysis of the United Nations framework in the economic and the social sectors, in terms of programme-planning, budgetary practices, inter-governmental structure and supporting staff in the Secretariat, as they have evolved over the last forty years and more. All the programmes and the global issues they deal with, were initiated by consensus and in response to the needs emanating from the growing interdependence of the international community. Even a cursory glance at the various programmes listed in the preceding chapter makes it clear that all of them are very important and designed to meet the objective of international cooperation for development as promised in the United Nations Charter. The question then is: is all well with the UN system and is there scope for reform and revitalization? Certainly there is. The larger question is what the 'reforms' seek to achieve. Should the objective be solely to seek efficiency and cost-effectiveness or should reform and revitalization also include efforts to recapture the sense and purposes of the United Nations in a world that is increasingly weaving the destinies of all peoples to an unprecedented degree of interdependence of welfare and mutual vulnerability?

The quest for efficiency, viability and cost-effectiveness has been a continuing process from the very inception of the UN system. Ad hoc committees, instituted for the purpose, have recommended procedural and institutional reforms and structural changes which were duly carried out. One specific instance, during the last ten years, is that of the

Committee on Conferences which has actively and successfully been engaged in providing the optimum apportionment of conference resources, facilities and services, while rationalizing the documentation system. Thus, beginning 1981, the periodic meetings of almost all the inter-governmental bodies have been reduced to the minimum—a session of eight working days in two years.

Measures to bring about the desired reform in programme-planning and related matters were also initiated. Reference here, in particular, is to the measures initiated by the Secretary-General, in 1984, in response to General Assembly Resolution A/37/234 of 21 December 1982, which formulated the regulations and rules governing programme-planning, the programme aspect of the budget, monitoring, implementation and methods of evaluation (ST/SGB/204). These rules and regulations, endorsed by the General Assembly, have been progressively implemented. Again, the fact of the Secretariat becoming top-heavy had already claimed the attention of the Secretary-General and member-States of the United Nations, in the early 1980s, and the former initiated the efforts to streamline its structure. Furthermore, the Joint Inspection Unit, which includes at least four nationals from the countries, making major contributions to the United Nations budget, has been actively engaged in in-depth investigations followed by reports for necessary action with a view to maintaining the efficiency and cost-effective functioning of the UN system. Other subsidiary bodies such as the CPC and the ACABQ have been doing their part as per their respective mandates towards the same objective. Yet suddenly, the demand for reform and reorganization in the name of efficiency and cost-effectiveness acquired crisis proportions in 1985–86.

UN UNDER ATTACK

What has rocked the United Nations since 1985–86, has not been a bolt from the blue, but a calculated onslaught built up, bit by bit, through sustained attacks on the organization. It is common knowledge that once the Reagan-Bush administrations took over, concerted and well-planned efforts have been directed at shaping the United Nations to American conformity or else paralyzing its functioning. First the United States' right-wing unleashed anti-UN fulminations in which the Heritage Foundation took a lead. Its studies and reports, distorting facts and figures, demonstrated that what was happening in the United Nations was directed against all that the United States of America stood for.[1] US Ambassador Jean Kirkpatrick simultaneously took to aggressive rhetoric and a confrontational stance against the developing countries.[2] The US administration held out threats of withdrawal, boycotted select UN agencies and unleashed a barrage of attacks through its media and officials. It spelt out such taunts as to suggest that the United Nations could leave New York to find a home elsewhere and that the US delegation would be there to bid them a fond farewell 'as they sailed off into the sunset'.[3]

The writing on the wall as to what was in the offing was clear. One Indian diplomat not only discerned as to what was behind the US denunciation of the United Nations but also made a public statement to that effect. Addressing a public meeting in Geneva in September 1984 he succinctly noted:

> There is a massive publicity drive launched by the media ... Think Tanks have been mobilised to provide underpinning for this attack.

---

[1] See for instance, *A World Without A UN* Washington, D.C.: The Heritage Foundation, 1984. This study argues, inter alia, that a world without a UN will be a better world. Also see *Report on U.S. and the U.N.: A Balance-Sheet* by the same Foundation. Since 1982, the Heritage Foundation has brought out a series of publications denouncing the United Nations. It is interesting to note that Ambassador Charles M. Lichenstein who served as deputy to Jean Kirkpatrick at the United Nations (1980–84) and made himself 'popular' by his taunting remark of the 'United Nations' ship moving into the setting sun ...' has been a Senior Fellow at the Heritage Foundation, since 1984. Also see, in particular, an objective study by the US–based Academic Council on the United Nations System (ACUNS), which brings forth the point that in addition to right-leaning forces, the pro-Israel lobby dominates the US Congress, while the UN is presented as an anti-Israel institution. Donald J. Puchala and Roger A. Coate, *The State of the United Nations, 1988* Hanover, NH: ACUNS, 1989, pp. 19–22.

[2] See, in particular Seymour Maxwell Finger, 'Reagan-Kirkpatrick Policies and the United Nations', *Foreign Affairs*, Winter, 1983–84, pp. 436–57. Ambassador Kirkpatrick broke all diplomatic norms by sending letters to a number of non-aligned states demanding an explanation of their conduct in associating with the communique of the non-aligned countries of 28 September 1981, at Havana, which she reagrded as containing fabrications and vile attacks against the United States. Text in Richard Jackson: *Non-aligned, the United Nations and the Super Powers* New York: Praeger, 1983, pp. 300–01.

[3] This observation was made by Ambassador Charles Lichenstein on 19 September 1983 at a meeting of the United Nations and Host Relations Committee. Also see *Ibid.*

The stuff that is churned out by these Think Tanks and so prominently publicised by the media are seldom based on facts and are often simplistic and misleading in their analyses.

Being a diplomat he did not refer to the United States by name, but the text of his speech is explicit and the tenor of his criticism as trenchant as the US attack on multilateralism. Continuing his speech at the meeting he observed:

This attack on multilateralism is being projected as a desire to seek managerial and administrative reforms in the UN organization. However, the fact is that this is an attack on the very raison d'etre of the United Nations, on the very necessity of multilateral cooperation. If their intentions were only to seek managerial/administrative reforms, this could easily have been done in the various intergovernmental bodies that operate in these organizations concerned ... The fact, however, is a massive publicity drive launched by the media to deride and weaken the UN multilateral system.[4]

Despite such protests, the attack on the United Nations continued, making the UN bureaucracy nervous. The Secretary-General made several placatory remarks to please the United States in the hope that the criticism would die down. The next 'logical' step for the US after the softening process, was to raise the cry of reform, not in the political field but in the social and economic sectors of the United Nations. This had the advantage of legitimacy, as members were of the view that the United Nations was in need of reforms. The developing countries, unhappy with the inadequate role of the world body, added impetus to the movement. Gradually, the media built up the need for reform. What provided momentum to the demand, was a JIU report emphasizing the need for reform—a report, whose circulation as a UN document and its content, subsequently became contentious.[5]

[4] The speech, made by Muchkund Dubey, the Permanent Representative of India to the United Nations Office, Geneva, is reproduced in *Mainstream*, New Delhi, October 1984.

[5] The JIU report entitled 'Some Reflections on Reform of the UN' (JIU/Rep/85/9), was circulated among members of the General Assembly on the occasion of the fortieth anniversary of the UN under the symbol A/40/998 Corr.1. It forcefully argues that reform in the economic and social sectors of the UN system was indeed indispensable and that the present UN system was based on fallacious conceptions. The report was given extensive publicity in the US press even before its distribution to member-States.

DEMAND AND RESPONSE

While building up the demand for reform and reorganization, the US administration also simultaneously applied financial pressure, amounting to an ultimatum, that unless 'reforms' were carried out, the United States would paralyse the functioning of the United Nations by witholding its contribution. The attack acquired an additional threat in 1985 when the US Congress passed a resolution to cut its contribution to the regular budget to a maximum of 20 per cent, unless changes were made in the UN voting and budgetary practices. The Congressional decision called for the cut, if the UN failed, by October 1986 to introduce weighted voting and give major contributors more influence in budgetary decisions. It is true that most of the major contributors delayed or withheld, beginning the 1980s, their contributions to the regular budget. Whether they did so because they were influenced by the continued attack on the UN system through the western media or had their own grievances, is not clear. What is clear is that no member-State issued the kind of ultimatum that the United States' demand for reform amounted to.

When the ultimatum was served, the United Nations was already on the brink of bankruptcy. The additional cut in the contribution of the United States (25 per cent of the entire budget), threatened, as the Secretary-General noted in September 1985, with 'sudden prospects that the United Nations may not be able to carry out its mandated work-programme or meet its financial obligations'. (Doc.A/40/1102, Corr.1 and 2). It was as if the United Nations was being held to ransom and the General Assembly reacted with accelerated alarm by establishing the Group of High Level Inter-Governmental Experts to

---

It turned out that the report was prepared by one inspector (Maurice Bertrand) without any specified mandate and against the understanding on the subject by fellow inspectors. The majority of inspectors have disassociated themselves from the report as they were not consulted. How the report was circulated as a General Assembly document remains a moot point. It should also be noted that when the report was sent to the various participating organizations, it was not given consideration as it was issued in violation of the rules.

It is interesting to note that the author of the report, soon after its publication, joined the UNA–USA project on UN Management and Decision Making as a senior consultant. He was also named a member of the Group of 18. This largely explains the similarities contained in the various studies of the UNA-USA and that of the reports and recommendations of the Group of 18.

of the United Nations (the Group of 18). It called for its report by
September 1986—a month before the deadline set by the US Congress.

Group of 18: A Damaging Report

The Group of 18 met in four sessions, from February to August 1986,
for a total period of eight weeks and submitted its report and recommendations in August.[6] It admitted to the fact that the time
constraints under which it had to work did not allow for a comprehensive study of some of the extremely complex problems put before
it. Its Chairman also noted that not all the relevant subsidiary organs
of the General Assembly submitted the information and comments on
matters pertaining to the groups work, as envisaged in General
Assembly Resolution 40/237 which established it.[7] The rush in com-
pleting its report without thoroughly doing the job it was assigned to
do gave rise to the obvious, that both the General Assembly and the
Group of 18, beseiged by the continuing financial crisis, were submitting to the dictates of one member, who held the power of the
purse.

The Group of 18 made, in all, seventy-one recommendations[8] for
'improving' the efficiency of the administrative and financial functions
of the United Nations. In doing so it succumbed, it seems, to US
pressure, upholding most of the criticism levelled against the organisation. In its introduction, it noted, without citing any supportive evidence,

[6] *GAOR*, Forty-first Session, Supplement no. 49 (A/41/49).

[7] Ibid., para 11. Also see, *Report of the Fifth Committee*, Forty-first Session, agenda
item 38, UN document A/41/795, 5 November 1988, paras 2–13.

[8] It is interesting to note that the United Nations Association of United States of
America (UNA-USA) had also undertaken a comprehensive study on UN management
and decision-making. The studies were prepared mostly by American scholars and there
was an advisory panel of twenty-three members; nine panallists from the US, five from
other OECD countries and nine from the countries of the developing world. Its studies
and reports followed similar approaches to the ones noted and recommended by the
group of 18, with one important difference. The UNA-USA study envisages a high
power ministerial group of not more than twenty-five member-States out of which at
least ten would have permanent seats, a recommendation which did not find a place in
the report of the Group. See, United Nations Management and Decision Making
Project, *A Successor Vision: The United Nations of Tommorrow*, UNA-USA, 1987.

To what extent the American studies, media reports and pressure from the Reagan
Administration worked is also reflected in the fact that the Secretary-General, in his
introduction to the 1987 report on the work of the organization, made somewhat similar
proposals to those contained in the UNA-USA study. See, *GAOR*, Forty-second
Session, Supplement no. 1, Add. 1.

'parallel growth in the inter-governmental machinery' and that the multiplication of the committees, commissions and expert groups resulted in the 'overlapping of agenda', 'duplication of work' and 'an overly complex structure' which suffered from lack of cohesion and made coordination difficult. Again, without specifying particular instances, the report read that the 'number, frequency and duration of conferences and meetings has reached a point of presenting difficulties to all member-States' and that the 'considerable resources allocated for such conferences and meetings are not put to maximum use', which amounted to wastage. Paragraph three of the Report recommended substantial reductions in the number of conferences and meetings and that their duration be shortened without affecting the substantive work of the organization. It found that the Secretariat's, 'structure has become too complex, fragmented and top heavy' and that the 'qualifications of its staff, in particular in the higher categories, are inadequate and the working methods are not efficient' (paragraph four).

Some of the criticism, for instance, with regard to the Secretariat structure being top heavy, was true. So was the reference to the over-staffing and proliferation of the inter-governmental bodies. However, while it was inevitable in such a vast organizational setup, for the Secretariat and the inter-governmental mechanism to have grown unwieldy, it was not through a self-propelled process, but in response to the needs resulting from the ever-escalating phenomena of inter-dependence. In any case, both the General Assembly and the Secretary-General had already taken the necessary steps to streamline the Secretariat and rationalise the inter-governmental structure in 1982. Indeed, the process of reform and restructuring has been an ongoing concern. What made the scathing observations of the Group of 18 most unfortunate was that they overtly highlighted issues peripheral to those involving the current crisis for reform and reorganization. Perhaps the most damaging part of the report was the exaggeration of some of the weaknesses of the UN system, which provided a sort of justification for the witholding of contributions to the regular UN budget by certain member-States.

Consideration by the Assembly

The forty-first General Assembly (1986) which considered the report, met under the shadow of the most serious financial crisis in UN history, threatening not only its immediate solvency, but also, as many feared, its long term viability. It was obliged to endorse the Secretary-General's economy measures to counteract the $85 million shortfall projected for 1987. And it found itself helpless to remove the widely held fear that there would not be enough cash to pay the salaries of the Secretariat staff in January 1987.[9] The worst defaulter, the United States, which owed more than $300 million refused to make any commitment on the time-schedule of its payment. It was in these circumstances that the Assembly began its consideration of the report of the Group of 18, which contained recommendations for major organizational changes, reduction in Secretariat staff and the consensus system in the budgetary process. Reaction to the report was sharp and divisive of UN membership. It was widely feared that the so-called consensus would provide a veto to major contributors, leaving the proverbial sword of Damocles hanging over future programming of the world body.

The Assembly resorted to an unusual procedure. It was decided that the report of the Group of 18 would be considered in the plenary session and that during this consideration the Fifth Committee would undertake a 'factual' examination of the Report and submit its findings to the plenary. What followed was an exhaustive consultative process. After debating the report from 10–15 October, the Assembly plenary turned it over to the Fifth Committee to undertake 'examination of its recommendations and submit its findings to the plenary'.[10] After receiving the Fifth Committee's report the President of the Assembly formed a small contact group to identify areas of agreement and divergence. This was followed by a larger consultative group of twenty-seven members to narrow the outstanding differences. Thereafter, a negotiating group was constituted which elaborated an agreed draft Resolution (A/41/L.49). The draft was then considered by a Committee of the Whole before presentation to the plenary. The resulting text (A/41.L/49/Rev.1) was sponsored by nineteen member-States, including the five permanent members of the Security Council and India, Japan and West Germany among others and adopted on 19 December, without a vote, as Resolution 41/213.

---

⁹ *UN Chronicle*, February 1987, p. 26.

¹⁰ Doc. A/41/795, 5 November 1986. Unlike the usual practice, no draft resolution was initiated and discussed at the Fifth Committee level. The Committee discussed the report of the Group of 18 at nine formal meetings held between 16 October and 5 November accompanied by eleven informal meetings and several rounds of informal consultations. Eventually, it merely made comments on each of the recommendations of the Report for consideration at the plenary.

In adopting the text of the Resolution the Assembly decided that the seventy-one recommendations as agreed upon and contained in the Report of the Group of 18 should be implemented, subject to certain qualifications. At the same time it reaffirmed the requirement of all member-States to fulfil their financial obligations, as set in the Charter, 'promptly and fully'. The Assembly also approved the reforms in the budgetary process, setting out eleven specific recommendations as contained in Part II of Resolution 41/213.

Financial Pressure Unabated

The issue of the non-payment or delayed payment of assessments remained a foremost concern of delegates throughout the debate and negotiations on the contents of the draft resolution. Several delegates of the Group of 77 made it clear that the US pay its arrears before they voted for any recommendation for reforms. The representative of the Bahamas spoke for many when he said, 'The organization should not be held hostage to the peculiarities of governments [and] no country, large or small, should be allowed to be in arrears'.[11]

On 4 December, Controller J. Richard Foren, told the Fifth Committee that the organization had received a payment of $100 million from the United States but that did not change the overall picture of the organization's financial crisis. The amount received would enable the UN to meet its day-to-day requirements only until January 1987. He also noted that the arrears of the US, as of December 1986, amounted to $284 million.[12] Earlier, the Secretary-General reported that the situation 'defeats rational forward planning and carries with it the strong possibility of the sudden interruption of programmes and Secretariat services'.[13] Despite the urgency, the US representative did not make any commitment to the payment of arrears. Obviously, the US wanted the recommendations of the Group of 18 to be endorsed first. To demonstrate the power of its purse, the US did dole out $100 million to 'save' the United Nations from bankruptcy until January 1987. The events make it clear that the measures contained in Resolution 41/213 of 19 December 1986, to carry out the so-called reforms to improve the efficiency of the administrative and financial functioning of the UN, were adopted through an improvised procedure in trying and abnormal circumstances.

---

[11] *UN Chronicle*, February 1987, p. 23.
[12] *Ibid.*, p. 26.   [13] Ibid; p. 9.

REFORMS AND THE FOLLOW-UP

Planning and Budgetary Procedure Revised

The specific recommendations of the group of 18 on programmes, planning and the budgetary process aroused great controversy and were considered to be the most crucial issues of the reforms suggested. In Section VI of its report the Group's critical assessment stated that the medium-term plan, the programme budget and the monitoring and evaluation systems were meant to constitute an integrated process, through which wide agreement should evolve on activities to be financed by the regular budget of the organization. Intriguingly, the Group did not question the validity of the medium-term plan or the methods of monitoring and evaluation. Instead it asserted that they were not properly used and that the regulations and rules were insufficiently applied. In making this criticism, the Group did not cite any specific instance.

The recommendations for programme planning and budget processing included three sets of competing proposals.[14] The first gave the twenty-one–member CPC the responsibility of advising the General Assembly, not only on programme content but also on the level of budget resources, and proposed that the CPC be renamed the Committee for Programme, Budget and Coordination. Its members were to be elected on the basis of expert capacity, but the Committee would keep its inter-governmental character. The second proposal differed from the first in as much as that while agreeing that the CPC would consider the programme aspect of the budget and of the medium-term plan, it would not be granted the right to advise the Assembly on the level of the budget. The third solution sought to entrust the functioning of both the programmes and the budget to a single inter-governmental expert body that would also have the right to recommend the overall limit of the budget. The CPC and the ACABQ were to be replaced by this single body.

All three proposals emphasized that the budgetary recommendations and decisions be made by consensus. What intrigued the larger membership of the United Nations was the emphasis on what was already the usual practice.[15] Hitherto, the budgetary process had

---

[14] *GAOR*, Forty-first Session, Supplement No. 49, pp. 27–35.

[15] While the dictionary meaning of the word consensus is the collective, but not unanimous, opinion of a group of persons, the term is used in the organizations of the UN in a slightly different sense. It implies a conclusion or decision which is not opposed by any member-State. It is significant that in the UN political process, consensus

begun with the Secretariat preparing the programme budget, keeping in view the directives of the General Assembly and other inter-governmental bodies. The CPC (an inter-governmental committee) would examine the programme content and the ACABQ (a committee of experts acting in their individual capacities) would examine the administrative and financial aspects of the programme budget. The final decision was taken by the General Assembly on the recommendation of its Fifth Committee. It should be noted that the Fifth Committee. It should be noted that the Fifth Committee, where the rule of one-member one-vote prevails, has invariably endorsed the recommendations of both the CPC and ACABQ; changes, if any, have been only peripheral. The ACABQ and the CPC have made recommendations by consensus. It is a different story that countries such as the United States and the USSR would participate in the process of consensus evolving and then cast negative votes in the Fifth Committee and the plenary.

The specific provisions as spelled out in Resolution 41/213, provided a wider mandate to the CPC. The Committee was given a key role in planning and programming as well as in the budgetary process. It retained its old name however, thus not accepting the Group's proposal that it be named the Committee for Programme, Budget and Coordination, and its inter-governmental character. It was also to be involved with the budgetary process from the initial stage. While maintaining that the CPC continue its existing practice of reaching decisions by consensus, the Resolution also reiterated complete adherence to Articles 17 and 18 of the UN Charter and full respect for the principal UN organs dealing with planning, programming and the budgetary process.

The new guidelines suggested that the Secretary-General in off-budget (even-numbered) years submit an outline of the programme budget for the following biennium indicating a preliminary estimate of resources to accommodate the proposed programme of activities. The priorities were to reflect general sectoral trends, real growth whether positive or negative, comparison with the previous budget and the size of the contingency fund. The contingency fund was introduced as a new item in the budget to express a percentage of the overall level of

denotes both a process of negotiation and its result—a practice designed to achive the elaboration of a recommendation by means of negotiation and its adoption without a vote.

resources. The percentage was included to accommodate the additional expenditure derived from the legislative mandate not provided for in the proposed budget.

The CPC, acting as a subsidiary organ of the General Assembly, was to consider the Secretary-General's programme budget outline and submit to the Assembly through its Fifth Committee, its conclusions and recommendations. On the basis of the Assembly's decision and the recommendations, the Secretary-General was to prepare his budget programme for the following biennium. Thus, the difference in the old practice and the reforms suggested was that the CPC as well as the Assembly were to be involved in the preparation of the budget from the onset. The Resolution especially emphasised that the new practice would not prejudice the mandate or functions of the ACABQ. In the budget (odd-numbered) years, the Secretary-General was to submit his proposed programme-budget to the CPC and the ACABQ in line with the existing procedure. Both Committees were to examine it in accordance with their respective mandates, and then submit their conclusions and recommendations to the Assembly through its Fifth Committee. The Assembly would then give final approval to the budget.

On the surface the changed process looked only modestly different from the preceding practice. The crucial change, however, emanating from the new process, lay in giving the members of the CPC—an intergovernmental body—a say in the content and level of resources of the budget. Hitherto, the sixteen-member expert Committee, the ACABQ, while examining the administrative and financial aspects of the budget would look to the mandate and check the requirements before making recommendations by consensus, never resorting to voting. It was doubted that the same process could be practiced by the CPC. As an inter-governmental body, making recommendation on budgetary allocation there would be no decision reached in the event of a disagreement between the major contributors and others. The new procedure adopted reaffirmed the prerogative of the Assembly as provided in Article 18 of the Charter; annexed to the Resolution is an opinion from the UN Legal Counsel that the Resolution does not in any way prejudice the provisions of Article 18 of the Charter or the rules or procedure of the General Assembly. The provisions assure each member-State one vote and provide for a two-third majority vote on budgetary questions. .

The system expected member governments to demonstrate understanding and act with vision and a sense of commitment. If the major powers were unreasonable in withholding support for certain programmes, the majority would resort to its voting power. Conversely, if the majority was unreasonable and used its voting power to pass a budget onerous to the major contributors, the major powers could resort to withholding funds. Either way programme implementation and even functioning, would have been delayed.

The standard, therefore, was to be reasonable. Whether this would be made to work was aptly noted by the then *Assembly President*, Humayun Rashid Chowdhry from Bangladesh: 'The changes introduced in the budgetary process in an effort to seek the much-eluded broadest agreement will have to undergo the acid test of practicability'.

Subsequent biennium budgets: The General Assembly, in Resolution 3043 (XXVII) of 19 December 1972, approved the introduction of a biennial budget cycle on an experimental basis. In Resolution 3195 (XXVIII) of 18 December 1973, the Assembly adopted the first programme budget of the organization for the biennium 1974–75. The same year it considered the first medium-term plan covering the period 1974–77. Subsequently, the regulations and rules of programme planning, the programme aspects of the budget, the monitoring of implementation and methods of evaluation were progressively developed and codified by the Assembly in its Resolution 37/234, dated 19 December 1982.[16]

The second medium-term plan was worked out to cover a six year period, 1984–89, while the next plan was expected to cover the subsequent six year period from 1990–95 and was to be adopted by the General Assembly at its Forty-third session in 1988. The financial crisis and subsequent developments, however, did not allow any worthwhile exercise in that direction. Furthermore, General Assembly Resolution 41/213, which embodied part of the recommendations of the Group of 18, called for certain procedural changes with regard to the adoption of the plan so that both the CPC and the ACABQ could examine it from its inception. Under the circumstances there was no scope for the adoption of the next medium-term plan by 1988. The Secretary-General therefore proposed the continuation of the expenditure based on the previous medium-term plan, for another two years, and that the next plan could cover the period 1992–97. While

---

[16] The Group of 18 did not question the validity of the instruments nor their evolutive character, but asserted that they were not properly used and that the regulations and rules were often ignored or insufficiently applied.

accepting the Secretary-General's proposal, to which of course there was no alternative, the General Assembly also agreed, at the insistence of the major contributors, that there be no increase, in real terms, in the budget of the next two bienniums and that the growth rate remain at zero.

The preparation of the biennium budget for 1988–89 followed a highly unusual exercise. The initial estimates were prepared, to quote the Secretary-General, 'during a period marked by threat to the financial viability of the organization and by a reassessment of its role and activity'.[17] He also noted that what was proposed was essentially a transitional programme budget based on activities of perennial character, the organizational structures and strength of staff (already reduced by 11 per cent) as they were at the end of 1986. The level of resources requisitioned in the programme budget 1988–89, in real terms, was below the appropriations for 1986–87. Both the CPC and the ACABQ, as had been the practice in the past, recommended the biennial budget by consensus and the Fifth Committee and the plenary of the General Assembly adopted it without any substantial change (Resolution 42/226, 21 December 1987). However, voting did take place and the budget proposals were adopted by a vote of 146 for, one against (Israel) and three abstentions (Australia, Japan and the United States).

The programme budget for the biennium 1990-91 was the first to be adopted in accordance with the procedure contained in Resolution 41/213. The report of the Secretary-General indicating priority settings and an outline of the programme budget for the biennium was presented by him (in document A/43/524) in August 1988. It was considered by the CPC and the ACABQ and on their recommendations, the budget estimates were adopted by the General Assembly through Resolution 43/214. The Resolution reaffirmed the basic rationale for the new feature of the budgetary process. It also decided on a preliminary estimate of $1767.06 million to be used by the Secretary-General as a basis for the appropriation for the biennium budgets. The General Assembly further decided to establish a contingency fund, as per the recommendations of Resolution 41/213, at a level of 0.75 per cent of the primary estimate i.e., $15 million.

The revised estimates were presented in 1989. The amount indicated a slight increase (0.4 per cent) which was vehemently resented

---

[17] Proposed programme budget for the biennium 1988–89, GAOR, Forty-second Session, Supplement number 6, A/42/6, Introduction, Part-I.

by some of the major contributors to the UN budget, especially the USA and USSR.[18] Although most of the members appreciated the reasons given by the Secretary-General for the nominal increase, a number of representatives from the developing countries expressed their disappointment at the negative growth rate of the budget in the two consecutive bienniums. It was noted that while the expenditure of the regular budget, as a result of inflation and currency fluctuations, had increased by 10.91 per cent, the level of extra-budgetary resources showed an increase of 17.72 per cent in nominal terms compared to the previous bienniums. It was therefore clear, the representative noted, 'that while certain members asked for zero growth in the regular budget, it was not because they were short of resources'.[19]

Uncertainty continues to cloud future programming and planning, specially in the economic and social sectors which are a crucial part of the activity of the United Nations system. Whether member-States act with vision and a sense of commitment to the principles of the Charter particularly those embodied in Article 55—something which has been conspicuously absent over the decades—remains a moot point.

CPC expanded: An indication of the situations likely to confront the world body on budgetary matters, arose when the expansion of the Committee on Programme and Coordination came into question. When the CPC was given a vital role in programme planning and the budgetary process, proposals were made, at the Forty-first Session of the Assembly for its expansion from twenty-one to thirty-six members to ensure broader geographical representation. The US representative, in particular, was not willing to support the expansion. Eventually, consideration of the proposal was deferred to the Forty-second Session. After protracted negotiations, a consensus was reached to expand membership to thirty-four on the basis of equitable geographical distribution: nine seats were reserved for the African states; seven for the Asian states; seven for Latin American and the Caribbean states; seven for the West European and others and four for the East European states. The proposal was expected to be adopted without

[18] GAOR, Forty-fourth Session, Fifth Committee, Summary Record, twelfth meeting, 16 October 1989, para. 1–11; and Ibid., fourteenth meeting, 19 October 1989, para. 22–28.

[19] *Ibid.*, Fourteenth meeting, 19 October 1989, para. 1–11. The views excerpted here are from the statement of India's representative to the United Nations, C.R. Charekhan.

voting, but the United States, having participated in the negotiations and consensus evolving, refused to go with the consensus and cast a negative vote. Voting was 152 for, one against (United States) and no abstentions.[20] The one negative vote acquires a significance of its own in recalling that the United States contribute 25 per cent of the budget.[21]

Conference Services and Related Issues: The Group of 18's highly critical observations of the conference services, the too frequent meetings of the inter-governmental bodies with their overlapping and 'duplication of agenda', resulted in its first seven recommendations relating directly or indirectly to the services and their related issues. The recommendations suggested that the General Assembly and the Economic and Social Council rationalise their structures, that no new subsidiary organ be created without discontinuing the existing ones and that the distribution of agenda among the main committees of the Assembly and between the committees and the plenary be reviewed. The Group also recommended that the high cost of holding meetings of the principal organs of the United Nations demanded that the available services be used to the maximum. It was clear that the Group of 18 had indulged in generalities to uphold the criticism made by the

[20] General Assembly Resolution 42/450, 17 December 1987.

[21] The United States has continued to cast negative votes or abstain, although with less frequency, on draft Resolutions worked out through a process of consensus. For instance on the question of the Fulfilment of the target for Official Development Assistance (Resolution 43/197 of 28 December 1988), voting was 148 for, none against, one absent (USA). On the question of the External Debt Crisis and Development (Resolution 43/198 of 28 December), voting was 150 for, one against (US), one absent (Japan); on Trends of Transfer of Resources to and from Developed Countries and their impact on the economic growth and sustained development of those countries (Resolution 44/232 of 22 December 1989), voting was 147 for, one against (US) and no abstentions. Again, at the convening of the Special Session on International Economic Cooperation, in particular, the Revitalisation of Economic Growth and Development of Developing Countries (Resolution 43/231 of 7 March 1989), the single negative vote was cast by the United States. More recently, the United States cast the single negative votes at two consecutive Sessions on a Resolution regarding the format of the publication of the *World Social Situation*. In 1990, the voting on Resolution 45/87 of 14 December 1990 was 146 for; one against (USA) and four abstentions (Germany, Israel, Japan, and United Kingdom). In 1991, on Resolution 46/95 of 16 December, on the same subject the voting was 157 for, one against (USA) and five abstentions (Belgium, Germany, Israel, Japan and the United Kingdom).

developed countries particularly the United States, for reasons stated earlier. Much of the criticism, however, proved to be unwarranted.

The fifth recommendation proposed that the number of conferences and meetings of inter-governmental bodies be significantly reduced without affecting the work of the organization. The matter was referred to the Committee on Conferences[22] by the General Assembly with the proviso that full respect for the mandate of the other legislative organs be maintained and that its work programme remain unbiased. As in the past the Committee continues to do its part to ensure the optimum utilization of conference servicing resources by scheduling conferences and meeting throughout the year to eliminate 'peaks and valleys' in the programme, by avoiding the overlapping of meetings and ensuring that requests for conference services correspond adequately to requirements. What added a new dimension to the Committee's work, were several sessions, held to consider ways of strengthening its role and also of establishing itself as a permanent inter-governmental body. The latter aspect was obviously a follow-up of the Group's recommendations that the Committee on Conferences be 'strengthened'. What followed was the adoption of General Assembly Resolution 44/222 B of 21 December 1988 which provides for a wider mandate and retains the Committee as a permanent subsidiary organ of the Assembly, composed of twenty-one members.[23]

[22] The Committee on Conferences was initially established in 1974 (Resolution 3351 (XXIX) with a view to propose, *inter alia* an annual calender of conferences. Its mandate was expanded in 1977 (Resolution 32/72) to include acting on behalf of the Assembly in dealing with departures from the approved calender that had administrative and financial implications, recommending measures to provide the optimum apportionment of conference resources, facilities and services, including documentation and advising the Assembly on means to ensure improved coordination of conferences within the UN system. The Committee, an inter-governmental body, composed of twenty-two members, was named by the President of the General Assembly in consultation with the five regional groups and invariably its membership included France, Germany, Japan, USSR, UK and the US.

[23] The Committee functioned, since 1974, on an ad hoc basis. It generally has wenty-two members appointed by the President in consultation with various regional groups to maintain an equitable geographical balance in its composition. However, the representation of the various regional groups varied; West Europe and others generally had six members and East Europe, three. It invariably included France, the Federal Republic of Germany, Japan, the USSR, the UK and the United States. When the question of reconstituting the Committee as a permanent subsidiary organ of the General Assembly, with a wider mandate, camp up, the developing countries sought an equitable geographical representation. The consensus worked out was that membership be reduced to twenty-one and that the geographical distribution be as follows: six

Just how superfluous some of the recommendations of the Group of 18 were is reflected in the first, which proposed that conferences and meetings be staggered throughout the year. The Committee of Conferences, already engaged in the task, had met with a considerable degree of success in streamlining the pattern of meetings so as to obtain the optimum utilization of resources and conference facilities. The Group also recommended that conferences and meetings be significantly reduced. In doing so, the Group failed to recognize the fact that the reduction to the minimum level had already been in practice over the years, especially since the financial pressure on the UN mounted. As far back as 1979 the Economic and Social Council, by its Decision 1979/81, laid down that the regular sessions of the functional commissions and its standing committees be limited normally, to a duration of not more than eight working days. Further more, several of these bodies meet only once in two years. It is, therefore, not surprising that notwithstanding fresh efforts by the Committee on Conferences, the calender of conferences and meetings for the biennium 1988–89 does not reflect a diminished level of meeting activity compared to 1986–87.

It is interesting to note that while the Group of 18 in its Report reiterated the strengthening of the role of the United Nations, it recommended that the Economic and Social Council 'be invited to hold one annual session' instead of two. Consideration of the recommendation was postponed until the Special Commission of the ECOSOC on the in-depth study of the United Nations inter-governmental structure and functions could complete its work. When the Special Commission reached an impasse and failed to make recommendations, the Council examined the question of revitalization of itself at its second regular session in 1989. Subsequently, the Council adopted Resolution 1989/114 on 28 July 1989 which focuses on the revitalization of its work. Thus the ECOSOC continues to hold two sessions. The arrangement is fully justified as it enables it to take up the consideration of reports from the various functional commissions

---

Africans; five Asians; four Latin Americans; two East Europeans and, four West Europeans and others. Some of the western powers, especially the United States, were against the change. Eventually the Resolution was adopted by a vote of 129 for and four against (Israel, Germany, the United Kingdom and the United States) and fourteen abstentions. The President of the General Assembly, as before is authorized to name the twenty-one members.

and subsidiary bodies. It has also taken steps to rationalise its biennial agenda and organizational work.

While most of the inter-governmental committees continued to meet once in two years, the Commission on the Status of Women's request to change its cycle of meetings from biennial to annual was endorsed by the ECOSOC and the General Assembly. The Commission has been meeting annually since its thirty-second session in 1988 as it considered that annual meetings best served its functions of monitoring the implementation of the Nairobi strategies for the advancement of women and the system-wise medium-term plan for women in development.[24]

As for the rationalizing and streamlining of the structures of the inter-governmental bodies of the General Assembly and the ECOSOC, the question had already been under the consideration of the relevant bodies. The Special Commission of the Economic and Social Council on the in-depth study of the United Nations Inter-governmental Structure and Functions in the economic and social fields, after fifteen months of work, failed to make any recommendations on restructuring. Negotiations, up to January 1992, remained inconclusive. The measures in recommendation seven of the Group of 18, aimed at controlling documentation, have been monitored by the Committee on Conferences. During its 1987 sessions the Committee had before it statistics provided by the Secretariat that revealed a trend towards a closer adherence to the thirty-two-page limit for reports of subsidiary organs set by the General Assembly in its Resolution 37/14(c) of 16 November 1982.[25] Here, mention is made of a recommendation which reflected US criticism directed at the expansion of UN buildings in Bangkok and Addis Ababa. The Group recommended that the construction of conference facilities should not be undertaken if sufficient resources were available. The General Assembly accepted the recommendation with the proviso that projects already approved by it (in Bangkok and Addis Ababa) be implemented. At its Forty-Second Session, the General Assembly adopted Resolution 42/211, paragraph

[24] For further details, see, the 'Review of the Efficiency of the Administration and Financial Functioning of the United Nations' Analytical Report of the Secretary-General on the implementation of General Assembly Resolution 41/213 (A/45/226, 27 April 1990), para 14–28.

[25] For details, see, GAOR, Forty-second session, Report of the Committee on Conferences, Supplement No. 32 (A/42/32) and Ibid., Forty-third Session (A/43/32); also, Reform and Renewal in the United Nations: Second Progress Report of the Secretary-General on the Implementation of General Assembly Resolution 41/213, Doc.A/43/286 of 8 April 1988, paras 44–48.

ten of which stated that the Secretary-General should proceed as
necessary on both the hitherto approved projects on the understanding
that no additional appropriation would be required in that regard in
the biennium 1988–89.

Changes in the Secretariat

The Group of 18's scathing criticism of the Secretariat staff and its
functioning made it seem as if all the ailments of the United Nations were
the result of the inefficiency of the Secretariat. Commenting on the
report, the Administrative Committee on Coordination succinctly noted,
'While the underlying causes of the growing budgetary problem are
political, the structural and administrative efficiency of the organization
has also been called into question'.[26] In one of its recommendations the
Group proposed a 15 per cent reduction in the overall strength of staff
members in the regular budget posts and a 25 per cent reduction at the
level of the under Secretary-General and the assistant Secretary-General.
The Assembly, while accepting the recommendation, felt that due efforts
be made to avoid negative effects on the implementation of programmes
and the existing legislative mandates. Resolution 41/213 stated that the
Secretary-General act on a pragmatic basis and 'with flexibility in order
to avoid inter alia the negative impact on programmes ... bearing in mind
the necessity of securing the highest standard of efficiency ...'. The same
emphasis on flexibility and the avoidance of a negative impact on programmes and the structure of the Secretariat was reiterated in General
Assembly Resolution 42/211 of 21 December 1987.

Ever since the US applied its financial pressure, the Secretary-
General followed the practice of not filling in professional positions
vacated by an incumbent at the conclusion of the term, or for other
reasons. The practice was adhered to with the result that by December
1986, there was already a reduction of approximately 12 per cent in
the professional staff. The freeze policy for new appointments has
variably continued. By 31 March 1988, the overall vacancy rate of
professionals was 13.8 per cent, while that of the general services
category was 6.9 per cent.[27] The number of posts in the top echelons

---

[26] Review of the Efficiency of the Administrative and Financial Functioning of the
UN: Comments of the Administrative Committee on Coordination on the Report of the
Group of 18, Doc.A/41/763, 24 October 1986.

[27] Figures cited in the Advisory Committee on Administrative and Budgetary Questions: First Report on the Proposed Programme Budget for the Biennium 1988–89
GAOR, Forty-second session, supplement no. 7 (A/42/7), pp. 9 and 18.

(USG/ASG) came down from eighty-seven in 1985 to fifty-six in 1987. The vacancy rate, as of 31 July 1988, for professionals and in the higher level posts reached 16.7 per cent, well ahead of the 15 per cent target to achieve the recommendation of the Group of 18, by 31 December 1989.[28] Thus the appropriations for the programme budget of the biennium 1988–89 were based on an overall vacancy rate of 15 per cent in professional staff and 10 per cent in the other categories.

By this time, however, the Secretary-General was obliged to hire additional staff especially to meet the new responsibilities of peace missions and in order to maintain an adequate level of manpower resources for the Department of Conferences and other essential services. In April 1990, he reported an overall reduction of 1,365 posts or 12 per cent approximately and a staffing table of 10,057, of which 9,959 were established and ninety-eight temporary, for the biennium 1990–91. The staffing table of 10,057 regular budget-funded posts for the biennium 1990–91, included forty-seven high level posts; one at the Director-General level, twenty-six at the under Secretary-General level and twenty at the assistant Secretary-General level. There were fifty-seven such posts originally approved at the beginning of the biennium 1988–1989. The reduction has therefore been of ten posts or 17.5 per cent.[29]

Despite the strict adherence to staff reduction, the Secretary-General candidly noted that the 'prolongation of austerity measures, including the freeze of the staff recruitment and restrictions on meetings has an adverse effect on programme implementation and on the Secretariat staff ...'[30] He repeatedly warned member-States that the capacity of the Secretariat had been stretched to the maximum and that, despite his best efforts, the various programmes especially in the economic and social fields had increasingly been postponed or terminated.[31] He also warned that post reduction of the size recommended would gravely disrupt, for example, conferences and documentation services essential to the conduct of discussions on issues on

[28] Review of the Efficiency of the Administrative and Financial Functioning of the United Nations: Report of the Advisory Committee on Administrative and Budgetary Questions, Forty-third session, Agenda item 49, Doc. A/43/929, 8 December 1988, para 8.

[29] *Ibid.*, para. 68-73.

[30] Report of the Secretary-General on the Work of the Organization, September 1987, *GAOR*, Forty-second Session, Supplement No. 1 (A/42/1), p. 16.

[31] For details, see Programme Performance of the United Nations for the Biennium 1988–1989: Report of the Secretary General, Document A/45/218 and Add. 1, 27 April 1990.

the international agenda.[32] The General Assembly also expressed its concern 'with the negative effect of the reduction of posts and of the recruitment freeze', but in the face of the continuing financial crisis, it is obviously helpless. It merely urged the Secretary-General to keep the situation under review with a view to lifting the freeze.[33]

The final action to be taken for the restructuring and functioning of the Secretariat awaited the results of the Special Commission established by the Economic and Social Council to carry out its in-depth study of the inter-governmental bodies in the economic and social fields. Meanwhile, the Secretary-General carried out a number of changes in the Secretariat structure. Following the twenty-ninth recommendation of the Group of 18, most of the functions of the offices of the Secretariat Services for Economic and Social Matters (OSSECS) were transferred to other departments and its personnel redeployed partly to the office of the Director-General, the DIEC, and to the office of the under Secretary-General for Political and General Assembly Affairs.[34] The office which was given an additional charge over what was to be known as Secretariat services, was renamed the Office of the under Secretary-General for Political and General Assembly Affairs and Secretariat Services. Interestingly enough, it has been assigned a separate unit known as the Division of Economic and Social Affairs.

The Fifth Committee, unhappy with the twenty-ninth recommendation, specifically stated that the General Assembly, at its thirty-ninth Session, had endorsed a JIU report commenting favourably on the work of the OSSECS (A/41/795, 5 November 1986, paragraph 44). At the Forty-Second Session of the General Assembly, support for the continuation of the OSSECS as a unit was reiterated by the Fifth Committee and the Group's recommendation criticized vehemently (A/C.5/42/SR.56–57, 59–61 and 65–67). Consequently, the General Assembly in its Resolution 42/211, paragraph 10(e) requested the Secretary-General to review his decision in the light of the Fifth Committee's argument. The Secretary-General worked out an interim arrangement wherein the integrity of the OSSECS, with reduced staff, was recognised but the unit remains a part of the office of the Political

---

[32] *Ibid.*, Forty-third Session, (A/43/1), p. 26.

[33] General Assembly Resolution 42/220, 21 December 1987.

[34] Traditionally, the post of under Secretary-General for the Political and General Assembly has always been occupied by a US national. The present incumbent is also an American, Joseph V. Reed.

and General Assembly Affairs which itself was renamed as noted earlier."[35]

The DIESA was also affected by the Secretary-General's reformatory measures in a number of ways. For instance, the functions previously performed by the office of programme-planning and coordination of the DIESA have been transferred to the Department of Administration and Management. Similarly, the social policy and development activities have been concentrated under the Director-General of the UN Office at Vienna, incorporating the Centre for Social Development and Humanitarian Affairs (CSDHA).

The fifty-fifth and fifty-seventh recommendations, perhaps the most meaningful proposals of the Group of 18, suggested that no post be considered the exclusive preserve of any member-State or group of states and that the ratio between permanent staff members and those on fixed-term appointments be reviewed with the objective of an adequate range between the two categories. Furthermore, they suggested that in order to ensure that the principle of equitable geographical distribution was faithfully reflected among the Secretariat staff holding permanent appointments, at least 50 per cent of the nationals of any member-State working in the Secretariat be employed on a permanent basis. The recommendation was specifically opposed by China and the USSR, who among several countries, the socialist in particular, had been treating the UN Secretariat posts of their nationals as on secondment. After deciding which of their nationals was to serve on a particular post and the length of the duration, one national was replaced by another. The recommendation, surprisingly, was not fully endorsed by the General Assembly. The Secretary-General was requested to continue to permit the replacement of candidates of the same nationality, within a reasonable time-frame, for posts held by staff members on fixed-term contracts, whenever it was necessary. The request was to ensure that the representation of member-States, whose nationals served primarily on fixed-term contracts, was not adversely affected.

Eventually, the expediency of mutual interests prevailed and the United Nations in its Resolution 45/239, 21 December 1990 affirmed that secondment was not in conflict with Articles 100 and 101 of the Charter and reaffirmed that the secondment of staff from government

---

[35] See the ACABQ, First Report ... Programme Budget 1988–89, *GAOR*, Supplement no. 7 (A/42/7), p. 86.

services to the Secretariat could be beneficial to both the organization and its member-States. With regard to the reduction of staff, the Secretary-General submitted reports[36] detailing the progress in implementing the recommendations of the Group of 18, specifying the structural changes in the Secretariat. Further 'reform and renewal in the United Nations' awaited the conclusions of the indepth study of the inter-governmental structure and the functions of the economic and social fields.

INTER-GOVERNMENT MACHINERY

The Group of 18, while admitting that, by itself, it could nòt carry out a study of the inter-governmental machinery, particularly in the economic and social fields, felt free, however, to conclude that it had multiplied and become too complex, thus creating the need to stream-line its structure. The Group recommended that a small high level inter-governmental body of experts be appointed by the General Assembly to carry out a study and make appropriate recommendations. At its Forty-first Session, the Assembly decided that this task be entrusted to the ECOSOC.

Special Commission's Indepth Study

Accordingly, at its organizational session in 1987, the ECOSOC, by its Decision 1987/112, established the Special Commission of the Economic and Social Council on the Indepth Study of the UN Inter-governmental Structure and Functions in the Economic and Social Fields open to the full participation of all member-States of the United Nations on an equal basis and invited governments to participate at the highest possible level in the work of the Commission. Altogether the representatives of 104 member-States[37] participated in the work.

[36] Reference here in particular is to the two progress reports (A/42/234 Corr. 1 and A/43/280 Corr. 2) which the Secretary-General submitted to the Forty-second and Forty-third Sessions respectively of the General Assembly and to the final report (A/44/222 Corr. 1) submitted to the Forty-fourth Session. The reports noted the maximum possible reduction of staff and restructuring of the Secretariat as recommended by Resolution 41/213 and that further restructuring of the Secretariat would be worked out in correspondence with the changes in the inter-governmental machinery, as and when agreed upon.

[37] No major member-State was conspicuous by its absence; only small states such as Bukino Faso, Botswana, Lesotho, Maldives, Saint Lucia, etc., or 'disinterested' ones like Burma (now Myanmar) kept themselves out of participation.

In recalling the eighth recommendation of the Group of 18, the ECOSOC indicated the purpose of the proposed in-depth study: (*a*) To identify measures to rationalize and simplify the inter-governmental structure, avoid duplication and to consider consolidating and coordinating overlapping activities and merging the existing bodies in order to improve their work and make the structure more responsive to present needs: (*b*) To develop a criteria for the establishment and duration of the subsidiary bodies, including periodic reviews of their work and mechanisms for implementing their decisions. The study also aimed at defining areas of responsibility and considering the establishment of a single governing body responsible for the management and control, at the inter-governmental level, of the United Nations operational activities for development: (*c*) To improve the system of reporting from subsidiary to principal organs and strengthen the cooperation of activities in the economic and social fields under the leadership of the Secretary-General.

The Commission[38] held nine sessions beginning 2 March 1987 to 23 May 1988. In addition to the thirty-six formal meetings, the membership continuously held informal sessions. Tons of documentation and notes were prepared by the Secretariat. The work of the Commission represented perhaps the most exhaustive study[39] on the economic and social framework of the United Nations ever attempted in the forty-five years of its history, but unfortunately, no meeting of minds took place among the member-States. From the outset, the objectives of the Special Commission raised controversy. Australia, the EEC and the United States, with slight variations, argued that the purpose of the

[38] It is intriguing to note that instead of leaving the question of electing its Bureau to members of the Commission, the Chairman of the Commission was appointed by the Economic and Social Council, or rather 'named' by the President of the Council, Eugeniusz Norworyta of Poland, by Decision 1987/112 of 6 February 1987. The choice fell on a career diplomat, Ambassador Abdel Halim Badawi of Egypt.

[39] The working papers made available to the Special Commission included detailed information of the agenda, the terms of reference of each subsidiary inter-governmental body's resolutions and decisions relating to the functioning of the inter-governmental machinery, since the adoption of General Assembly Resolution 32/197 of 28 December 1977. Furthermore there were working papers (No. 9/Add.1–23) on each of the major programmes in the economic and social fields and some forty working papers which contained synoptic summaries of views expressed during the discussion in the Speical Commission on the functioning of the inter-governmental machinery and subsidiary bodies of the ECOSOC and the General Assembly. For a list of these working papers, see Annex. VIII and Annex. IX of the Report of the Special Commission (E/1988/75, 1 June 1988).

exercise was to agree on the principles or direction of reform with a view to obtaining administrative and financial efficiency before settling down to the details of the inter-governmental structure. For them, the reform process should have aimed at improving the cost-effectiveness and efficiency of the UN structure and functions in the economic and social fields. On the other hand, the Group of 77,[40] and its members such as India, Brazil, Bangladesh, joined by China, Norway and the erstwhile USSR among others, argued that the purpose of reform was to make the UN more relevant in international economic cooperation and development and in promoting economic-social progress. In other words, the reform process, according to the majority, was to enable the UN organs and bodies to better address the urgent problems concerning the international community in the economic and social fields, enhance their capabilities in coping with the challenges of the future and revitalise them to better fulfil their mandates under the Charter and serve the member-States in general, and the developing countries in particular, more effectively.

As the Commission proceeded 'from the general to the specific', in its third session from April to May 1987, the differences between its members sharpened. At its fourth session in September that year, the Group of 77 presented an informal paper outlining its proposal for strengthening the ECOSOC, including its 'universalization'.[41] The latter proposal was not only opposed by the western powers and others, but also provided a ready tool to them for propagating what they called the 'unreasonableness' of the Third World countries. Unfortunately, a non-issue attracted more attention and consumed more time than important questions such as the operational activities in the economic and social fields and the relationship between the

---

[40] Tunisia's representative the then Chairman of the Group of 77, acted as its spokesman at the Commission.

[41] The informal paper presented by the Group of 77 on 1 September 1987, is in the Report of the Special Commission of the Economic and Social Council on the In-depth Study of the United Nations Inter-governmental Structure and Functions in the Economic and Social Fields (Doc.E/1988/75), 1 June 1988 (hereinafter cited as Report of the Special Commission), Annex. I, pp. 16–18.

Subsequently, with a view to identifying areas of agreement and disagreement, member-States and groups were requested to submit informal position papers. Accordingly, at the eighth session (April 1988), informal papers were presented by Australia, Canada, China, West Germany (on behalf of the European Community), Japan, Norway, Tunisia (on behalf of the Group of 77), USSR (on behalf of the East Europeans), and the United States. See, *Ibid*., Annex. II, pp. 19–61.

United Nations and the specialized agencies. The weakness of the Group of 77, having no secretariat (unlike members of the OECD or EC) of its own and no continuity of experienced advisers, was obvious. Evidently no spade work was done and the position papers presented revealed the lack of the expertise needed. The demand for the universalization of the ECOSOC could not be justified, both from the point of view of an effective Council or the interests of the developing countries; merely increasing its membership would not add to its authority. However, whether it was the Group of 77's initial proposal for universalising the ECOSOC or a tactical move by western powers, the roles of the General Assembly, the ECOSOC and that of the Trade and Development Board, and the inter-relationship between these organs, aroused much controversy.

While it was generally agreed that the ECOSOC has not been able to play the role envisaged for it in the UN Charter, there were differences of opinion regarding the reasons for its shortcomings. Almost all member-States in different languages and with different motivations, emphasized the need for strengthening the ECOSOC and that it should play the key role, not only in spelling out the various programmes, but also in the implementation, follow-up, and monitoring of UN policies, programmes and coordination. It was clear, however, that the western powers, in general, were not interested in giving a regulatory role to the ECOSOC, or for that matter to any UN body, in fiscal and monetary matters, or on international trade and development issues. The United States, variably supported by the western powers, made it explicitly known that in the limited area which should be the concern of the United Nations, the ECOSOC could be strengthened as a central organ for in-depth discussions on economic and social issues and coordination, but this only by 'trading off' the role of the General Assembly and the Trade and Development Board.

As far as the restructuring of the inter-governmental bodies through rationalization and streamlining was concerned, it was widely agreed that the ECOSOC subsume a number of subsidiary inter-governmental bodies and that its sessional committees[42] be increased from two to three, the third dealing exclusively with operational activities. However, the questions of which inter-governmental bodies be subsumed by the

---

[42] The two existing sessional committees of the ECOSOC are the Economic Committee and the Social Committee.

ECOSOC or terminated altogether and of providing it adequate resources with which to meet its additional responsibilities resulted in sharp differences between members of the Special Commission.

The subsidiary inter-governmental bodies, identified by the developed countries as the ones whose mandates be terminated or subsumed by the ECOSOC or transferred to some other inter-governmental body were:
1. The Inter-governmental Committee on Science and Technology for Development (the EC, Japan, Norway, and the USA).
2. The Inter-governmental Committee on the Development of Utilisation of New and Renewable Sources of Energy (Australia, the EC, Japan, Norway and the USA).
3. The Committee on Natural Resources (the EC, the USA and Japan).
4. The Commission for Social Development (the EC, the USA, and Japan).
5. The High Level Committee for TCDC (the EC and Norway).
6. The Commission on Transnational Corporations (the USA).

The member-States or Groups which made the proposals are noted respectively in brackets.

Deadlock: The Group of 77 was agreeable to the termination of some of these subsidiary bodies, provided that the United Nations' concern with the activities covered by these bodies was maintained and that the ECOSOC would be authorised to take over their functions and convene meetings of experts to advise them as and when required. The United States, however, was the most determined among the western powers, to terminate them altogether. What was surprising was that all the programmes were initiated after protracted negotiations, expert reports and through a process of consensus, to which the United States as well as the other western powers, were a party. No one, including the representative of the United States, questioned their validity. Furthermore, as discussed in Chapter three, the programmes covered by the inter-governmental committees threatened with termination and their support structures in the Secretariat have given a purposeful direction to the developmental activities of the United Nations and have been responsive to the changing needs of the international community, especially those of the developing countries.

It should also be noted that the continuance or otherwise of an inter-governmental body is invariably linked with the future of corresponding programmes and the Secretariat structure. Departments or units are so structured as to meet the services of a particular inter-governmental body which in turn provides the guidelines and authorisation to the Secretariat, department, and unit for the operational activities of the programmes. What was obvious, from the informal discussions was that the market economy countries believed that the UN programmes for the development of new and renewable sources of energy, natural (non-agricultural) resources, and science and technology, and the monitoring of the role of the Transnational Corporations, amounted to encroachment in areas which should remain the exclusive domain of private entrepreneurship—areas which should be subject to bilateral relations between a specific developing country and developed country or that of the TNCs. Instead of saying so explicitly, however, their attempts were directed at dismantling the inter-governmental machinery corresponding to these programmes.

Interlink

The three entities of an inter-governmental mechanism, an operational programme and a Secretariat structure are intertwined. Once a programme is approved, it needs a supporting staff in the Secretariat, which in turn, functions under the directive of an inter-governmental machinery whether it is the ECOSOC itself or a specific committee instituted for the purpose. If the inter-governmental machinery is dismantled and its functions are not subsumed by another inter-governmental body such as the ECOSOC, there can be no supporting staff in the Secretariat and the concerned programme cannot be operational.

The case of the much maligned Committee on Natural Resources is an example of interlinking. It covers an area of activity which has been a subject of vital concern to the developing countries since the early 1950s. It was then that the question of the sovereign right of member-States to utilize and exploit its natural resources was raised by the developed countries. As most of the developing countries had, during the colonial era, given the right of exploitation to extra-territorial entities, the industrially advanced countries insisted that the sovereign rights conform to the international obligations already undertaken or the existing agreements signed with external powers or multinational corporations (later named Transnational Corporations). The issue was eventually settled, at least in theory, with the adoption of the Declaration of the Rights and Duties of the States promulgated in 1974. A related and very pertinent issue has been that the developing countries did not have the own technical knowhow to fully exploit and utilise their natural resources. Here the United Nations was expected to fill in the gap with technical assistance in the form of advice, the training of personnel and, in some cases, by lending the service of experts and adequate equipment. In 1970, the ECOSOC instituted a Standing Committee on Natural Resources for overall policy guidelines on various programmes, advisory services to governments and the reviewing arrangements for coordinating the UN activities in natural (non-agricultural) resource exploitation. With the institution of the Department of Technical Cooperation and Development (DTCD) in 1977 in the Secretariat and subsequently the Centre for Transnational Corporations (CTNC) and the Centre for Science and Technology for Development (CSTD), the programme for the development of natural resources acquired new dimensions. The work was mainly done by experts serving in the Secretariat, while the Committee reviewed the programmes and extended formal authorisation of their operations by virtue of being a subsidiary body of the ECOSOC.

It was the financial squeeze, by some of the major contributors to the United Nations, which called for the decision to deprive members of all inter-governmental bodies, with some exceptions, of travel facilities and subsistence allowances at the UN's expense. Thus as and when the Committee on Natural Resources met, the representatives of the fifty-four members constituting it, rarely sent their experts from their capitals. Most of the member-States simply deputed a member of their Permanent Missions to participate in the Committee's work.

True, the Committee's 'inadequate and low level' of representation was the argument presented by the developed countries for its termination. What was not noted was that the programmes were prepared in consultation with experts of the governments concerned and experts of the Secretariat (i.e., the DTCD)—a practice that characterised the work of most of the specialized agencies. It is also obvious that a 'minister-level' representative who attends the meetings of the specialized agencies has no more expertise on the subject than, for instance, a second Secretary of the Permanent Mission who attends meetings of the Committee of Natural Resources. While the other argument called for economy-measures, the Committee was already meeting just once in two years for eight working day sessions and the total cost of servicing its meetings (including travel of one staff member from each of the five Regional Economic Commissions) came to $20,000.

Thus, it was not financial constraints which lowered the so-called low level participation of members of the Committee, but other considerations which were behind the demand for its elimination. The termination or otherwise of the Committee and that of the inter-governmental Committee on New and Renewable Sources of Energy and its related bodies would be closely linked with the discontinuance of the DTCD in the Secretariat and the programme of Technical Assistance under the regular budget. Likewise, the termination of the other inter-governmental bodies, without making alternative arrangements, would amount to the termination of the UN' operational activities in the areas concerned. By its ninth session, in May 1988, the Special Commission had reached an impasse. The last-minute efforts of the Chairman, to work out a compromise, failed. Consequently, the Chairman prepared a brief report, and the position papers of the various members and groups of delegations were annexed to it for consideration by the Economic and Social Council at its session in July 1988. The ECOSOC passed on the report to the General Assembly for consideration at its forty-third Session. The discussion and informal negotiations that followed failed to yield to any agreement and, to date, the impasse continues.[43]

The more unfortunate part of the discussions and negotiations of the Special Commission, was its summary as prepared by the Chairman, which also turned controversial and was considered biased. In brief, he identified the major issues which prevented an agreement as being: (*a*) the precise definition of the role and responsibility of the General Assembly, the ECOSOC and the Trade Development Board; (*b*) the consequential adjustment in the scheduling and work programmes of the General Assembly and the ECOSOC; and (*c*) the question of restructuring the subsidiary bodies through rationalization and streamlining.

While the summarization was objected to by the Group of 77 in,

---

[43] The General Assembly, while continuing to be seized of the matter, passed on the buck to the Secretary-General requesting him to hold consultations with all member-States to seek their views on ways and means of achieving a balance and effectively implementing the second and eighth recommendations of the Group of 18, and to submit a report at its subsequent session (Resolution No. 43/174 of 9 December 1988). The exercise was repeated at the Forty-fourth session (Resolution 44/103 of 11 December 1989) and at the Forty-fifth Session (Resolution 45/177 of 19 December 1990). The situation did not change at the Forty-sixth Session either when the General Assembly, without discussion, decided (Resolution 46/467, 20 December 1991) to defer its consideration to the next session.

discreet terms, the delegation from Mexico took the initiative in insisting
on placing the objections on record for inclusion in the Report of the
Special Commission and the text of the Chairman, dated 21 April and
23 April (Annexure III of the Report) and 4 May 1988 (Annexure IV
of the Report). The Mexican representative held the view that the texts
had not been adopted, and that they contained views whose articu-
lations alone called into question the very existence of the organization
and the authority of the General Assembly. He also said that the
articulation of such views threatened the vital interests of the developing
countries and did not help strengthen multilateralism in the economic
and social fields.[44]

Facade and Reality

The fifteen month-long discussions and negotiations which characterised
the proceedings of the Special Commission were quite revealing. What
until recently, was a suspicion—that the demand for reforms in the
organization to seek the efficiency and efficacy of the economic and
social sectors of the United Nations, was merely a facade—became
reality. What was projected in the name of improving efficiency was,
indeed, a well-planned and concerted effort to jettison the whole basis
of the functioning of the multilateral system of cooperation evolved
during the 1960s and the 1970. It was evident from the discussion and
position papers presented at the Special Commission, that the objective was to prevent the United Nations from acquiring role in the
monitoring and regulation of international economic relations. It was
also clear that some of the major market economy countries which
dominate the existing international economic order, found it expedient
to their own interests to try to dismantle, under the pretension of
reform and reorganization, whatever mechanisms and political processes the world body had acquired to regulate and influence changes
in the existing international economic system. The United States, in
particular, took the stand that reforms, if any, and not fundamental
changes in the existing economic order, should be effected on their

---

[44] This statement, made by the delegation of Mexico on 23 May 1988, is reproduced
as Annex. 10 of the Report of the Special Commission (E/1988/75).

own terms and outside the framework of the United Nations. Hence the target of its attacks were those particular programmes and structural arrangements of the United Nations system which they regard as an encroachment on their hegemonistic domain. These include programmes and their corresponding inter-governmental machinery and Secretariat support structures responsible for science and technology for development, for monitoring the role and activities of transnational corporations, for the development of natural resources and new and renewable sources of energy and for technological cooperation among the developing countries.

The work of the Special Commission was the most exhaustive and indepth study of the UN structure in the economic and social fields ever attempted. The Chairman and members of the Bureau of the Commission held several informal consultations with the executive heads of the inter-governmental organization of the UN system and working papers were prepared by the Secretariat, identifying the agenda, composition, terms of reference and functions of each of the subsidiary bodies.[45] The Commission then proceeded to discuss and scrutinise the functioning of the various bodies, one by one, from its fifth to seventh sesssion (January-March 1988). To facilitate the work of the Special Commission, the Secretariat also prepared synoptic summaries of views expressed on the functioning of the inter-governmental machinery and subsidiary bodies. That there was no convergence of views was mainly due to the fact that the market economy countries on the one side and the developing countries on the other, held different opinions on the objectives and content of reforms.

What was, however, revealing was that the study clearly proved that the oft-repeated complaints (also endorsed by the Group of 18 without even having done a preliminary study and therefore 'constituting' part of the term of reference of the Special Commission) of parallel growth in the inter-governmental machinery, overlapping of agenda and duplication of work, was found to be highly exaggerated, if not altogether unwarranted. Indeed, right from the beginning, as noted by the Secretary-General,[46] the United Nations has been involved in reviewing the inter-governmental structure and corresponding Secretariat support staff.

[45] See, supra, n. 37.
[46] Review of the Efficiency of the Administrative and Financial Functioning of the United Nations: Report of the Secretary-General, Doc.A/45/714, 20 November 1990, para 31–35.

The Commission failed to make any recommendations on the reforming and restructuring of the economic and social structures. This was mainly because the developed countries, led by the United States, sought to eliminate or minimise those UN programmes evolved during the 1960s and 70s—a period, that the Secretary-General noted, 'represented a phase in which multilateral cooperation expanded and led to institution building at the United Nations', to deal with 'development issues as well as social questions by way of drawing greater attention of the member-States'.[47]

At its meeting on 29 April 1988, the Special Commission requested the Chairman to prepare a text to facilitate the process of negotiations. In response, the Chairman placed before the Commission, on 4 May 1988, his draft conclusions and recommendations for consideration and negotiations.[48] The text included proposals for the discontinuation of some ten inter-governmental bodies including the ones relating to science and technology for development, natural resources, the development and utilization of new and renewable sources of energy, with the proviso that the ECOSOC would convene as and when required, meetings of experts to advise on matters to be subsumed by it, which were hitherto dealt with by the inter-governmental bodies. This was a big concession to the developed countries and yet they refused to accept it as a working paper on which negotiations could be held.[49] They insisted on circumscribing the role of the General Assembly on economic and social matters and curtailing the duration of its Second and Third Committee Sessions.[50] Again, while they argued that

[47] *Ibid.*, para 36.

[48] See, Report of the Special Commission, E/1988/75 Annex. IV, pp. 99–106.

[49] The Group of 77 was the only one which expressed its willingness to accept the Chairman's draft as a working paper for further negotiations. The other groups, especially of the western countries found an excuse as the draft had endorsed Group's demand for the universalization of the ECOSOC.

[50] Some of the market economy developed countries have insisted that the duration and agenda of the two Committees of the General Assembly be curtailed. If this proposal is accepted, it will amount to decreasing the role of the General Assembly in social and economic matters. Such proposals ignored the fact that the General Assembly, under the provisions of the Charter, is concerned with all international problems—that of peace, security, disarmament, human rights, economic and social development—and that all these problems are intertwined. The General Assembly is the principal forum and all-pervasive apex body of the United Nations system for policy-making in all areas of UN activity. Furthermore it is in the Committees that issues are discussed, interactions are intensified, draft resolutions prepared, compromises effected and agreed upon. Again, the agenda of the second and third Committees are already very heavy. The two

the basic thrust of the reforms and reorganization should be the strengthening of the ECOSOC and insisted that a number of subsidiary bodies be subsumed by the Council, they were not willing to equip it with the resources commensurate to its expanded responsibility. They even insisted that the ECOSOC reduce its annual work to one session of twenty-eight working days instead of two sessions, as is the current practice. A typical observation of the developed countries, regarding this bears citation.

[It is] our firm conviction that the aim of *increasing the effectiveness and efficiency of the ECOSOC would be served by a net reduction in the resources required for the consideration of social and economic issues in the UN.*[51]

The comment was just an echo of what US Secretary of State George Shultz observed in February 1986: 'The best way to improve the efficiency and effectiveness of the United Nations is to reduce its budget'.[52]

It is obvious that the market economies do not even want to discuss matters which are of vital interest to a larger section of the international community constituting more than two-thirds of the world's population, and which would bring out the unfairness, inequity and deficiencies in the existing international economic [dis]order in which they have a vested interest. The traditional function, as envisaged in the UN Charter, of UN multilateralism which is to harmonise national policies in the larger interest, has been condemned as statism. Indeed, since the advent of the Reagan-Bush administration, the United States increasingly took the position that not multilateralism, as practised through the United Nations, but the competitive market economy system can bring about economic development. Its typical approach is that 'The key to development is not found through agreed conclusions at an international meeting or even through transfer of resources. The

---

Committees have therefore, in recent years, opted for a biennium programme agenda. Hence to reduce the duration of the sessions of the two Committees, as was suggested, would seriously undermine the General Assembly's consideration of economic and social problems.

[51] Informal position paper circulated by the delegation of Australia, *Report of the Special Commission*, E/1988/75, p. 20, emphasis added.

[52] Cited in B.G. Ramcharan, *Keeping Faith With the United Nations* (Dordrecht: Martinus Nijhoff, 1987), p. 67.

key is domestic economic policies which encourage private enterprise'.[53]

Thus, what is under attack is the very core of the multilateral system of the UN. While this may appear to be a one-sided view it is also the way the Secretary-General looks at the development. Placed as he is, in a very sensitive position, the Secretary-General has to tread the razor's edge to maintain his non-partisan role and weigh words carefully before expressing an opinion. Despite going out of his way to please the United States, in the hope of lessening its criticism and so that it would save the United Nations from bankruptcy, he could not ignore the gravity of the situation. In his introduction to the Annual Report of 1987 he noted:

> The financial crisis which made necessary the austerity measures and encouraged the reforms that are now being implemented stemmed from more profound causes than dissatisfaction with the administrative efficiency of the United Nations. Deep-seated political differences gave rise to *a turning away* in some quarters *from multilateralism and to the rejection by some member-States of adopted* programmes.[54]

NORTH-SOUTH TUG OF WAR

As the United Nations community started recovering from the shock treatment meted out by the United States, on the eve of its fortieth anniversary it once again found itself confronted by the North–South issues—a clear demonstration of the fact that these issues cannot be wished away and constructive action needs to be taken, in the mutuality of interests, through cooperative efforts and that the politics of confrontation can only further aggravate the already deteriorating situation.

[53] Excerpt from a speech made by the US Assistant Secretary of State for International Economic Affairs to the UNCTAD's Trade and Development Board, on 25 March 1985, cited in B.G. Ramcharan, *Keeping Faith With the United Nations*, pp. 54–55. The latter part of this study deals with this again.

[54] Introduction to Annual Report of the Secretary-General on the Work of the Organization, *GAOR*, Forty-second Session, Supplement 1/Add. 1, para 55 (emphasis added).

Unfortunately, such politics, although with less intensity as one side appears to be on the defensive, continue to characterize UN deliberations on key economic issues.

For nearly two years (1985–87), when the question of reform and reorganization dominated the work of the Secretariat and that of the decision-making organs and their subsidiaries, the North–South issues were kept in cold storage. What followed was clearly a renewal of the tug of war between the developed countries of the North and the Group of 77 representing the South; the North, led by the United States, has been pulling all its 'weight' to keep the United Nations out of its involvement with development issues and the other side is trying desperately, making use of its voting power as before, to keep the United Nations very much involved in its struggle to seek a better position in the international economic environment. The North, well organized as it is, believes it does not need the UN system to safeguard its economic interests; indeed, it finds the UN studies, reports and discussions on development issues of 'nuisance value'. The South, representing a motley group of states at varied levels of development does need the United Nations. The UN process and procedure of discussion, expert reports and studies accompanied by protracted negotiations and the frustrations that have followed have made the developing countries conscious of their peripheral status in the existing international economic system and of their commonality of interests. The world body has helped them evolve some degree of solidarity among themselves and to make use of the instrumentality it provides, in their quest for change in the rules of the game governing the world economic system. If the United Nations is marginalized, they have no forum for the redressal of their grievances.

There is more to the situation. The relevance and the future of the United Nations as a global organization is at stake. It cannot effectively perform its role in the area of peace and security, a role which it has acquired in recent years with renewed vigour and wide support, if it fails to do its part in the economic and social fields. That the two areas of UN activity are intertwined needs no emphasis. However, as the developments over the recent years indicate, the side holding the real power including the purse strings is gaining more ground in this tug of war than that holding the voting power.

Pressure for preferred ideology of market economy: From the study of the Special Commission, it is clear that the demand for reform and the subsequent pressure applied, was directed, not at revitalising the UN functioning in the economic and social sectors, but at drastically limiting its role to areas of activity which are of interest to the major contributors of the UN budget such as drug control, the environment, population control, human rights (civil and political only) and refugees. As regards international cooperation in areas of vital interest to the developing countries such as science and technology for development, trade, money and fiscal matters, the powers that be in the existing international system, would like to see that the developing countries are obliged to opt for private enterprise and a free market economy and internal reforms to facilitate foreign investment. Aid and assistance, if any, according to them, should be subject to bilateralism or 'poly-centralism' as confined to the USA, the European Community and Japan rather than the multilateralism as evolved in the UN system."

While the United States mounted its attack, in 1985–86, on the UN multilateral system, demanding reform and reorganization, it also attempted to use the UN forum to impose on others, especially the developing countries, its preferred system of development. In July 1986, the US introduced a draft resolution in the ECOSOC to recommend the promotion of private enterprise which would invite foreign investments and provide an increasing role for the transnational corporations. The developing countries resisted the effort and through various amendments and revisions, had the substance of the text diluted. What emerged from the US initiative was General Assembly Resolution 41/182 of 8 December 1986 on the Role of National Entrepreneurs in Economic Development which referred to entrepreneurship, both in the private and public sectors, as a viable strategy for development.

The United States' efforts towards its ends continued, however, more so when revolutionary changes began to unfold in the economic and political systems of the East European countries, including the USSR. The worsening of the economic plight of the developing countries particularly, as a result of massive debt burdens, also placed them in desperate situations and more dependent on the major developed

---

[55] Multilateralism as evolved in the UN system does not imply that no decisions can be taken in multilateral forums unless all the countries participate in the decision-making. What it implies is that decisions taken should be in the interest of all and that no interest-group should be left out of the decision-making process. It implies that there should be no attempt to impose preferred development strategy or a set of measures applicable to all countries. Thus the policies adopted should not seek to promote sectarian interests and multilateralism should be able to take care of the interests of countries pursuing different social economic systems and which are at different stages of development.

See, Muchkund Dubey, A New Dynamic Multilateralism, *Development*, Journal of the Society for International Development, 1989/4, pp. 73–76.

countries. Not only the smaller Third World countries but also the larger nations such as Argentina, Brazil, India, Indonesia, Mexico and Nigeria, among scores of others, found themselves at the mercy of the market economies for immediate relief from their growing debt burden. The circumstances prompted the United States to launch another initiative to obtain UN legitimacy for its own economy system. It succeeded in getting a mention of the market economy system as a viable strategy for development in the Programme of Action adopted at the Second UN Conference on the Least Developed Countries,[56] the International Development Strategy for the Fourth International Development Decade[57] and in the Declaration on International Economic Cooperation, particularly in the Revitalisation of Economic Growth and Development of Developing Countries.[58]

All the declarations, however, featured other strategies also and as prominently, to the disliking of the United States and some of the other developed countries. Directing their efforts at a specific resolution on the encouragement of private enterprise, the US piloted, through the Economic and Social Council, in July 1990, and subsequently at the Forty-fifth Session of the UN General Assembly, a Resolution entitled Entrepreneurship. It also succeeded in obtaining the sponsorship of some of the developing countries and the East Europeans, including the erstwhile Soviet Union, although the text was revised and some of the 'emphasis' considerably diluted. As adopted, the Resolution includes 'the need for an effective and efficient public sector in, inter alia establishing or improving conditions favourable for private enterprise'. The concepts of 'market-oriented approaches', and 'facilities for foreign enterprises' remain the major thrusts of the Resolution. It also requests the Secretary-General 'to incorporate, in subsequent issues of the *World Economic Survey*, a chapter regarding the role of entrepreneurship as a key element of growth and development'.[59]

The demand for reforms by the United States not only sought the dismantling of the programmes and inter-governmental structure evolved during the 1970s, but include efforts to undermine the objectives of the two institutions, the UNIDO and the UNCTAD which

---

[56] See A/45/695 and A/Conf.147/Misc.9 and Corr. 1 and Add. 1, 14 September 1990.

[57] General Assembly Resolution 45/199 of 21 December 1990.

[58] General Assembly Resolution S-18/3 of 1 May, 1990.

[59] Resolution 45/188 of 21 December 1990. The Resolution was adopted by 138 votes for, one against (Cuba) and no abstentions.

were established on the demands of the developing countries in the 1960s.[60] As noted by an analyst, 'there is a resolute and concerted effort to impose on these organizations, roles based on a preferred strategy of development' and to deny them 'the functions which rightfully belong to them and which they were discharging so competently until a few years ago'[61]

US financial squeeze unabated: Notwithstanding the Secretary-General's final report on the implementation, to the maximum, of the reforms recommended by Resolution 41/213, there has been no respite from financial insolvency. The United States continues its financial squeeze, by witholding or delaying its dues, obviously to seek further reforms to its liking, as so far, the negotiations on the restructuring of the inter-governmental machinery and programmes in the economc and social fields remain inconclusive.[62] The United States has also, (upto December 1991) refused to make any commitment or indicate a timeframe for the payment of the money it owes to the regular UN budget. Instead, over the last six years, as and when the United Nations reached the fringe of bankruptcy, it paid some of its arrears at the fag end of the years.

[60] The third institution, namely the United Nations Capital Development Fund as discussed in Chapter I (see pp. 38–39) had already been moulded to serve objectives other than the ones with which its establishment was sought.

[61] Muchkund Dubey, n. 53, p. 74. It is pertinent to note that western criticism against the UNCTAD has mellowed since 1986. Thanks to A. McIntyre's interim stewardship and subsequently that of Kenneth Dadzie who took over as the UNCTAD Secretary-General in 1986, structural changes in the Secretariat and the orientation of the UNCTAD reports have considerably been affected on lines desired by the western powers. A number of senior researchers and officials were transferred from one division to the other and placed on assignments which were not to their liking. As a result some ten senior officials have left the UNCTAD Secretariat.

[62] As noted earlier (see *supra* p. 206) the Secretary-General submitted two progress reports on the implementation of Resolution 41/213 and the final report, indicating details of the reduction of the Secretariat staff and the implementation of recommendations relating to the administrative and financial functioning of the United Nations. He further noted that he was awaiting the outcome of the study on the restructuring of the inter-governmental machinery. As the report of the Special Commission on the subject had not made any specific recommendations, the matter was again taken up by the General Assembly as its Special Session in 1990. Its deliberations were inconclusive. At the Forty-fifth Session, the General Assembly decided to continue to pursue the objectives of Resolution 41/213, particularly those that had yet to be decided upon i.e., the changes in the inter-governmental machinery. The Secretary-General was asked to continue to report on the subject. Accordingly he submitted yet another report (A/46/633, 12 November 1991), but discussions at the Forty-sixth session again remained inconclusive.

Outstanding Arrears as of 31 December 1984-92

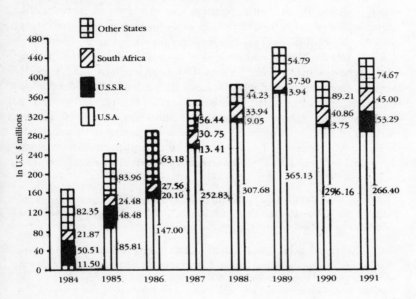

Source: UN Docs. ST/ADM/SER. B/279-371

Note: Contributions are payable in January each year. However payments are unduly delayed. As of February 1992, the total outstanding arrears amounted to $1249.898 million of which United State share is $565.026 million: USSR (Russia) including Belarus (Bylorussia) and Ukraine $159.97 million; South Africa: 49.044 million and others: $ 505.847 million. With effect from 28 December 1991, Russia became successor to the State of USSR. It should be noted that out of 15 constitutent republics of USSR which have all now become independent, three were already original members of the United Nations. Out of the remaining 12, which declared their independence in 1991, 11 have joined the United Nations — Estonia, Latvia, Lithuania in September 1991, Armenia, Azerbaijan, Kazakhstan, Kyrghyzatan (formerly Kirgizia), Moldova, Tajikistan, Turkmenistan, Uzbekistan on 2, March 1992 (the remaining one, Georgia, which is currently engulfed in a civil war is likely to join the United Nations later). Their respective scale of assessment with retrospective effect, will be determined by the General Assembly on the recommendations of the Committee of contributions sometime in the later half of 1992. The assessment thus made will be deducted from the current assessment rate for the Russian Federation of 9.41 per cent.

Once the General Assembly adopted the set of recommendations for reform (Resolution 41/213 of December 1986), by consensus, all the major contributors, with the exception of the United States, started clearing their arrears and have also been regular in paying their apportionments each year. Thus from 1988–1991 no arrears were outstanding against Canada, France, Germany, Japan and the United

Kingdom, to mention a few. The Soviet Union also cleared its dues and continued to make regular payments of its apportionment until 1991. Despite its domestic political and economic upheavals, the member-States made a contribution of $48.6 million (i.e., its arrears plus 50 per cent of its total apportionment of $96 million for 1991). Canada and the Nordic countries have not only been regular in paying their apportionments right on time (January) but have readily made advance payments as and when urgency demanded. Several developing countries, including India, have been more or less regular in making their payments. A large number of them, however, have defaulted on account of balance of payment problems. One perennial defaulter has been South Africa.[63] It has not contributed its apportionments since 1975 and by February 1992 its arrears amounted to $49 million.

---

[63] South Africa refused to pay its contribution beginning 1975 as a protest against the ruling of the President of the General Assembly, in 1974, when non-approval of its credentials by the General Assembly implied that it be deprived of participation in the Assembly.

This is one of the several instances which showed that the developing countries very often act and react at the United Nations with more exuberance than discretion. It was in 1970 when the General Assembly was taking up, in a routine manner, the report of the Credentials Committee and was on the point of adopting a resolution approving the report to the effect that the credentials of all the delegations were found in order, that the representative of Tanzania moved a snap amendment inserting the phrase, 'with the exception of the delegation of South Africa'. Once Tanzania moved the amendment the majority of the member-States, in a recorded vote, could not but vote for it to demonstrate their opposition to the policy of apartheid. This was an unprecedented move as the credentials of the South African delegation were found in order (in the sense that they were duly signed by the competent functionary of South Africa) by the Secretary-General and by the Credentials Committee. After obtaining legal opinion, the then President of the General Assembly (Edvard Hambro) ruled that such an amendment amounted to moral denunciation of the policies of apartheid and had no other legal implications. The same political move was repeated year after year until 1974 when the President of the General Assembly on a point of clarification sought by African members gave his ruling to the effect that since the General Assembly was master of its own rules and could deny, to a member, participation in its proceedings. He also ruled however, that such a position was not tantamount to explusion of a member-State which could be effected only on the recommendations of the Security Council. Since then South Africa has not participated in General Assembly proceedings and has refused to pay its contribution. Article 19 of the Charter, which provides for the denial of voting rights if a member is in default of its arrears amounting to two years of its apportionment, cannot be enforced here as South Africa has already been deprived of its voting right by virtue of its non-participation.

One fails to understand the rationale behind the amendment moved by the representative of Tanzania. He knew well that the action could not force South Africa to change its policy of apartheid. On the other hand, the United Nations has been deprived of an amount which has accumulated, as of 1992, to $49 million.

Reporting on the financial situation[64] in October 1991, the Secretary-General expressed his 'profound concern' that, 'at a time the world community has entrusted to the United Nations new and unprecedented responsibilities, the organization should continue to find itself on the brink of insolvency'. He noted that as of 30 September, the unpaid assessed contributions to the regular budget totalled $723.5 million. Of this amount, $389.9 million was owed for the current year, and $333.6 million for the years prior to 1990. In addition, the unpaid assessed contribution towards peace-keeping operations totalled $518.2 million. He also noted that the financial crisis continued to cast its shadow over the UN for the last six years and that his repeated pleas to member-States for payment of their dues remained largely unheeded. He stressed that he had, once again, sent letters to all member-States conveying 'a stark alternative'. In his letters of September 16 1991 he warned, 'Either we manage to address the financial problem, or the United Nations will be rendered incapable of performing its far-reaching functions especially in the maintenance of peace and security'. By November 1991, the organization once again reached a point where it had no funds available to carry on its operational activities for more than a couple of weeks. The United States then made part payment in two instalments, still leaving outstanding arrears of $266.4 million and delaying its payment for 1992, an amount of $565 million.

Extra-Budgetary Funding

Another intriguing aspect of the pulling of budgetary strings is that while the United States continues to withhold substantial parts of the money it owes towards the regular UN budget, it is using its 'money-power', in conjunction with some members of the OECD, to influence programming and support structures in the Secretariat to promote its preferred ideology through contributions to the extra-budgetary fund. The same member-States, which insist that the regular budget maintain zero growth, are willing to put more money into extra-budgetary resources. In the biennium 1990–1991, its resources amounted to $2.7 billion and showed an increase of 17.72 per cent in nominal terms, compared to the 10.9 per cent increase in nominal terms of the regular budget. The regular budget, in real terms, showed a decrease of 0.4

[64] *The Financial Situation at the United Nations*: Report of the Secretary-General, Document A/46/600 of 24 October 1991.

per cent over the preceding biennium; the increase in the actual amount were the results of inflation and currency exchange fluctuations. As the Indian representative noted, 'It was clear that when certain member-States asked for zero-growth it was not because they were short of resources'.[65]

Thus for the biennium 1990–1991, while there was a reduction in the regular staff of the Secretariat, 2549 posts were funded by extra-budgetary resources. This represents an increase of 637 posts or 33 per cent from the beginning of the biennium 1988–89.[66] It is an open secret, although this fact is kept off the record, that those who contribute funds to extra-budgetary sources not only indicate the priorities of the programmes on which the funds are used, but influence the appointments of the Secretariat staff for them. Over the years the representatives of several governments and members of the ACABQ have expressed their concern over this occurence, but the trend, continues unabated. The development amounts to the very negation of multilateralism and is not in accordance with the common interests of the international community. The funding also indicates, as the representative of Finland aptly noted, the 'sliding away from the principle of collective responsibility in the financing of the United Nations'.[67] The programmes that member-States should pass only unilaterally, are being implemented and legitimized through the United Nations. The influencing of appointments has severely disrupted the principle of the 'equitable representation' of the staff of the Secretariat. Indeed, most of the senior officials (assistant and under Secretary-Generals) who were axed were nationals of the developing countries. The nationals of the industrialized advanced countries whose appointments were terminated, not only enjoyed the option of finding better positions elsewhere but of reappointments to programmes financed by extra-budgetary resources.

[65] *GAOR*, Forty-fourth Session, summary records, fourteenth meeting, 19 October 1989, p. 2.

[66] Report of the Secretary-General, Doc.A/44/226 17 April 1989, para. 74.

[67] *GAOR*, Forty-fourth Session, Summary Records, Twelfth meeting, 16 October 1989, p. 7.

The question of extra-budgetary funding came up again for discussion at the Forty-fifth Session and the Secretary-General was asked to submit a detailed report at the next Session, which he did (see document Extra-Budgetary Resources of the United Nations: Report of the Secretary-General, Doc.A/46/545, 4 November 1991). The General Assembly deferred its consideration (Decision 46/467, 29 December 1991) to its Forty-seventh Session.

Struggle for change: As noted earlier, the developing countries, notwithstanding the Group of 77 and the Non-aligned Movement, have no institutional forum other than the United Nations from which to seek changes in the international economic environment which has been operating against their interests. The United States' ultimatum of 1985 caught the Group of 77 unprepared and placed it on the defensive. They yielded to the mounting pressure for reform and reorganization and agreed to defer the consideration of some of the key issues vital to their interests relating to money, finance, trade and development. The question of global negotiations has remained in cold storage since 1984. Unlike the preceding years, no efforts were made to even keep it alive by requesting the President of the General Assembly to hold informal consultations for the launching of global negotiations.[68] Nevertheless, the Group of 77 has not given up its struggle for change. As a counter move to US efforts to deny the United Nations a role in key economic issues, the Group has, time and again, moved draft resolutions and had them adopted, with specific references to the New International Economic Order (NIEO) and the United Nations Charter of Economic Rights and Duties of States.[69]

At the Forty-fourth Session, in an unprecedented event, the United States and the USSR jointly sponsored a Resolution enhancing international peace and security and international cooperation by 'reaffirming'

[68] In 1979, the General Assembly decided to convene a special session which would lead to the launch of a round of global and sustained negotiations on international economic cooperation for development, which would include major issues in the field of raw materials, energy, trade, development, money and finance. The special session met intermittently from January to April 1980 accompanied by intensive informal negotiations. However, when all the members agreed on a text as the procedural framework for global negotiations, the United States, supported by the United Kingdom and the Federal Republic of Germany, did not. Efforts to revive the negotiations continued at all subsequent sessions of the General Assembly by its President. There were also some discussions and debates following the report by the President at the end of the session. However, since 1985 even this exercise has not taken place, but the developing countries have refused to remove the item from the agenda of the General Assembly. Each year the General Assembly deferred consideration of the item to the next session as it did at the Forty-fifth Session (45/435 dated 21 December 1990) and at the next, (46/443, 20 December 1991), deferring it to the Forty-seventh Session.

[69] See, General Assembly Resolution 44/170 of 19 December 1989, which was adopted by 131 votes for, one against (United States) and twenty-three abstentions (mostly OECD members). Also see General Assembly Resolution 46/280, entitled Economic Measures as a ... of Political and Economic Coercion against Developing countries, which when voted upon was ninety for, thirty against with nine abstentions.

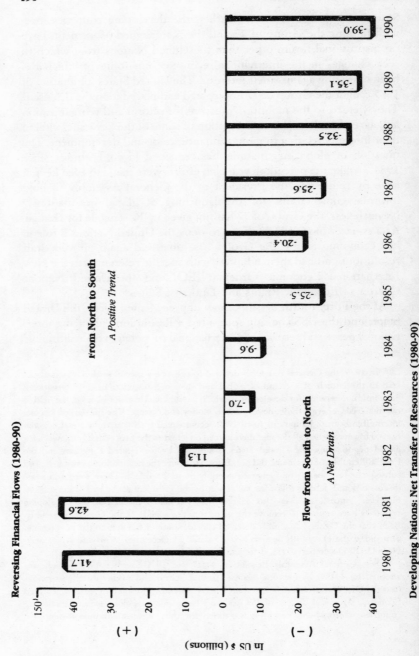

Reversing Financial Flows (1980-90)

from North to South
A Positive Trend

Flow from South to North
A Net Drain

In US $ (billions)

(+)

(−)

41.7   1980
42.6   1981
11.3   1982
-7.0   1983
-9.6   1984
-25.5 1985
-20.4 1986
-25.6 1987
-32.5 1988
-35.1 1989
-39.0 1990

Developing Nations: Net Transfer of Resources (1980-90)

the validity of the Charter and calling upon member-States to intensify their efforts within the UN framework. No additional sponsors were sought, or permitted, on this important issue, perhaps to demonstrate the new-found solidarity of the two superpowers.[70] The Resolution (44/21, of 15 November 1989) was, of course adopted with a vote. A couple of weeks later the developing countries presented a draft resolution on the strengthening of international peace and security which, inter alia, stated that its maintenance was closely linked with the equitable management of world economy, effective arms control and disarmament measures, the protection of the environments and the promotion of human rights. The western countries did not, ob-viously, care for the reference to the 'equitable management of world economy' and the United States voted against it while the other western powers, mostly members of the OECD, abstained.[71]

The 1980s witnessed a fast deteriorating economic situation in the developing countries. Various official reports indicated that, beginning the decade, the net transfer of resources of the developed countries as a group turned negative, and it has remained so ever since. Indeed in a perverse shift of net financial flows and partially as a result of the debt crisis, each year, since 1983, the developing countries have actually transferred more financial resources to the industrialized countries of the North than they have received in new funds.[72] Furthermore, the sharp decline in prices of primary commodities, the high rates of interest initiated by the United States and followed by other major market economy countries, the sharp fluctuation in exchange rates

[70] The joint draft was announced at a Press Conference jointly held at UN head-quarters on 3 November 1989, by US Assistant Secretary of State, John Bolton and USSR Deputy Foreign Minister Vladimir Petrovsky. See *UN Chronicle*, March 1990, p. 72.

[71] General Assembly Resolution 44/126 of 15 December 1989. Voting was 128 in favour (including the USSR and other East Europeans), one against (USA) and twenty-four abstentions.

[72] The main UN Secretariat Document that contained analysis and policy recom-mendations regarding the net transfers are: Net Transfer of Resources from Developing to Developed Countries, Report of the Secretary-General, 13 May 1987 (A/42/272); Report of the Secretary-General: 22 June 1988 (E/1988/64; World Economic Survey, 1985; World Economic Survey, 1986, 1989 and 1990; External Debt Crisis and De-velopment; Report of the Secretary-General, 16 October 1989 (A/44/628); Debt and Management adjustment; Report by the UNCTAD Secretariat, 19 February 1990 (TV/B/C.3/234). External Debt Crisis and Development: Report of the Secretary-General. Doc.A/45/380, dated 8 October 1990. Annual Reports of the Secretary-General ..., 1989, 1990, 1991.

and the mounting debt burden made the situation insurmountable for the developing countries.

In 1987, the Group of 77 attempted to renew its efforts towards convening an international conference on money and finance for development. To begin with it requested the Secretary-General to draft a report on Current International Monetary Issues. The report of the Secretary-General (Doc.A/43/749 and Corr.1) provided the basis for the convening of an international conference to discuss the whole gamut of money and finance for development, but no dates were suggested. The US, joined by the other developed countries, opposed the move; the arguments advanced were that the United Nations should first set its house in order and a zero-growth rate in the regular budget be maintained. Convening a conference, they felt would merely raise expenses without seeking any useful purpose. The Group of 77 yielded to the economic and political pressure and agreed to postpone the consideration of the draft resolution to the Forty-fourth Session of the General Assembly, but insisted that the Secretary-General continue to monitor the international monetary situation and prepare an updated report. The United States, supported by other members of the OECD, was not willing to support even this brief resolution. At this point, the Group did not yield and eventually the Resolution was put to a recorded vote and adopted by a vote of 127 for, nineteen against and five abstentions.[73] The developing countries, did however, recognise the futility of convening the conference without the support of the industrialized countries and agreed that its consideration be postponed to the Forty-fifth Session and then again to the Forty-sixth Session.[74]

In 1988, when the General Assembly was all set to adopt a resolution from the preparation of an international development strategy for the Fourth United Nations Development Decade, the draft of which was evolved through a consensus, the United States alone decided to cast a negative vote. The voting was 151 for, one against (the United States) and no abstentions (Resolution 43/182 of 28 December 1988). Subsequently, the draft of the strategy adopted in 1989 and 1990 included, at US insistence, a reference to market economy approaches for

---

[73] General Assembly Resolution 43/187, 20 December 1988. The negative votes included those of members of the OECD; the Scandinavian countries were among those who abstained.

[74] General Assembly Decision 45/441, 21 December 1990; Also see report of the Second Committee A/45/849/Add. and text of the draft Resolution in Doc.A/C.2/45/L.4.

development. The Resolutions were adopted without vote.[75] At the same Session in 1988, the General Assembly voted on a Resolution proposed by the Group of 77 which called for international cooperation for the eradication of poverty in the developing countries. The United States again decided to cast the lone negative vote.[76] Yet another example of the US' attitude was evident in the context of the reverse flow of financial resources. The Group of 77 put forward a Resolution which would request the developed countries to at least adhere to the oft-repeated promises of Official Development Assistance averaging 0.7 per cent—a promise which has never been kept especially by the major market economy countries. The United States put its thumbs down, again. The voting was 148 for, none against, with the United States abstaining.

More evidence of the inflexibility of the United States was revealed by its attitude to the debt burden of the developing countries. By 1990, the figure had reached a mind-boggling $1.3 trillion, the debt service charges alone consuming a major part of hard-earned foreign exchange. The United States, since the problem accelarated, conveyed its conviction that the debt burden should remain the exclusive concern of the Group of Seven or actually the Group of Five—the United States, the United Kingdom, the Federal Republic of Germany, Japan and France—to which the creditors, both governments and commercial banks largely belong. In other words, only the creditors could decide what should be done, and so far nothing concrete has taken shape, without even giving an hearing to the debtor countries as a group. The Group of 77, wishing for an open discussion on the problem which is closely linked to issues involving trade, money and finance, tried to bring the question before the United Nations General Assembly. In 1988, the Group again proposed a draft Resolution which would lead to a general discussion in the General Assembly on the ways and means of finding a solution to the crisis emanating from the debt burden. The United States and the other market economy countries made their disapproval obvious. The Resolution was then revised to requesting the Secretary-General to appoint a special representative to hold consultations with governments, banks and multilateral institutions with a view to extricating the developing countries

---

[75] General Assembly Resolution 44/169, 19 December 1989 and Resolution 45/199, 21 December 1990.

[76] Resolution 43/195 of 20 December 1988. The voting was 128 for, one against (United States) and twenty-one abstentions.

from the debt crisis. The United States refused to support the revised Resolution, but only Japan, amongst the OECD countries, abstained from voting. When put to the vote, the Resolution (43/198 of 20 December 1988)[77] received 150 for, one against (the United States) and one abstention (Japan).

Another issue of vital interest to the developing countries is the earning of foreign exchange by the export of primary commodities. Price fluctuations, however, have often been detrimental to their interests. Hence, efforts were made to establish a Common Fund for commodities with a view to stabilizing prices by financing global stock operations during periods of acute shortage or surplus and dealing with the problem by supporting improved production and marketing techniques. The agreement reached in 1981 could not become operative because the required number of ratifications, funding and support from the major market economy countries was not forthcoming. In June 1989, the target was reached and the Common Fund Agreement did become operative, but the major trading countries kept themselves out of it. When Resolution 44/218 of 22 December 1989 welcoming the entry of the Agreement into force and requesting the states who had not yet ratified the Agreement to do so, was urgently voted upon, it received 146 votes for, none against and two abstentions (the UK and the USA). At its next session in 1990, General Assembly Resolution, 45/200 of 21 December, adopted without a vote, made similar pleas and also decided to include the 'question of commodities' in the agenda of the Forty-seventh Session.

Widening Gap

While the United Nations, over the last decade, went through its financial emergency resulting from the delay or non-payment of dues by member-States and then, beginning 1985, was engulfed in a frenzy of reform and reorganization, the real problems, which have had drastic consequences in the day-to-day lives of the common people, were relegated to the background. The number of people in the developing countries living below the poverty line enduring

---

[77] The Secretary-General as a follow-up to the Resolution appointed Italy's former Prime Minister Bettino Craxi as Special Representative. He submitted a detailed report (A/45/380) which conveys some concrete suggestions. Whether they are acted upon very much depends on the banks. Transnational institutions and the governments belonging to the market economy countries. Also see *supra*, p. 243, note 70.

hunger, disease and no shelter, increased to more than a billion in the 1980s, compared to 700 million in the 1970s.[78] The UNICEF reported that more than 40,000 children died everyday, during the 1980s,[79] as a result of what is referred to as invisible malnutrition which affects one quarter of the developing world's children. It quietly lowers their resistance. In cause and consequence, it is inextricably interlocked with illness and infection which both sharpen and are sharpened by malnutrition itself. The UNICEF report suggested that it could be overcome, specifically by calorie intake, if only 20 per cent of the grain kept in cold storage to maintain market stability in Europe and America, or 25 per cent of what is fed to cattle in the developed countries to get juicy meat, is directed to meet the needs of hungry children. Indeed, the pet food industry in the North, providing fillet of beef to dogs and cats has crossed the $30 billion mark.

It is true that the developing countries, having attained sovereign status should look after the welfare of their own people. It has become increasingly difficult, however, to manage their responsibilities in a world economy where they have no control over the external economic environment which runs counter to their national interests and aggravates their difficulties. The countries of the South, caught in the debt trap, found their burden further aggravated by the United States, followed by the European countries, increasing interest rates. Decisions were taken primarily on the basis of respective domestic situations and in utter disregard of the interests of the developing countries. A report of the Secretary-General (A/Ac.233/5) issued in January 1990 indicated that the industrialized countries frequently took decisions which have resulted in drastic consequences for the developing countries. For the developed countries, the 1980s marked an era of sustained economic growth. As a group, their gross domestic products expanded by an annual average of 3.3 per cent over the period 1986–89 compared to 2.2 per cent during the first half of the decade. Some developed countries such as Japan have fared particularly well. For many of the developing countries, however, the period has been viewed as a decade lost for development. The long-term downward trend in the prices of commodities, on the one hand, and the proliferation of tariffs, export

---

[78] Report of the Secretary-General A/44/467, 18 September 1989: Also see Annual Report of the Secretary-General, 1991 (Section VIII), pp. 15–16.

[79] For details of the adverse effects on women and children in the developing countries as a consequence of the deteriorating economic situation see UNICEF Annual Reports, State of the World's Children, 1984–91.

restraints and other trade barriers imposed by the governments of North America and western Europe on the other, have led to the sharp deterioration of their terms of trade.

External debtedness has emerged as one of the main factors of the economic stagnation of the developing countries. The total burden, as noted earlier has crossed well over the $1 trillion mark.[80] Even excluding the richer oil-producing developing countries, the amount reached $39 billion in 1990 alone. The cumulative figure over eight years is nearly $190 billion. The massive transfer of resources from the developing to the developed countries deprived the former of the much-needed resources for development. This has had its own social and economic consequences. Living conditions in Africa, Latin America, the Caribbean and large parts of Asia have deteriorated, and their economic and social infrastructures have eroded to the extent of impairing stability and prospects for growth and development.

Revival of Negotiations?

As noted earlier, the launching of global negotiations remained in cold storage since 1984 largely due to the United States and the other industrialized countries, refusing to accede to the demands of the New International Economic Order with which the negotiations were linked. Studies and reports, however, including those issued by the United Nations Secretariat, the UNCTAD, the GATT and the OECD indicating the dismal social and economic situation prevailing in the developing countries, did lead to a series of discussions years later. Several international conferences and Round Tables, at non-governmental levels, attended by UN experts and diplomats were held in 1988–89, to discuss the ways of dealing with the hard and chaotic realities of the world economy. The consensus reached reflected the crux of the problem to relate to the question of reform and revitalization of the United Nations in the economic and the social fields. While emphasizing this need, however, it was agreed that the stalemate in the North–South dialogue had contributed to the marginalization of the United Nations. It was recognized that structural

[80] In its two-volume report on debt, World Debt Tables 1990–1991, the World Bank estimates that the total external debt of all developing countries reached some $1.34 trillion by the end of 1990, an increase of about 6 per cent during the course of each year. Also see Report of the Secretary-General, Net Transfer of Resources from Developing Countries (A/45/487) submitted to the Forty-fifth Session (1990) of the General Assembly and *World Economic Survey 1991*, pp. 68–72.

and procedural reform would not, in and of itself, overcome the difficulties and frustrations resulting from the lack of cooperation between the North and the South. What was needed, was a renewal of efforts to make a fresh start in North–South negotiations by obtaining the widest consensus of ways with which to revitalize the United Nations in the overall management of the world economy.[81] The former Chancellor of the Federal Republic of Germany, Willy Brandt, stressed the need for a North–South Summit.[82] Thorvald Stoltenberg, Norway's foreign minister also observed, 'I believe there is a growing need for a more binding international cooperation in the 1990s. A North–South Summit under the aegis of the United Nations could explore the basis for a more effective system of global macro-economic coordination between [the] industrialized and developing countries'.[83] The reiteration of their beliefs prompted not only the Group of 77 but also the Scandinavian countries and other groups at the United Nations to review the situation with a view to initiating concrete steps by the international community.

General Assembly Special Session: After intensive and extensive negotiations, the Group of 77 initiated a proposal for convening a special session of the United Nations General Assembly to discuss the overall issues relating to international economic cooperation. At the initial stage, an overall consensus, for the proposal was reached, although the United States continued to express its scepticism on the utility of convening such conferences. Nonetheless it was hoped that the United States would go along with the other developed countries in joining the negotiations and the preparatory work for the conference. After

[81] Reference here, in particular, is to the International Round Table, Moscow, 5–9 September 1988 on The Future Role of the United Nations in an Inter-dependent World held in cooperation with the USSR Association for the United Nations and the UNITAR. For a brief report on the Round Table see Michel Doo Kingue in *Development*, 1989/4, pp. 63–66 and Khadija Haq, 'Issues Before the Upssala Round Table on the Future of the United Nations' in ibid., pp. 5–7.

[82] 'The World, Ten Years After the Brandt Commission' paper prepared for the International Symposium on the Crisis of the Global System, organised by the Vienna Institute for Development and Cooperation, September 29 1988, Vienna.

[83] *Towards a World Development Strategy Based on the Growth Sustainability and Solidarity: Policy Options for the 1990s*, Report presented to the OECD Development Centre, twenty-five anniversary symposium, 8 February 1989. Reprinted in ibid., 1989/1, pp. 7–14.

intensive debate and negotiations in the Second Committee, the consideration of the draft resolution for the convening of the special session was postponed to the resumed session of the forty-third session of the General Assembly. However, when the resolution was put to the vote at the session on 7 March 1989, the United States cast a negative vote. The voting was 123 for, one against (the United States), with no abstentions. In an explanatory statement that followed, the President of the General Assembly said it was necessary to take stock of the significance of the transformation of the world economy and to consider the pressing issues of cooperation and the international economic situation so as to address both in the light of their interrelatedness. He expressed the hope that the special session, to be convened from 23 to 27 April 1990, would also serve as a forum for a dialogue and negotiations between the North and the South.

The Secretary-General, in his annual report on the work of the organization, drew further attention to 'the widening economic and technological gap between the developing and developed countries and the continued stagnation, if not regression' in many of the developing countries, particularly Africa and Latin America. Without referring to the oft-offered advice of the industrialized countries to the developing nations of opting for market economy approaches, he noted: 'It would be inaccurate to assume that the present lop-sided growth patterns are due in all cases to inherent differences in under-lined potential for unsound policies' nor should one 'expect these persistent imbalances automatically to correct themselves'. He referred to the large number of developing countries he had visited and stated,

I have been deeply impressed by the strenuous efforts these countries were making against formidable odds, for the welfare of their peoples. However, the external economic environment aggravates difficulties they faced in the process of development. I believe that it is now essential to resume a broad-based North–South dialogue on international economic cooperation that takes fully into account the views of all countries. The special sessions of the General Assembly scheduled for early next year can provide an excellent opportunity for it.[84]

---

[84] Report of the Secretary-General on the Work of the Organization, DPI, 1003, September 1989, pp. 24–25. Also see ibid., 1990, pp. 28–34 and ibid., 1991, pp. 15–17.

The expectations of the Secretary-General were belied. The negotiations that followed indicated that the United States in particular regarded it as inopportune and fruitless to discuss crucial issues at such a large gathering. When the Preparatory Committee, open to all member-States convening the special session, met in January 1990, the United States and the other developed countries attended the meetings and the informal negotiations, but it was clear that there could be no convergence of views.

During the five-day session from 26 February–2 March, the Preparatory Committee approved a provisional agenda and work programme for the Eighteenth Special Session of the General Assembly. It was also agreed that the focus of the session would be on the 'reactivation of economic growth and development in the developing countries', and that the delegations would 'strive for consensus on matters of substances. Two texts for discussion were proposed, one by Bolivia, on behalf of the Group of 77, and the other, by Canada. The fifty-seven–point draft introduced by Bolivia stressed that the peace dividend—resources released by disarmament—be used to promote global economic growth and development. The draft also proposed a substantial increase in net resource flows, over a long term rather than a short-term development approach, the correction of fiscal deficits in the United States and the other developed countries and the attainment of Official Development Assistance at 0.7 per cent. The other measures recommended sought to reverse the deterioration of commodity prices, the integration of the East European countries into a market-driven economy and a 'durable and comprehensive solution to the external debt crisis in the developing world'. The Canadian representative observed that the draft should have contained stronger references to population, human resources and environmental issues and that the problems of the developing countries should not have been depicted in a North–South context.

Ireland, speaking on behalf of the European Community, said that its views on international economic cooperation diverged from those of the Group of 77 in several respects. The twelve Community member-States believed in 'a decisive break with the failed policies of the past' and called for a draft declaration to make it clear that the developing countries were primarily responsible for their own progress. The European Community also felt that the draft make references to the role of democratic institutions, the relevance of market-oriented growth and the development of human resources. China found the draft of the Group of 77 comprehensive on the whole but wanted specific reference to the unbalanced economic growth in the developed and developing world and that this imbalance could be corrected by, among other things, lowering interest rates and placing greater emphasis on multilateralism.[85]

The Eighteenth Special Session of the General Assembly met in April 1990. Initially the session was to last for just five days but it continued for another three. The compromise draft was adopted by consensus. Its wide-ranging thirty-eight-point Declaration on International Economic Cooperation, particularly the Revitalization of Economic Growth and Development of the Developing Countries,[86] was hailed by General Assembly President, Joseph N Garba of Nigeria, as a watershed in the history of international economic cooperation who noted that 'it took ten years to achieve it'.[87] The adopted text contains wide-ranging programmes to guide economic policies in both the developed and the developing countries through to the end of the century and beyond. The Declaration refers to the need for the revitalization of economic growth and social development in the developing countries as the most important challenge of the 1990s. It calls for favourable external conditions for the developing countries and states that 'this major challenge has to be addressed in the context of increasing interdependence and integration in the world economy'.

The first part of the document provides an assessment of the 1980s, highlighting the increasing deterioration of the socio-economic situation in the developing countries and the lop-sidedness of the prevailing economic system. It outlines the challenges and opportunities for the 1990s and sets specific commitments and policies for all governments—of the developed and developing countries alike—in the areas of debt, development aid, the environment, the open trading system, stable commodity markets and a large role for the United Nations in helping revitalize development. While emphasising that the developing countries bear the responsibility of the welfare of their people, it also stresses the elements of growing inter-dependence and the pressing need to improve the international environment and form an equitable trading system in order to ensure the success of national

---

[85] The summarised version of the meeting of the Preparatory Committee, 26 February-2 March 1990, has been excerpted from *UN Chronicle*, June 1990.

[86] General Assembly Resolution, S-18/3, 1 May 1990 contains the text of the declaration.

[87] Text of the Declaration, General Assembly Resolution, S-18/3, 1 May 1990.

policies. Reiterating the hard fact that 'the major industrialized countries influence world economic growth and the international economic environment profoundly', it says that 'the coordination of macro-economic policies should take full account of the interests and concerns of all countries, particularly the developing countries'.

The declaration stresses that the major challenges before the international community, for the 1990s, are the eradication of poverty and hunger and the greater equity in income distribution and development of human resources. It further states that the developed countries 'enhance the quantity and quality of their aid' and implement the agreed international target of 0.7 per cent of their GNP as ODA, with 0.15 per cent to the least developed countries. On the key issue of whether or not the United Nations should be the forum for discussions, negotiations and agreements on matters relating to money, finance, trade and development, the Declaration reaffirms that the UN system 'has a large role to play in international cooperation for revitalizing development in the 1990s'. It calls upon all member-States to make the UN system 'more effective and efficient' and emphasizes that the world body is 'a unique forum in which the community of nations can address all issues in a integrated manner'.

While the contents of the Declaration and the exhortations therein, are not different from scores of such instruments 'carrying pledges solemnly made' during the 1960s and 1970s, much of it is just rhetoric. Of course, it contains new slogan-phrases as, for example, 'development with human face', 'adjustment with growth and human development', the full utilization of human resources to stimulate creativity, innovation and initiative' and 'flexibility, creativity and openness[88] as integral part of our economic system', but it goes without saying, that mere words or phrases, however innovative in their meaning, by themselves do not make any impact. The question that remains a moot point, is, whether or not those who have acquired the ascendency in the prevalent international economic [dis]order are actually willing to act for equitable management of the world economy. One redeeming feature of the Declaration, so far, is that the concept of UN multilateralism, which had been in a convulsive state through the 1980s, survived, albeit in solemn pledges and in theory.

The all-pervading question that arises in the 1990s is whether or not

---

[88] Peter Fromuth, ed., *A Successor Vision: The United Nations of Tommorrow* (Lanham, M.D.: UNA-USA, 1988), pp. xv-xxiv.

there is a thaw in the frozen North–South dialogue. The question holds the key to the basic issue of reform and revitalization of the UN system in the economic and social field just as East–West relations have been fortuitous in peace and security matters. Regrettably, recent developments in North–South relations, far from showing any improvement, indicate further deterioration. Notwithstanding the Declaration of International Economic Cooperation, containing pious hopes and laudable ideals, adopted at the Eighteenth Special Session of the General Assembly, no worthwhile measures were taken to improve the economic plight of the developing countries. Intriguingly, improvements in East–West relations have further strengthened the North and aggravated the economic servitude of the South to it.

The former Secretary-General Perez de Cuellar, while pleading anew the need for building 'a sense of partnership between the developed and developing countries' to resolve global economic issues, again drew attention to the growing 'intensified alienation' between an increasingly affluent and 'homogenous North and increasingly impoverished and desperate South' which if allowed to persist, 'would be a tragedy of great proportion'.[89] In his last Annual Report presented on the eve of the Forty-sixth Session of the General Assembly the outgoing Secretary-General yet again drew specific attention to the 'rising affluence and increasing poverty [as a] pronounced and paradoxical feature of the present world scene'. He warned that 'no system of collective security will remain viable unless workable solutions are sought to the problems of poverty and destitution afflicting the greater part of the world. A reinvigoration of the North–South dialogue' he pleaded, 'has now become more urgent than every'.[90] However, as in the preceding sessions, efforts to revive the dialogue were frustrated by the powers that be. The General Assembly was obliged 'to defer consideration', without even a discussion, of the item relating to the launching of global negotiations to the Forty-seventh Session.[91]

    Excerpts from a speech by Javier Perez de Cuellar delivered in Bonn, Germany, 2 July 1991 and reproduced in *UN Chronicle*, December 1991, p. 3.

    Annual Report of the Secretary-General on the Working of the Organization, 1991, Section VIII, p. 15.

    UN General Assembly Decision No. 46/443 dated 20 December 1991. Also see *supra*, pp. 148–50.

5

An Overview

The preceding chapter analyzed the recommendations of the Group of 18, the follow-up by the General Assembly in its Resolution 41/213, the institutional and procedural changes effected and what transpired at the Special Commission which was entrusted with the task of undertaking an indepth study of an UN inter-governmental structure and functions in the economic and social fields and making appropriate recommendations. This chapter is an overview of the entire set of issues relating to reform and reorganization and analyzes, in the context of the emerging political environment, what is desirable and, at the same time, feasible to improve the functioning and effectiveness of the UN system.

As noted earlier, reform has been, from the inception of the organization, more or less a continuous process, in grappling with the endemic institutional problems of coordination, effectiveness and efficiency. For the most part, the reforms and procedural changes were attempted in an ad hoc and incremental manner. There have been junctures, however, at which member-States felt it necessary to look at the inter-governmental structure as a whole and make more systematic changes leading to an overall or partial restructuring of the institutional arrangements. For instance, the adoption of General Assembly Resolution 2688 (XXV) of 11 December 1970 was the result of attempts to enhance the United Nations' development system Another major effort at reform took place in the mid-1970s when three years of deliberations led to the adoption of Resolution 32/197, in December 1977, for the restructuring of the economic and social sectors.

CONSEQUENCE OF REFORMS: CLOUD OF UNCERTAINTY

Unlike the earlier efforts, however, the exercises for reform that began in 1985–86 have so far been carried out under the threat of financial bankruptcy and acute political pressures, clouding in uncertainty the future of the world organization and posing a serious challenge to its relevance and viability. As the Secretary-General, in his analytical report on the implementation of Resolution 41/213 has candidly noted, the very fact of withholding financial contribution and linkage of the withholding to the demand for financial administrative reforms, vitiated the atmosphere surrounding the consultations prior to the adoption of Resolution 40/237, which led to the appointment of the Group of 18. In the suspicion-charged background, 'the underlying tensions during the work of the Group and the short period given' to it to complete its task, 'it was hardly surprising that the recommendations did not necessarily rest, in all cases, upon documented facts and scientific operation'.[1]

The staff of the Secretariat, which provides the mainstay of the organization, was demoralized, a widely known fact that the Secretary-General was obliged to draw specific attention to, in several of his reports. In a more recent one, he specifically noted that the reduction in the Secretariat staff was arbitrarily set and that 'the process of post-reduction was in itself disruptive, by the attention it required from programme managers and by its obvious effects on the attitudes and morale of the staff'. He also noted that the organization has been hampered by

> an acute financial crisis, coupled to some extent by an express lack of confidence from some Governments in its ability to perform its role. It had to devote a large amount of its energy to cope with a situation of daily financial uncertainty while being criticized for its

[1] Review of the Efficiency of the Administrative and Financial Functioning of the United Nations: Analytical Report of the Secretary-General on the Implementation of General Assembly Resolution 41/213(A/45/226, 27 April 1990), para 243-245. The Secretary-General submitted two progress reports A/42/234 & Corr. 1, and A/43/286 & Corr. 1, on the implementation of the reforms as recommended by Resolution 41/213 to the Forty-second and Forty-third Sessions of the General Assembly and the final report A/44/222 & Corr. 1 to the Forty-fourth Session (1989). The Report cited above was referred to as a supplement analytical report to the ones already submitted.

alleged uncontrolled growth, inefficiency, undue complexity, fragmentation and lack of effectiveness.[2]

Many of the charges and criticisms made against the organization,
which led to the demand for reform, have proved to be exaggerated if
not baseless. It is unfortunate that precious resources were wasted in
correcting excesses which did not exist. For instance there has been no
reduction in the quantum of documentation or in the number of
meetings as per the annual calender of conferences and meetings.[3] The
reason for this is simply that they were already brought down to the
minimum before the renewed exercise for 'reform' began in 1986–87.

What prompted the United States to raise a hue and cry for reform
is now an open secret. Efforts to mould the United Nations' programmes and activities to its liking are being initiated. Allegations of
excessive staffing were made. As a result of 'reform', the strength of
the regular staff has been considerably reduced. On the other hand,
the strength of the staff financed by extra-budgetary resources has
increased. Thus the strength of the Secretariat staff remains more or
less the same. The difference is that the funds and staff are devoted
now to preferred programmes which are not necessarily in keeping
with the needs of the international community as a whole. Priorities
have become topsy turvy. Several UN programmes under the mid-
term Plan (1984–89 extended until 1991) designed to assist development in the developing countries have either been abandoned or
postponed, for lack of funds.[4] Furthermore, there has been no relief
from financial uncertainties. The United States, responsible for 25 per
cent of UN funding, continues to withhold or delay substantial parts
of its contribution. The one new element, if at all it can be said to be
new, is that budgetary provisions are made by consensus,[5] and that the
CPC an inter-governmental body, has acquired more say on the
contents of budget proposals.

The continuing stalemate on the restructuring of the inter-governmental machinery, has created a hiatus in the role of the United
Nations in the economic and social fields. Neither has there been any

---

[2] *Ibid.*, para.78.

[3] A/45/226, n. 2, para. 16–20, 36–37. Also see *supra*, pp. 121–23.

[4] This point has been discussed in detail earlier. See, in particular, supra, pp. 51–53
and 115–18.

[5] See supra pp. 116–18.

agreement on the content and objectives for reform and the restructuring of the UN system. The provisions in the Charter which provide the framework for UN programmes and objectives in the economic and social fields are very clear, but, as the deliberations of the Special Commission indicated, some member-States of the developed countries were unable to distinguish between the validity of the issues and objectives and the relevance of the structure established, to address it. They did not question the validity of the issues and objectives, but were not willing to support what was implied, i.e., the structures. 'This has resulted', to quote the Secretary-General, 'in a situation where the United Nations is constrained to address present day issues as well as those which are emerging, without the appropriate mechanism or deliberative or decision-making capacity'.[6]

Political developments, especially since 1988, have unfolded some promising changes in the international environment such as the ending of the Cold War and a remarkable demonstration of the United Nations' capability in conducting a variety of successful operations aimed at managing peaceful resolutions of conflicts in various parts of the world. In sharp contrast to these developments, the North–South divide and its related problems have become more acute and present a serious challenge to the United Nations' future as a world organization.

THE CHANGING UNITED NATIONS

Political institutions as they develop, very often take forms different from the ones mapped out for them at the time of their inception. The United Nations, at forty years and plus, bears the point. In 1945, the world body was envisaged by its three chief architects, the United States of America, the United Kingdom and the Soviet Union, as, a British analyst put it bluntly, 'a consortium which would enable them to rule the world for the foreseeable future... '[7] Once the three Allied

[6] Review of the Efficiency ... The United Nations Intergovernmental Structure and Functions in the Economic and Social Fields: Report of the Secretary-General (A/45/714, 20 November 1990), p. 44.

[7] Martin Woolacott, 'The UN Today: Power Broker's Deadly Failure', *The Guardian* (London), 7 March 1982. The privileged position which the three chief architects had acquired for themselves was also extended to China, at US insistence, and to France, at the insistence of the United Kingdom. See K.P. Saksena, 'Forty Years of the United Nations: A Perspective', *International Studies*, vol. 2, no. 4, December 1985, pp. 290–91.

powers fell out with each other and split into the so-called East and West, the United States assumed the leadership in guiding the United Nations along the direction of its choosing. It is common knowledge that the United States successfully used the United Nations' instrumentality (at least during the first decade of its existence) as if it was an extension of the US Department of State.

The expansion of the role of the General Assembly, constituted on the principle of the sovereign equality of member nations, came about after the framework of the United Nations was planned. The original framework placed the General Assembly, compared to the Security Council, in a secondary role, but certain factors combined to give it a pivotal position in the UN system. At the San Francisco Conference, the participating member-States, other than the big five wielding veto powers in the Security Council, combined their efforts under the leadership of Australia, to successfully demand a much wider role for the General Assembly. The United States in the context of its emerging rivalry with the Soviet Union and aware of its political and military ascendency among the members of the United Nations, encouraged the demand. Consequently, the provisions of the Charter especially Article 10, gave the General Assembly the overall jurisdiction on discussions and recommendations on any matter of international concern, whether relating to peace and security or economic development and social welfare. Furthermore, with the East–West Cold War severely undermining the effectiveness of the Security Council, the United States, in order to circumvent the Soviet veto, helped build up the power and influence of the General Assembly and boosted the 'democratic' principle of one state, one vote. From the point of view of the United States, there was, at the time, no discrepancy between idealism and national interest. Its military and economic power had successfully lined up three-fourths of the member-States on its side, thus assuring its domination of UN policies and voting patterns in the General Assembly.

The United States' 'control' of what John Stoessinger calls 'an automatic two-thirds majority'[*] in the United Nations, lasted till the late 1950s, when the influx of Asian and African states to its membership changed the scenario. Thereafter the United Nations gradually

---

[*] *The United Nations and the Super Powers* (New York, Random House, 1970) 2nd Ed., p. 13. It should be noted that a two-thirds majority was needed for the adoption of recommendations on important matters by the General Assembly. The United States' at least until 1955, could always muster support of three-fourths of the UN membership with whom it had built up defence alliances.

emerged as a unique institution the first and only one of its kind, to embrace all the territorial units and political entities of the world.[9]

Thus over the years, the complex interplay of political forces with countervailing influences, shaped the United Nations into an entity different from what it was designed to be by its founders in 1945. Not that it became more effective than before but it was no longer subservient to, or controlled by, any particular power or group of powers. Some did talk of the 'tyranny of the majority' or 'the hegemony of the super powers' but the fact is that until recently, the United Nations belonged to no one in particular but to all.[10] As of now, it has around its table, representatives of not only those who fought world wars among themselves in the past but also of those who have clashed in the post-war period. All kinds of antagonists and various contending interests are represented and that includes the haves as well as the have nots of the present global economic system.

It is not surprising, therefore, that the processes of the United Nations which provide the mechanism for reconciling contending interests, resolving differences and harmonizing the actions of member-States have become more challenging as well as more frustrating than ever. That the world body has attained a forum and character different from what was envisaged at the time of its inception has been the root cause of the disenchantment of its chief architect and consequential to the current crisis. The emergence of the United Nations mechanism as a non-partisan entity, no longer subject to manipulation, should have been regarded as a welcome development, instead of being criticized.[11] Another variation from the original design

[9] Apart from the member-States, the two Koreas, which joined the UN in 1991, were there as observers as are Switzerland and a number of smaller states as well as extra-territorial organizations like the Palestine Liberation Organization(PLO). These observers do not have the right to vote but they do participate in the debates and discussions and in 'corridor diplomacy'. Again, almost all the major regional organizations such as the European Community (EC), the Organization of African Unity (OAU), the Arab League, the Islamic Conference Organization and the Non-Aligned Movement (NAM) Coordinating Group etc., have acquired observer status and form part of the diplomatic milieu of the United Nations.

[10] It should be noted that at its inception, 'original' membership to the United Nations was strictly confined to those who had signed a declaration of war against the Axis Powers—Germany, Italy and Japan. Even neutral countries such as Sweden and Ireland, were not invited to the San Francisco Conference.

[11] Several western writers on the subject, have viewed this development as an indication of the growing weakness of the United Nations. For instance, a UNA-USA study refers to the development as an 'identity crisis' of the world body. It categorically asks,

which has not been favourably received dates back to the Yalta Conference of 1945. Stalin is reported to have said, at the time, that he was prepared to protect the rights of the small state, but would never agree to any Soviet action being subject to judgement, to which the Big Three agreed.[12] Over the decades, however, the United Nations developed procedures which enabled it to call upon any state, however mighty (including the USA and the USSR) to explain or justify its conduct or acts or omission or commission before the world forum (the General Assembly) obliging all others to stand up and be counted for or against the alleged violation of the accepted norms of international behaviour. The procedure has, of late, also seen the United States finding itself in the dock.[13] The member-State, which contributes 25 per cent towards the cost of maintaining the forum, has found it difficult to tolerate the venting of criticism and grievances against it in the very arena it sustains.

Intriguingly enough, the major target of reform and reorganization has not been the political processes of the United Nations, but its administrative and financial functioning. Again, it is not the political structure but the inter-governmental machinery in the economic and social and related programmes, which has been subjected to the demand for reform. As analyzed in the first chapter the United States painstakingly worked out, in 1944–45, a United Nations framework in the economic and social fields which would ensure its growing ascendancy in the world economy to persist. The Charter, no doubt, contains commitments to the ideals of the promotion of higher standard of living, economic and social progress and development, and the solution of international economic, social and related problems, but as succinctly noted by the Director of the UNA-USA United Nations

---

'Whose United Nations' and suggests that since the United Nations belongs to no one particular group of states, it should delimit its objectives and role as enshrined in the Charter, especially in the economic and social fields and keep such global issues, as emanating from the North–South conflict, out of its purview. Peter Fromuth, 'The United Nations at 40: The Problems and Opportunities', in *A Successor Vision: The United Nations of Tomorrow*, Lanham MD: UNA-USA, 1988, pp. 81–105.

If the global forum of the United Nations is not the place, where else, one may ask, can such crucial issues of our time be discussed and attempts made to resolve them?

[12] Ruth Russell, *A History of the United Nations Charter* (Washington, D.C.: Brookings, 1958), pp. 519–44.

[13] Notable examples in recent years have been the question of Grenada, and the complaints of Libya, Nicaragua and Panama. Also see Saksena, *Forty Years of the United Nations*, n. 7, pp. 289–317.

Management and Decision Making Project, 'in the economic realm ... the United Nations was envisaged by the industrialized nations (of the West) as *a means to extend and reinforce the post-war status quo*'.[14]

As discussed earlier in Chapter 1 the powers controlling the existing international economic system, for decades, successfully kept the role of the United Nations limited to a non-factor in the regulation of international economic relations. It was only beginning the late 1970s that new processes and institutional arrangements appeared, encroaching on, with one step followed by another small step, the domain which the industrialized states hitherto treated as their exclusive preserve, and where the United Nations' activities could exercise some influence in bringing about the needed change in the existing economic system. That the industrialized countries, in general, and the United States in particular, did not want the United Nations to assume any measure of influence in international economic relations was the main reason behind the hue and cry for 'reform and reorganization'.

RADICAL CHANGES IN THE INTERNATIONAL ENVIRONMENT

The last couple of years have unfolded such radical changes in international political environments as, perhaps, never before been witnessed since the end of the Second World War.

Until recently, the United Nations was being referred to as irrelevant in dealing with pressing world problems. Moreover, it was teetering and tottering under the threat of financial bankruptcy (a situation which still as of February 1992, continues unabated) and wrenching under the strains of demands for administrative and financial reforms. The situation has not changed much in this regard, either; although international media had glossed over this dismal state of affairs.

What has changed dramatically is the sudden transfiguration of international environments and "rediscovery" of the United Nations as an organization pivotal to the resolution of international conflicts that not long ago appeared intractable.

[14] Fromuth, n. 11 of this chapter, pp. 1–3. Emphasis added. He also notes that this strategy permitted a number of measures accommodating the concerns of the Third World such as formation of the UNCTAD and the UNIDO etc., but to the extent only that such new institutions did not effect a dent in the existing international economic system. pp. 83–84.

Ending of the Cold War: What has added momentum to the United Nations' role in the field of international peace and security largely emanates from the cessation of tension and antagonism between the so-called East and West. The two superpowers, representing the opposite ends of Europe,[15] initiated in 1987, an assiduous search for the basis of a stable peace and cooperation between them. They reached agreements on many issues and the period beginning 1988, witnessed the peaceful resolution of several conflict situations, through the instrumentality of the United Nations, in various parts of the world.

Both the East and West 'rediscovered' the United Nations, as indispensable for the promotion of international cooperation. In September 1989 the five permanent member nations of the Security Council, represented by their foreign ministers, held exclusive deliberations at UN headquarters and issued a statement in which they announced their agreement to seek positive changes in the international political climate from confrontation to the relaxation of tensions and reiterated that the United Nations had a central role to play in the maintenance of peace and security.[16] In early November 1989, the Berlin Wall was dismantled and the formal ending of the Cold War was announced. As a demonstrative example of the close cooperation between the two superpowers, the Soviet Union and the United States, for the first time in history, jointly sponsored a resolution in the General Assembly which sought to strengthen the United Nations' role in maintaining international peace and security.[17] The years 1988–91 also witnessed leaders of both the East and the West addressing the General Assembly in the context of the UN commitment to peace and of ushering in a new era of hope and promise. The leaders included heads of state, such as Ronald Reagan, Margaret Thatcher (who had followed the Reagan line on UN denigration, until

[15] Europe is used here not in geographical but civilizational sense of the term. Also see Chapter I, *supra* n. 27.

[16] Over the period, the holding of meetings of the five permanent members (excluding non-permanent, elected members) of the Security Council became a regular feature. So has the Foreign Ministers' meeting of the Five, in September, become an annual feature. For an excerpt from the joint statement issued by the five Foreign Ministers on September 27, 1991, see *UN Chronicle*, December 1991, p. 43.

[17] Resolution 44/213 of 15 November 1989 entitled, Enhancing International Peace, Security and International Cooperation in Various Fields in all its aspects in Accordance with the Charter of the United Nations. The Resolution was adopted without vote. Also see, *supra*, pp. 149–50.

1986), Mikhail Gorbachev, Francois Mitterand and George Bush. The commitments augured well for the United Nations and for world peace. The United Nations was being increasingly asked to play an important role in humanitarian efforts around the globe and to oversee the peaceful resolution of conflicts, organize elections, and, as and where necessary, to ascertain the views of the people concerned. These were welcome developments indeed.

Disintegration of the USSR

The most significant event, since the inception of the United Nations, has undoubtedly been the demise of one of its three chief architects, the USSR, in 1991. On Christmas eve, Mikhail Gorbachev appeared on national television and announced his resignation as President of USSR, thus ending the existence of a mighty superpower. The same day President Yeltsin of the Russian Federation formally informed the UN Secretary-General, that Russia was taking over the Soviet seat in the Security Council and would assume all its rights and obligations. He also sent along a sample flag of the Russian Federation. On December 28, the red Soviet flag was replaced by the blue, red and white colours of the Federation. A few hours later Yuily Vorontsov, the former Soviet Ambassador, presided over the Security Council consultations, for the first time, as the Russian Ambassador.[18] While the disintegration of the Soviet Union will certainly have far reaching ramifications on the operational system of the United Nations, it is too early to visualize and conceptualize the consequences as events are still unfolding and no clear picture has emerged so far on the future of the landmass which, until the other day, contained one of the two super-powers of the world.

---

[18] The pole from which the Soviet flag had fluttered stood bare in the morning. In the afternoon UN security guards raised the Russian flag and it began fluttering among those of the other member nations. There was no formal ceremony as happened in the past when the flags of new members were raised. Some legal experts held the view that the change may require an amendment to the Charter which specifically mentions the Soviet Union as a permanent member with the right to veto, but no member raised an objection. This was so because the other permanent members of the Security Council had agreed to the change. Neither did the remaining constituents of the erstwhile USSR question the claim of the Russian succession to the seat. Obviously, the permanent members did not wish that the occasion be used to press for reform in the Security Council with an increase in the number of members as the developing countries had been demanding. *Times of India*, 29 December 1991.

Revitalizing UN Peace and Security System

Once the two superpowers reached an understanding they also recognized the fact that although they could resolve and reduce their differences through negotiations outside the United Nations, they did need the organization to come to grips with issues concerning other nations, which in one way or another impinge on their relationship as well. The conclusion of the Geneva Accord, concerning Afghanistan, in April 1988, bears the point. The Accord represented the culmination of diplomatic activity sustained over the years, through the United Nations, in the effort to secure a peaceful solution of the conflict[19] and provided the basis for all Afghans of their right to self-determination. It was the first instance of the world's two mightiest military powers coming together as co-guarantors of an agreement negotiated under the auspices of the Secretary-General of the United Nations. The Accord was followed by the institution of the United Nations Good Offices Mission for Afghanistan and Pakistan (UNGOMAP) to monitor its implementation, including the withdrawal of Soviet troops from Afghanistan.

Developments relating to conflicts in other areas were demonstrative of the same political linkage. In August 1988, a ceasefire was secured in the eight–year long Iran–Iraq war in compliance with Security Council Resolution 598 of August 1987. Consequently, a United Nations Iran–Iraq Military Observer Group (UNIIMOG) was successfully deployed to observe the ceasefire.[20]

In Namibia, it was eventually the United Nations Transition Assistance Group (UNTAG) which successfully arranged elections,[21] leading

[19] In December 1979 the Soviet Union intervened militarily in Afghanistan and installed a new government. The Security Council could not take any action because of the veto exercised by the Soviet Union. The General Assembly in 1980 requested the Secretary-General to find a solution to the problem and to appoint a special representative to assist him in the work. What followed was intensive diplomatic activity often referred to as proximity talks. It was this sustained diplomatic effort which proved fortuitous, once the Soviet Union and the United States reached an understanding on Afghanistan.

[20] After protracted negotiations among the five permanent members, the Security Council unanimously demanded a ceasefire from both warring nations, who had been waging the bloodiest war against each other since September 1980. Iran refused to accept a ceasefire unless Iraq's guilt in starting the war was recognised. It was the understanding between the major powers not to supply arms to the warring nations which prompted Iran to accept the ceasefire in August 1988. The UNIIMOG having completed its task, was withdrawn by December 1990.

[21] As a sequal to the superpowers coming together, a crucial breakthrough was

to the establishment, on 21 March 1990, of a new government of the Namibian people under the presidentship of Sam Najuma of the SWAPO. Namibia was admitted to the UN in April 1990.

In Central America, the United Nations played a significant role in resolving the conflict in Nicaragua. The United Nations Observer Mission (ONUVEN) monitored the preparation and holding of free and fair elections in February 1990. The success of this endeavour led to a central role for the organization in the peaceful transfer of power in a region where, in the past, such transfers have been the exception rather than the rule. The international commission for Support and Verification (CIAV), of the United Nations played a key role in the voluntary demobilization of members of the Nicaraguan resistance. The task of receiving and destroying the weapons of its members and verifying the ceasefire which made possible their demobilization, was discharged by the United Nations Observer Group in Central America (ONUCA).[22]

Thus, as against the thirteen UN peace-keeping operations launched during the first forty-three years of the organization's existence, five were mounted in 1988–89 and four initiated during 1990–1991. Never

---

effected by two agreements signed simultaneously at UN Headquarters on 22 December 1988; a tripartite agreement (S/20346) between Angola, Cuba and South Africa and a bilateral agreement (S/20345) between Cuba and Angola. The agreements called for the withdrawal of South African military forces from Namibia, the withdrawal, to Cuba, of 30,000 Cuban forces from Angola, the implementation of Security Council Resolution 431 and 435, 1978 for Namibian independence beginning 1 April 1989 and free and fair elections in Namibia under UN supervision. The *UNTAG* completed its mission in February 1990.

[22] Since early 1980s the political situation in Central America was in turmoil and the government of Nicaragua had brought several complaints against the United States for alleged acts of aggression, including naval blockades. In August 1987, at the initiative of the President of Costa Rica, an agreement was signed amongst the five Presidents of the Central American states spelling out a 'procedure for the establishment of a firm and lasting peace in Central America'. However, it could not be implemented. In 1988–89, following an understanding between the Soviet Union and the United States, the United Nations' pursuit of peace in the region resulted in the launching of the UN Observation Mission for the Verification of Elections in Nicaragua (ONUVEN) on 25 August 1989. This was followed by the institution, on 6 September 1989, of the International Support Verification Commission (CIAV)—a combined task force set up by the United Nations and the Organization of American States. A third key element of what became the major international peace-keeping effort was the establishment of the ONUCA. It led to the successful conclusion of the UN supervised election and steps to demobilize the Nicaraguan Resistance Group (FNLN) in El Salvador in February–March 1990 with assistance from an extended mandate for the ONUCA.

before were such precedents set as were done, in different ways, in Namibia, Angola and Nicaragua and most notably in Central America in El Salvador, which is in the offing. Indeed, the organization is conducting missions that were unthinkable in the era of the Cold War. It should be noted, however, that although the ending of the Cold War radically changed the international political environment, the United Nations entered the post-Cold War era as an element of continuity, of constancy, in the midst of a state of flux. All peace-keeping operations, in one way or another, were made possible because of its continued involvement with conflict situations and the implementation of plans based on negotiations with the parties concerned and initiated much before the Cold War ended.

Peace settlements that have made notable headway during 1990–91 include those in E1 Salvador and Western Sahara. In the latter area the UN Peace Settlement Plan,[23] as approved by the Security Council, was launched on 6 September 1991 with a formal ceasefire between the forces of Morocco and the Frente Popular Para la Liberacion de Saguia el-Harma y de Rio de Oro (POLISARIO). The despatch of military observers marked the first stage of the UN Mission of referendum in Western Sahara known by its French acronym the MINURSO. The Mission was formally established by the Council on 29 April 1991 to oversee the implementation of the UN settlement plan which was worked out in cooperation with the Organization of African Unity. The next step is the holding of a plebiscite to let the people of Western Sahara decide whether they want to join Morocco or opt for independence.

The Security Council, on 30 September 1991, reaffirmed its strong support for the urgent completion of the peace mission instituted by the UN Observer Missions in El Salvador and known by its Spanish acronym ONUSAL. Its immediate task is to bring about an agreement between the Frente Farabundo Marti para la Liberacion National (FMLN) and the government of El Salvador, the surrender of arms by

[23] Western Sahara formerly known as Spanish Sahara on the west coast of Africa has been in turmoil and violence since 1976. The United Nations has been actively involved in restoring peace in the region. After protracted negotiations, in which the representatives of the Secretary-General of the United Nations and of the Organization of African Unity (OAU) played a significant role, an agreement was reached between the two warring sides, the POLISARIO and Morocco. The peace settlement plan and the UN Mission (MINUSRO) were formally approved by the Security Council on 29 April 1991.

the FMLN and the conduct of fresh elections[24] for the formation of a new government.

Perhaps the most ambitious and challenging role which the United Nations has accepted is in Cambodia. For more than a decade, it has been involved in finding a solution to the volatile situation that characterized the country specifically since 1979. Eventually, through a complex process of negotiations which acquired fresh impetus with the ending of the Cold War, a peace accord was signed at a conference convened in Paris in October 1991.[25] The participants included the five permanent members of the Security Council. Under the agreement the United Nations accepted the responsibility of sending a massive peace-keeping force, including military and civilian personnel numbering more than 3,00,000 to oversee the implementation of the agreement. The terms include the obtaining of a ceasefire between the warring forces, the rehabilitation of more than 3,00,000 refugees living in camps on the Thai–Cambodian border, the conducting of free and fair elections and taking over the responsibilities of the government of the Cambodian administration relating to foreign affairs, defence, internal security, information and finance. The mission, to be known as the United Nations Transitional Authority in Cambodia (UNTAC), is estimated to cost more than $3 billion over the next two years. While awaiting the approval of the finances involved by the Security Council and subsequently by the General Assembly, on the recommendation of the Secretary-General, the Security Council has already authorized the sending of the UN Advance Mission in Cambodia (UNAMIC). Since September 1991, the Security Council has also been actively involved in resolving the ongoing civil war in Yugoslavia and has recently initiated steps for sending an approximately 10,000-strong peace-keeping Force to the country.[26]

[24] As noted earlier, Central America has been increasingly engulfed in a chain of viciously violent events including civil war in El Salvador, since the early 1980. Consequently, some 300,000 El Salvadoreans have sought refuge in neighbouring Guatemala and Nicaragua, adding to the violence and turmoil in the region.

[25] For the background and text of the agreement, see *Agreements on a Comprehensive Political Settlement of the Cambodian Conflict*, New York: UN Department of Publication, January 1992.

[26] Security Council Resolution 727 of 9 January 1992. Also see Secretary-General's Report, S/23363 of 5 January 1992. The relevant documents on Yugoslavia are in the *Review of International Affairs* (Belgrade), issue numbers: 995–1001, August 1991 to January 1992.

The radical changes as well as the revitalization of the UN peace and security system have been made possible by the ending of the antagonism between the USA and Russia which has been increasingly replaced by agreements between the two. Indeed, it is the agreement between the United States, the unchallenged superpower and Russia, or, more appropriate, the compliance of the latter with the directives of the former, that has formed much of the present international scenario. August 1990 witnessed yet another remarkable development when, for the first time in the history of the United Nations, enforcement measures were recommended to seek the vacation of the military occupation of Kuwait by Iraq.[27]

One is reminded, however, of an observation which V K Krishna Menon of India is reported to have made in 1954. While challenging a remark of the President of the General Assembly to the effect that great power harmony was quite enough to hope for the solution of a certain subject, Menon stated that he did not concur that 'because the United States and the Soviet Union agree, all problems are resolved'. He concluded by warning that 'The time might come when they will agree at our expense'.[28]

Menon's comment may sound cynical but it is not without relevance in the context of current political developments. The erstwhile Soviet Union is no longer in a bargaining position vis-a-vis the United States and, engulfed as it is in domestic turmoil, cannot afford to be an antagonist. At this juncture its options are limited to cooperating with the United States or pursuing a passive foreign policy. Either way, whether out of choice as in the past, or of necessity today, Russia's acquiescent policy is in keeping with Menon's prophecy as far as the third world is concerned. The former Soviet President, Mikhail

---

[27] In the case of Korea from 1950–53 the United States, having obtained rump sanctions from the Security Council, launched in the name of the United Nations and the use of UN flag, military action against North Korea. The action was opposed by the Soviet Union. Military action against Iraq's occupation of Kuwait is the first undertaken with the concurrence of the five permanent members of the Security Council. However, the Secretary-General aptly noted that this also was not a UN war. For elaboration of the points, see, in particular, K P Saksena and C S R Murthy, 'The United Nations and the Gulf Crisis' in A H H Abidi and K R Singh, eds., *The Gulf Crisis*, New Delhi: Lancers Books, 1991, pp. 20–40.

[28] Quoted in the *New York Times*, 19 November 1954. Cited in Ross N. Berkes and Mohinder S. Bedi, *The Diplomacy of India: India's Foreign Policy in the United Nations*, London: Oxford, 1958, p. 2.

Gorbachev, was on record for having said that the Soviet Union would not pursue a foreign policy contrary to US interests.[29] Indeed, beginning 1991, the Soviet Union was not only not doing anything contrary to the United States' interests but was largely a passive spectator to what the United States and its allies were planning or doing in managing world affairs through the United Nations. Gorbachev's successor, Boris Yeltsin, also demonstrated his loyalty to and dependence on the United States. After the coup that failed, both Gorbachev and Yeltsin as well as the leaders of the republics of the erstwhile Soviet Union looked to western leaders, and US President George Bush in particular, for support. It is interesting to note that when Yeltsin and the Presidents of Byelorussia and the Ukraine worked out the formation of the Commonwealth of Independent States at their meeting in Minsk (7 December 1991), the Russian President, before announcing the formation, first telephoned the White House to inform the US President of the agreement and sought his approval. Much later, the President of Byelorussia dialed Moscow to inform Soviet President Gorbachev.[30]

New World Order in the Offing?

In this radically changed situation, the United States having no power or group of powers to challenge its supremacy, is all set, it appears to usher in a new world order. It was in his nomination acceptance speech as a Republican candidate, in 1988, that President George Bush first referred to a new world order. Since then the term has become such rhetorical commonplace, at least in the United States, that it is often enshrined in capital letters as New World Order or even abbreviated to NWO. No blueprint has been spelled out, but from the various utterances of President Bush and other policy makers in the US administration and media, it can be taken to mean collective law enforcement. This was evident in the Security Council verdict against Iraq, when the US acted as policemen after obtaining a rump sanction

[29] On the eve of his meetings with President George Bush in June 1990, the Soviet President gave an exclusive interview to *Time* magazine wherein he painstakingly argued that US and Soviet interests converged in meeting the many imminent and crucial global problems. He is quoted to have said, 'In any area of Soviet foreign policy, if we are doing something that harms the interests of the United States, then that policy cannot be successful'. *Time*, 4 June 1990, p. 14.

[30] *Time* magazine, 23 December 1991, p. 11. Also see 'An exclusive interview: Boris Yeltsin', *Newsweek*, 6 January 1992, pp. 11–13.

from the Council and carried out its task without bothering about the framework or the political processes of the United Nations.

True, Iraq's president blatantly violated accepted norms and what was wrong should have been set right. But by whom and by what means is what has been questioned. The Charter lists conditions for moving from economic to military sanctions. These were ignored. How the members of the Security Council were pursuaded to give a positive vote is an open secret. Again, the Charter provides for a Military Staff Committee, under the joint control of all five permanent members of the Security Council. Right from its inception, however, the Committee has remained inoperative through the four frozen decades of the Cold War. The famous Security Council Resolution 678 of 1990, authorising the use of military might against Iraq was so carefully worded as to avoid mention of the Committee. There was no UN control of the Coalition forces that killed an estimated 500,000 to 1 million Iraqis—both civilians and military personnel—and, through carpet bombing, destroyed the industrial and communication infrastructure of the country, pushing it back to a pre-industrial age.

President Bush says that the United States does not intend to act as the world's policemen, out at the same time insists that 'lawlessness' should not be allowed in the New World Order and that 'military action against Iraq provided a warning in this regard'.[31] President Bush is also quoted as having said, 'For the foreseeable future, no other nation or group of nations will step forward to assume leadership. And as the twentieth century gives way to the twenty-first .... what country's name will it bear? I say it will be another American century'.[32] President Bush's National Security Advisor, Brendt Scowcraft put the concept of the NWO succinctly by assertaining that 'with US leadership and Soviet compliance', the United Nations would 'live upto its Charter ideals of policing the world and penalising the wrongdoers'.[33]

The rest of the world, especially the Third World countries have viewed these developments and many of them have, in discreet terms, expressed their apprehensions. Prime Minister Mahathir Mohamad of Malaysia has been more blunt. According to him American 'dramatic' new clout will be used to 'shore up a sagging US economy'. Pressure on other countries, he believes, will be 'political as well as economic and military adventures'. In October 1990, Mahatir told *Time* magazine

[31] *Time* magazine, 1 April 1991, p. 19.
[32] *Ibid.*
[33] *Ibid.*

that people 'now live in fear of the United States. Believe me. If you are friendly with the United States, that is fine. But if you annoy them they can take action like they did in Panama'.[34] The Malaysian Prime Minister's statement echoes Menon's apprehensions expressed more than thirty-five years ago. But while the latter spoke of two super-powers, the question that arises today whether the United States intends to impose its hegemony over the others as it has emerged as the only superpower.

Here one cannot ignore the fact that the United States is an open society and has a democratic system of government. There is not much scope for an unwarranted use of American military might. Such an exercise could prove to be counter-productive, as was demonstrated by the Vietnam war. The US administration did not so much lose the war on the battlefield as it did on the domestic front. Thus, how and whether the United States acts as a policeman or as police chief, as it did in the Gulf region, is likely to depend on the geographical location of the conflict situation and also on public in the US. There have been, however, innumerable instances when public opinion in the United States was swayed by intensively orchestrated propaganda. Why its nationals, representing hardly 5 per cent of the world's population, should have an exclusive say on matters which are of vital concern to the international community as a whole, raises a more pertinent ques-tion. Is it possible for the United States to control and gear the machinery of the United Nations into activity of Washington's choice? With its objective in the economic and social fields already clear, it is becoming apparent that it would like to take the same role in the field of peace and security. Whether it can do so as it did in the first decade of UN existence under less favourable circumstances[35] remains to be seen.

However an analyst of the Royal Institute of International Affairs in London believes that if the United States, which attempted to play the role of a world policeman, gave it up at a time when it was much stronger compared to other countries, there is even less reason for it to work now. The French President Francois Mitterrand holds the view that 'a Pax Americana is unrealistic'. As he sees it, 'no one can claim that from now no one country decides for all'.[36]

---

[34] Ibid.

[35] Compared to the first ten years when the United States had a rival power in the Soviet Union, it has no such challenge now or in the immediate future.

[36] Time magazine, 1 April 1990. p. 21.

While the United Nations has evolved into a different body from what it was during the first decade, it has not, acquired the mechanism to provide protection against the determined depredation of the strong. It has, however evolved an extensive armoury of diplomatic and parliamentary devices that could maximise and mobilise forces which, in any given situation, favour just and peaceful action. Much depends on the major powers and larger membership of the United Nations. What may appear difficult, if not impossible, for one member-State to resist the arbitrary use or misuse of power, a collective membership could act firmly through the instrumentality which the United Nations provides, to stop a possible transgressor. It is in this context that the question of what form the United Nations takes in the immediate future is of great significance.

'REFORMS' CONTEMPLATED

Security Council

With the ending of the Cold War, the Security Council has acquired, to a considerable extent, the role which was envisaged for it by the architects of the Charter. In all conflict resolutions in the recent past, the Security Council has played a key role except in the case of Panama. Over the last few years, the exclusive informal meetings of the five permanent members to work out a line of policy of unanimous concurrence—essential for any decision by the Council—have been more frequent. However, ever since the number of elected members was raised to 10 in 1966, unanimity constitutes for the five, four affirmative votes for a decision as compared to two in the original arrangement.

The question of revising the membership of the Security Council, gained momentum again in the last few years. Many UN members now numbering 175 have expressed the view that the Security Council be reshaped to reflect today's world. The question acquired an urgency ever since the Security Council, beginning August 1990, increasingly resorted to the enforcement measures of Chapter VII of the Charter. The former Secretary-General Perez de Cuellar aptly noted that action in this specific field of activity should not only be just but should also be seen as such. He emphasized that agreement among the Council's permanent members must carry with it the willing support of the majority of nations.[37]

The existing pattern of representation in the Security Council has become extremely lopsided in view of the radical political changes and the coming together of the East and West of Europe. Thus the Europeans and others now have seven seats, four permanent and three nonpermanent. The Third World countries, pressing for an equal representation, are seeking a further expansion of Security Council membership on the basis of an equitable geographical distribution of seats.[38] Furthermore, both Japan and Germany, who are now among the top four contributors to the UN budget, would like to find a place among the permanent members of the Council. Japan currently contribute more than 12 per cent of the budget. Germany's annual assessed contribution to the United Nations, as of now, is considerably larger than either that of France or Britain. The question is what the criteria for permanent membership should be, whether on the basis of economic power or population. There is also a strong view that Brazil, India and Nigeria, by virtue of being the largest countries of their respective regions, should become permanent members.[39] This proposal, which seems plausible, would mean adding five new permanent members—Japan, Germany, Brazil, India and Nigeria. Unlike the present members however, no new member is to possess the veto power. If the proposal is accepted there would be three categories of members: Five veto-wielding permanent members; five permanent members without veto; and a number of elected non-permanent members.

It is obvious that whatever the nature of the reforms and reshaping of the membership of the Security Council are to be, opposition will come from those affected. While there have been mostly informal proposals and ideas floating around, Italy took the initiative in making a formal move in October 1991. The General Assembly, at its Forty-sixth session, had on its agenda an item initiated by the non-aligned

[37] *UN Chronicle*, December 1991, p. 43.

[38] In accordance with the amendment dated 17 December 1963, (Resolution 1991 A(XVIII)) which became operative from Januray 1966, the Security Council has the following pattern of the geographical representation: Two from West Europe and other states; one from the East European states; two from the Latin American states; and five from the African and Asian states. With regard to the Afro-Asians, the practice has been that two are elected from Africa, the two from Asia and the one Arab member-State is chosen alternatively from Africa and Asia.

[39] These and other set of proposals have been well analysed in John Newhouse, 'The Diplomatic Round', *The New Yorker*, 16 December 1991, pp. 99–102.

countries including India way back in 1979 entitled the Question of equitable representation of and increase in the membership of the Security Council. No formal discussion took place at that Session however, but the General Assembly decided (Decision No. 46/418, 11 December 1991) to defer consideration of the item and to include it in the provisional agenda of its Forty-seventh Session.

Intriguingly enough, when the disintegration of the Soviet Union took place and the Soviet seat was quietly passed on to the Russian Federation, no one raised an objection. It was obvious that the five existing permanent members did not care to share the right to veto with what could have been an additional member. Furthermore, as no revision of the Charter is possible without the concurrence of each of the five, it is difficult to predict how the negotiations for expansion will emerge in the years to come. What is clear is that there will be resistance to change, but the continuing expansion of the Security Council's role, especially in the area of enforcement measures, makes reforms desirable. As noted earlier, the Council should be enlarged so that decisions are not imposed, at the behest of the United Nations, by a select few.

Office of the Secretary-General

The office of the Secretary-General is another UN institution which has aroused considerable enthusiasm for reform towards building up a 'leadership role'. It should be noted that in the context of the ongoing exercise for reform of the administrative and financial functioning of the United Nations, there has been no official proposal for reviewing the role of the Secretary-General. Indeed, there have been no mis-givings as to the way the incumbent discharged his responsibilities. On the contrary, his role both as head of the administration and as catalyst and moderator in conflict situations has won high praise from all quarters. Nonetheless, there have been write-ups in the media and from research scholars of the western countries, where, intriguingly the emphasis has been on reform of the selection process and on a fixed term of seven years.

The attempt seems to be to change the practice followed for the last four decades, based on the recommendations of the Preparatory Commission (1945–46), which proposed that the Secretary-General be selected for an initial period of five years, from among nationals other than those of the five permanent members of the Security Council. The process of selection throughout has consisted of the Security

Council holding closed meetings to select a candidate. Once unanimity on a choice is reached among the Big Five, the selection is generally endorsed by the other members of the Security Council and by the General Assembly. What was being proposed[40] was a seven-year single term instead of five years and that a non-political committee should undertake the task of a world-wide political search to find a competent executive irrespective of nationality and professional background.

The western media picked up this concept and momentum was generated in support of the proposals. *Time* magazine fully supported the seven-year single term citing the study by two UN experts[41] and quoting the President of the UNA-USA who had argued; 'Why not consider business leaders, university presidents, even cultural leaders— people of executive quality?'[42] The *New York Times*, in its editorial, reiterated the argument, adding that the choice should not be confined to diplomats and that, 'serious consideration of former heads of governments, business executives or Foundation officials would add stature to the job and interest to the quest'.[43] Such proposals ignore the realities that the United Nations is neither a business enterprise nor a governmental agency. The Secretary-General has to run the organization not only efficiently and cost-effectively but also to meet the growing needs of the world community. The Secretary-General represents, more than any other functionary, the entity of the United Nations and the ideals and objectives enshrined in its Charter. At the same time he has to bear in mind that the United Nations is not a world government and that it has no coercive authority.

[40] The UNA-USA Studies initiated the proposal to build up a momentum for enhancing the leadership role of the Secretary-General. See in particular 'Leadership at the United Nations: The Role of the Secretary and the Member States' in Peter Fromuth, ed., *A Successor Vision: The United Nations of Tommorrow*, pp. 193–212. Also see, Thomas Franck, 'The Good Office Functioning of the United Nations Secretary General' in Adam Roberts and Benedict Kingsbury, eds., *United Nations, Divided World, The Role of the United Nations in International Relations*, Oxford, Clarendon Press, 1989, pp. 79–94.

[41] In 1991 as the term of the Secretary-General was to expire at the end of the year, yet another study, *A World in Need of Leadership: Tommorrow's United Nations* prepared by two retired senior UN officials, Brian Urquhart and Erskine Childers and sponsored by the Ford Foundation and the Dag Hammarskjold Foundation, persuasively argued for a seven-year fixed term for the Secretary-General as also for the top echelon of the Secretariat.

[42] *Time* magazine, 19 November 1990, p. 39.

[43] See text of the editorial reproduced in *UN Newsletter* (New Delhi), 27 April 1991, p. 2.

The Secretary-General operates under the Charter which represents international goals in a world of sovereign independent states where national interests remain dominant. The two poles of his world represent, at one extreme, the global objectives of the Charter and at the other, the pragmatic and on occasion downright selfish nature of national sovereignty. Working between these two poles, the Secretary-General cannot afford to lose touch with either. The effectiveness of the office depends much on the personality of the incumbent, the respect derived from his performance as an impartial harmonizer of differences and as a catalyst of the contending interests of the member-States. It is imperative for the incumbent to be familiar with the UN system and political forces at work at any given time. He has to remain in close contact with member-States to meet the growing needs of the world community. A Secretary-General who is too dynamic and acts in disregard of the wishes of the major powers as also the wider section of members could prove disastrous for the organization. The choice has invariably been, and should continue to be, from amongst nationals of member-States other than those of the five permanent members of the Security Council and whose background is well-known to those who have a decisive say in the selection. This is all the more necessary at a time when there remains only one superpower. The United Nations is passing through perhaps its most critical phase and it is too risky to introduce trial and error elements, particularly with regard to the office of the Secretary-General which holds the pivotal position in the organization.

At the time of writing this study, the selection process for the new Secretary-General and speculation as to the incumbent were still on. Talk of appointing some lofty, retired dignitary, such as Margaret Thatcher of the UK or Eduard Schwardnadze of the erstwhile USSR, arose, even as the names of several prominent Americans, including that of former US President Jimmy Carter, were being tossed about. The list of names grew steadily longer—much longer than in any of the past selection rituals. The African States pushed for one of their own arguing that their own continent was the only from which a Secretary-General had not been chosen, even through Africa's fifty-one members constituted a third of UN membership (which on 17 September 1991 had risen from 159 to 166). Acting together, they submitted an official list of six names, which was endorsed by the Organization of African Unity (OAU), including Boutros Boutros-Ghali of Egypt. President Hosni Mubarak joined in the lobbying for Egypt's candidate. The other candidates and their supporting heads of governments did not lag behind in their proposals either. Indeed, never before in the history of the United Nations had such open canvassing and lobbying been witnessed in the selection of the incumbent for the office of the Secretary-General.

The scores of ballots in the Security Council during the months of October and November, finally pronounced Boutros-Ghali the winner on 21 November 1991.[44] The recommendation of the Security Council was unanimously endorsed, as in the past, by the General Assembly (3 December 1991) and Dr Ghali took over the post with effect from January 1992. The sixty-nine year old former Deputy Prime Minister of Egypt, is a renowned scholar of international law and organization. He is also widely known for his part in the negotiations, held under US auspices, that led to the Camp David Agreement of 1978 between Israel and Egypt. He is an Arab and an African, a Coptic Christian married to a Jew, 'with a little more than European style'. As *Le Monde* puts it, 'he is the "hyphen-man", a perfect link between the West, the Third World and the Middle East'.[45]

Whether the choice is regarded as an anti-climax to the months of protracted negotiations, lobbying and suspense that preceded the selection, or his appointment is a triumph for the Third World in general and Africa in particular, or it is taken as a culmination of the successful manoeuvering of the power-that-be, perhaps the most significant aspect of Dr. Ghali's selection is that well-established norms have been adhered to. The incumbent is not a national of any of the five permanent member-States of the Security Council. The most important point is how he redeems the United Nations from its present financial plight and what remedial measures he initiates to relieve the world body of the aliments plaguing it since the mid-1980s. What remains to be seen is if, as his predecessor did but in vain, he can help bring about a meaningful dialogue between the two sides of the great divide—the North and the South—the most crucial problem confronting the United Nations today. The future will also tell if he

[44] A day before the crucial voting, Boutros-Ghali did what was essential for any candidate to be the winner. In his meeting with John Balton, the US Assistant Secretary of State for International Organization, Ghali was reported to have convincingly argued that he counted much on the United States, without whose support 'he could neither get the job nor continue as an incumbent' and that he 'would do nothing to contradict US interests'. *Newsweek*, 2 December 1991.

[45] Ibid.

can use his good offices to keep the United Nations on an even keel, as his predecessor attempted to do, though not very successfully, in a fast changing international political environment.

It is true that the powers and functions of the Secretary-General are limited; he has hardly any scope for viable political initiative without the specific authorization of the General Assembly or the Security Council. Nonetheless his office is adequately endowed with the capacity to resist manoeuvring of the UN apparatus by any power or group of powers to promote vested interests. He alone, among all the functionaries and organs, personifies and represents the entity of the UN and the principles and objectives enshrined in its Charter. His own assessment of a given situation and public pronouncements carry much more credibility, moral and political influence, than that of any head of state, howsoever mighty.

Peace-Keeping

The peace-keeping operations are one area of UN activity which has gained wide appreciation recently including the awarding of the 1988 Nobel Peace Prize. This new-found enthusiasm has led to proposals to extend its activity to include areas different from those in which it has operated so far. The enthusiasm is obviously the result of inflated impressions of recent events which have witnessed the launching of several new operations. It should be noted that the concept of peace-keeping evolved, beginning 1947, in to a situation where the peace and security mechanism, as envisaged in the Charter, became frozen as a result of the Cold War. In the given circumstances, the United Nations improvised pragmatic steps[46] for the observance of ceasefire and for keeping combatants apart so that negotiations for peaceful settlements could be successfully resorted to. The concept is unique in the sense that military forces are employed and not to serve the interest of any power or group of powers but to serve as a non-partisan instrument of peace and to prevent conflicts between peoples.

The striking success of operations over the last few years, as noted earlier, has encouraged reflections on the possible extension of the principle to new areas. Some governments went to the extent of

---

[46] For details see, *The Blue Helmets: A Review of United Nations Peace Keeping*, Revised Second Edition, New York UN Department of Public Information, 1990. Also, K.P. Saksena, 'Not by Design: Evolution of UN Peace Keeping Operations and its Implications for the Future', *International Studies*, vol. 16, December 1977. It is interesting to note that no peace-keeping operations were launched after 1978 until 1988.

believing that the concept of peace-keeping could also be used to combat international terrorism and drug trafficking.[47] The Indian representative, however, rightly argued for a cautious approach, saying that the operational concept should remain what it had been, that of a non-fighting, non-enforcing force, 'instituted with the specific consent of the host countries concerned, with the constant support and approval of the Security Council'.[48] Emphasizing the pacific character of the peace-keeping operations and that the 'consent of the parties concerned is crucial to their mandate', the Secretary-General aptly noted that 'such operations are to be distinguished from measures under Chapter VII of the Charter'.[49] As the concept was originated to meet the exigencies of conflict situations with a specific purpose, over the decades, more so in the recent past, it has demonstrated its usefulness in controlling armed hostilities and building up the necessary environment for the peaceful settlement of disputes and resolution of conflicts.Indeed,if there is any prospect of developing and sustaining a truly international concern for maintaining international peace and security, backed by collective action, the UN operations hold the key to the foreseeable future. At the same time it should be realized that peace-keeping operations are not the panacea for all international peace and security problems. Regrettably, no serious attempt has been made to take the necessary steps for removing the limitations that have manifested themselves over the decades. One limitation is that the concept has been operative largely in observing and maintaining a status quo. The operations in the Middle East and in Cyprus emphasize this aspect, but it is hoped that the ending of the Cold War will help improve the prospects of amicable settlements in these areas as well. Another serious limitation emanates from the fact that while member-States are quite enthused at the success of the peace-keeping operations, they are still reluctant to meet their financial obligations, among others. Year after year the UN has been denied the resources with which to meet its responsibility in this field, with contributions being

[47] See statement by Soviet representative to the Special Political Committee on agenda item 678, Comprehensive review of UN peace-keeping operations, 30 October 1989, USSR, Permanent Mission to the United Nations. Press Release, 30 October 1989.

[48] See statement of Indian representative in the Special Political Committee dated 1 November 1989. Permanent Mission of India to the United Nations, Press Release, November 1, 1989.

[49] Annual Report of the Secretary-General on the Work of the Organization, 1990, September 1990, p. 14. Also ibid., 1991, pp. 4–5.

delayed or withheld. There have even been instances of member-States, in utter disregard of their obligations, attempting to jeopardize or subvert UN operations. The most glaring example is that of Israel (1982) vis-a-vis the UN Interim Force in Lebanon (UNIFIL).[50]

Thus, instead of proposing new ventures in hitherto untried areas, the United Nations should first concentrate on providing adequate finances and logistic support, a reserve stock of basic peace-keeping equipment and supplies, and work towards an increase in working capital fund and dependable cash contributions. Furthermore, the current limitations in the operations should be surmounted, launching only those of a determinate character at clearly defined points of location and strategy.

Despite the difficult financial situation five new ventures were launched during 1991 and two more, UNTAC in Cambodia and UNPROFOR in Yugoslavia,[51] in early 1992. Both these ventures not only require huge financial resources but are tasks of a complexity and scope unprecedented in UN experience. In Cambodia, an unprecedented complex task has been entrusted to the United Nations at an estimated cost of $3 billion. No efforts have been made to ensure financial and logistic support. How financial responsibilities will be met can be gauged by the fact that the United Nations Advance Mission in Cambodia (UNAMIC) was instituted for a six-month period, from 1 November 1991 to 30 April 1992, at an estimated cost of $14 million. By January 31 1992 only $2 million had been collected (ST/ADM/SER.D 371, 6 February 1992).

The former Secretary-General Perez de Cuellar's note held a warning in that 'the disparity between responsibilities and resources can no-

---

[50] See in particular, Alan James, 'Painful Peace Keeping: United Nations in Lebanon', *International Journal* (Canadian), vol. 38, Autumn 1983, pp. 613–34.

[51] The civil war that erupted in Yugoslavia, in the summer of 1991, has since claimed a heavy toll of life and property. The situation became more complex when four of the six constituent republics declared their independence and two of them—Croatia and Slovania—were recognized as independent states by several European powers. While the United Nations and the majority of its members, including the United States of America, as of January 1992, continued to treat Yugoslavia as a single entity and to respect its territorial integrity, the members of the European Community were divided in their respective responses to the situation. The United States took the initiative in September 1991 and Cyrus Vance, former US Secretary of State, was given the onerous task of mediator while being named the United Nations' special envoy. While the United Nations peace-keeping force is supposed to protect life and property in the ongoing civil war, the responsibility of mediation between the warring forces is shared by the European Community and special envoy Cyrus Vance.

where be more crippling—and dangerous—as in this matter'. In a report on the financial situation, he expressed his 'profound concern that at a time when the world community has entrusted to the United Nations new and unprecedented responsibilities, the United Nations should continue to find itself on the brink of insolvency' (A/46/600, 24 October 1991). He pointed out that, as of September 1991, peace-keeping assessments due from governments amounted to $486.99 million. Addressing a personal letter to all UN members, the Secretary-General reiterated that unless the financial problem facing the United Nations was addressed, it would be rendered incapable of playing the role now expected of it in promoting and maintaining peace. There has been no respite, however. In January 1992, member-States owed more than $500 million to the peace-keeping account.[52]

Apart from the financial aspect, another disturbing element is that the long established practice of drawing personnel for peace-keeping operations from states other than those of the five permanent members of the Security Council is being increasingly ignored. The United Nations has been obliged to engage the armed forces of national governments which are willing to send in their contingents immediately and can afford to wait for the reimbursement of their expenses at a later stage. As this task can be performed by the major powers, it is not surprising, therefore, that the three-decade old established practice of excluding the five permanent members of the Security Council from the peace-keeping forces has been pushed aside. Financial insolvency has also forced the UN to be left with no option but to allow the United States and its allies to provide logistic support to missions in Iraq as in other areas of activity where peace-keeping operations are active or are being launched. Thus, the United States' U-2 surveillance flights over Iraq and its intelligence services provide the required information to the UN Commissions, which are obliged to depend on the reports.

Distinction Blurred

Of the utmost significance is the fact that the distinction between the UN activities listed in Chapter VI and in Chapter VII of the Charter has been blurred. The developments following the Gulf War are a glaring example of the distinction between peace-keeping and peace

---

[52] For details see Status of Contributions as at 31 January 1992, ST/ADM/SER/371, 6 February 1992.

enforcement measures being increasingly obliterated. For the first time, United Nations Iraq–Kuwait Observer Mission (UNIKOM) between Iraq and Kuwait has been instituted under Chapter VII of the Charter. The Secretariat has been assigned the complex responsibilities of Chapter VII, by the Council's decisions, which include: The demarcation of the boundary between Iraq and Kuwait through the mechanism of the five-member UN Mission; the elimination of Iraq's mass destruction capability through the Special Commission and the International Atomic Energy Agency; the management of the compensation fund; the arrangement of the return of Kuwait's property seized by Iraq; and the discharge of the other onerous tasks derived from Security Council Resolution 706 (1991).

Thus the UN Secretariat engaged itself in performing a complex task never before undertaken on behalf of the United Nations—a task whose legitimacy under the Charter is questionable, to say the least. Chapter VII of the Charter provides for collective enforcement only to the extent of thwarting acts of aggression and breaches of peace, i.e., the restoration of status quo-ante. Its provisions are not meant to impose or enforce political settlement, nor to undertake retaliatory or punitive measures. What is perhaps the most disturbing aspect of UN action after the Gulf War, which is bound to seriously undermine the non-partisan character of the organization and its credibility, is the choice of personnel acting in its name. The various missions in Iraq assigned the task of punitive measures are manned by the personnel of governments which comprised the Coalition Forces, and who have been given ad hoc appointments or sent on secondment to the UN Secretariat by the governments concerned. Never before have the objectivity and non-partisan role of UN personnel been questioned[51] as in the case of the missions in Iraq.

Greater Role in NWO

Notwithstanding such serious constraints, and there is no indication that they will be removed in the foreseeable future, the United Nations is being projected for a greater and more effective role in the maintenance of international peace and security. The Gulf War and its aftermath have obviously spurred the United States and its allies

[51] For details see Iraq's communication to the Secretary-General, S/23110, 2 October 1991.

(which now include not only the major western powers but the successor of its erstwhile arch rival, the USSR) to convert the United Nations into an instrument of the so-called New World Order.[54]

Various policy statements gave an indication of the new thinking. For instance, the Foreign Ministers of the five permanent members of the Security Council, in a joint declaration on 27 September 1991, pledged their commitment to a revitalized role for the United Nations in the building of a new world order. A more formal move in that direction came soon after the disintegration of the Soviet Union, when the first ever summit of the Security Council was convened on 31 January 1992, the initiative being taken by the Prime Minister of the United Kingdom, John Major (whose country held the rotating Presidency of the Council for the month). Fifteen heads of governments and states adopted, by consensus, a declaration which reconfirmed their commitment to promoting the collective security system of the Charter, further strengthening and making more efficient the capacity of the United Nations for preventive diplomacy, peace-making and peace-keeping, preventing the proliferation of weapons of mass destruction, and to protecting human rights. The Secretary-General was invited to prepare, by 1 July 1992, his analysis and recommendations on the ways of strengthening and making more efficient the capacity of the United Nations to discharge the responsibilities noted above.

The declaration adopted is long on generalities and short on detail. The Secretary-General was asked to recommend what the world body could do by way of preventive diplomacy to avert a conflict before it broke out. In short, he is expected to provide a warning signal to the Security Council. For the Secretary-General to be able to advise the Council an early warning system is needed a requirement which is not possible given the existing financial situation and lack of sophisticated surveillance. As candidly noted by Perez de Cuellar in his last Annual Report of 1991:

There is no mechanism or means available to the United Nations to maintain an impartial and effective global watch over situations of

[54] See in particular James Schlesinger, 'New Instabilities, New Priorities', *Foreign Policy* Winter 1991–92, pp. 3–24; Also Patrick M. Cronin, 'American Global Leadership After the Cold War: From Pax Americana to Pax Consortis', *Strategic Review*, Summer 1991, pp. 9–21.

potential or incipient conflict. Preventive diplomacy presupposes early warning capacity, which, in turn, implies a reliable and independently acquired data base. At present, the pool of information available to the United Nations is wholly inadequate. Lacking access to the technological means, such as space-based and other technological surveillance systems and without field representation commensurate with need, it is hard to visualize how the Secretariat can monitor potential conflict situations from an equally impartial standpoint.

As of now the United States alone (the former Soviet Union, also had the capability) has the surveillance capability to monitor developments all over the world. If the Secretary-General has to rely on US technology, the United Nations will have to accept the danger that the information would come through a prism with the potential for distortion. The same problem will arise with regard to those accused of acquiring weapons of mass destruction or of gross violation of human rights. The United Nations would have to depend on intelligence made available by members, especially those who have world-wide surveillance systems, raising again the possibility of bias. In such situations the effective use of preventive diplomacy would involve serious hazards. The gravity of the situation is compounded by the fact that preventive measures, even if adequately organized, may not always produce positive results. The question that arises is what to do then. It is well known that the provisions of the Charter (Articles 43–47) regarding the use of military force under the direction of the Security Council through its Military Staff Committee have remained inoperative. No attempt has been made to activate them, nor was there even a reference to the provisions of the recent first summit of the Security Council. Thus the pretence of the United Nations being in a position to take collective enforcement measures against an 'offending' state can hardly be kept up. Even when the Security Council was prompted to authorize military action to chasten a power guilty of transgression, as in the case of Iraq, once the action was authorized and undertaken by those who had the capability, the Council was powerless to exercise even a semblance of supervision or direction.

In the last forty years and more, the United Nations has authorized collective enforcement measures in only two situations—in Korea, from 1950–53 and in the Gulf, in 1990–91. In both cases the military operations were identified as taken by one state against another in collusion with its allies or 'clients', thus gravely undermining the Charter's concept of collective security. And in both situations, the military action taken violated the rule of proportionality and the application of the provisions of Chapter VII was overextended. The destruction of Iraq's military potential and its communication and industrial infrastructure which, for example, became a major objective of the coalition forces, had no Security Council sanction. What was worse was that the rules of humanitarian law, applicable in armed conflicts, were not complied with and the inhuman damage inflicted on the civilian population of the 'offending' state was ignored with impunity.

In sum, the path that the United Nations' Summit has perceived in providing a 'greater role' to the Security Council, is replete with more peril than promise for peace, stability, and justice. Indeed, there is a widely held apprehension that the plan of action which the Security Council Summit approved, in general terms, carries a hidden agenda for moulding the United Nations into an instrument of the New World Order as envisioned by the US. The 'greater role' could well mean the US acquistion of political manoeuvring and the freedom, through UN legitimacy, to impose its own values and world view on the vast majority of those member-States constituting the Third World."

DISMAY AND DISARRAY

It is ironical that while the United Nations is being projected for a greater role in the political and security field, the field of economic and social development—the very area of activity which prompted initiatives for the reform and reorganization of the system—has reached a stage of immobility. The fact that no arrangement of peace or stability will remain viable unless workable solutions are sought to the problems of poverty, debt and destitution afflicting the greater part of the world is being ignored. The major powers of the North, which, until the mid-1980s, were denouncing the UN system suddenly discovered its utility to promote what they believe in. Obviously

---

" See the editorial, *The Pioneer*, New Delhi, 1 February 1992.

intoxicated by the arrogance of power, they are serving their own vested interests in the areas relating to peace, security, human rights and the environment. They are also determined, it appears, to reduce the United Nations to a non-factor in matters which are of vital interest to the vast majority of nations. There is little recognition of the reality that global problems, whether they relate to peace or security, the environment or development, debt and poverty or human rights, are intertwined. One set of problems cannot be dealt with effectively without the cooperation of the North and the South in the other areas as well. The intensified alienation of the two approaches became more pronounced in 1988. The major powers of the North, while concentrating on enlarging the role of the United Nations in the field of peace-keeping and resolution of conflicts, paralyzed UN functioning in the economic and social fields. They refused to negotiate the restructuring of the inter-governmental machinery, except on their own terms, thus proving four years of protracted efforts in that direction to be an exercise in futility. There has been no agreement on the precise role the United Nations should play in the economic and social fields nor an understanding for a mechanism that could be devised for collective North–South efforts in constructively and cooperatively dealing with the problems that the South faces. The North has refused to share with the South the management of the world economy. Thus the United Nations which has regained its rightful multilateral role in the political field is still not considered appropriate for economic issues. Reporting on these developments at the General Assembly, the UN Observer noted:

> The debate in the General Assembly brought out the sharp contrast between a sense of progress and development in the political arena and a sense of frustration on the economic side. It appeared as if, 'the peace epidemic' has had no effect on the international economic environment—the real bread and butter issue.[56]

Joseph N Garba of Nigeria, the President of the forty-fourth Session of the General Assembly expressed the hope that the current superpower that would trickle down and make the world a better place for rich and poor alike and that global action would follow to remove 'the

[56] *UN Observer* (New York), 11 November 1988, p. 2.

pathos, poverty and despair in the Third World'.[57] Recent developments, however, indicate movements in the opposite direction.[58]

South in Bloc-Dominated Economy

As the world entered the last decade of the twentieth century, the
post-war economic order dominated by the United States came undone.
In its place a new world economy has emerged, dominated by the
three trading blocs which are controlled by the leading industrialized
powers. If the trend towards a tripolar system continues, the developing
countries of the South, which represent 75 per cent of the peoples of
the world, are bound to fall further behind in the process of development and the gap between the world's haves and have-nots will widen
further. These developments also pose a serious threat to the multilateral trading system, to the GATT negotiating framework and partly
explains why the Uruguay Round of Multilateral Trade Negotiations
which began in 1986, are still at an impasse.

The trend towards a bloc-dominated economy has been clearly
marked by two legislative developments: the Single European Act
adopted by the EC member-States in 1986 and the US Omnibus
Trade and Competitiveness Act of 1988. The EC decision, which
aimed at the formation of a single west European market by the end of
1992 and the lowering or elimination of barriers between the EEC
states, has raised fears of the creation of a 'fortress' Europe. The
Omnibus-Act calls upon the government of the world's largest trading
nation to negotiate with other governments, on a bilateral basis, for
improved market access to US exports. If negotiations with a nation
fail, the Act provides for retaliatory restrictions against the country's
imports into the United States. Threats to invoke the Super 301 and
Special 301 provisions of the Act against Brazil, China, India and
Thailand, in the last two years, are demonstrative of the harsh punitive
measures that can be and have been unilaterally used to protect
American trading interests. Unfortunately the continued marginalization, for the last ten years, of the developing countries in the world
economy have left most of them in a vulnerable position. The debt
trap and balance of payment problems have further aggravated their
plight. Taking advantage of the situation, the North has mounted

---

[57] *UN Chronicle*, March 1990, p. 15.
[58] *Ibid.*, December 1991, pp. 59–61. Also see *World Economic Survey*, 1991.

more pressure to further strengthen its hegemony over the South. Threats have been made and conditions imposed in trade and aid, under one pretext or the other, such as the Trade Related Investment Measures (TRIMS), Trade Related Intellectual Property Rights (TRIPS) and under the guise of environmental protection, to mention some.

Such developments have further intensified the alienation of the North and the South. No developing country has been powerful enough to resist by itself, the exploitative relationship that is being imposed, but as a collective entity, represented by the Group of 77, they have taken up the option of making use of the forum of the United Nations to vent their frustration. At the Forty-sixth Session of the General Assembly, China, as Chairman of the Group of 77, introduced a draft Resolution at the Second Committee (A/C.2/46/L.55) entitled Economic Measures as a Means of Political and Economic Coercion against Developing Countries. The Group called upon the 'international community to adopt urgent and effective measures to eliminate the use by some developed countries of unilateral economic coercive measures against developing countries for the purpose of exerting, directly or indirectly, coercion on the sovereign decisions of the countries subject to these measures'. Deploring the measures as incompatible with the Charter of the United Nations, the Group reiterated that the developed countries refrain from making use of their predominant position in the international economy to exercise political or economic coercion through the application of economic instruments with the purpose of inducing changes in the economic, political, and social policies of other countries. The recorded voting at the second Committee meeting, showed that the Resolution received 100 votes for, twenty-eight against and eleven abstentions. The developed countries of the North voted against the Resolution, but only the representative of the United States took the floor to openly denounce it. (A/C.2/46/SR.58). At the plenary session of the General Assembly, the Resolution (46/210, 10 December 1991) was adopted by a vote of ninety-seven for; thirty against and nine abstentions.[59] Interestingly enough, the number of affirmative votes declined to

---

[59] A similar Resolution (44/215, 20 December 1989) bearing the same title but milder in tone was adopted at the Forty-fourth Session. The voting then was 118 for, twenty-three against and two abstentions. It requested a report from the Secretary-General at the Forty-sixth Session. Accordingly the Secretary-General presented a report (A/46/567, 15 October 1991) which was taken into consideration in the adoption of the Resolution referred to.

ninety-seven and the socialist countries of eastern Europe either joined the developed countries of the North in casting negative votes or abstained. Those who abstained included the Ukraine and the erstwhile USSR. While not a single developing country cast a negative vote, some thirty of them however, found it 'politically convenient' to be absent at the time of voting.

The Secretary-General, in his 1990 Annual Report, warned that the 'intense competition among economic superpowers or blocs not only to gain economic advantage and to influence the shaping of the new rules of the game' would have serious consequences for the world economy.[60] These developments, he expressed the fear, are likely to 'lead to fragmentation of the international trading system, exacerbate existing trade tensions and further marginalise the majority of the developing countries'. He also expressed serious concern at 'the increased reliance on bilateral and plurilateral arrangements rather than on multilateral rules for trade liberalization'.[61]

There are, however, clear indications of growing rivalry among the major trading blocs. The United States responded to the EC's protectionist measures by launching what it calls the Caribbean Basin Initiative (CBI) to strengthen its trade relations with the Caribbean countries. It offers incentives to trade such as duty-free entry for Caribbean products into the United States and tax incentives for US business houses to invest in new plants in the Caribbean. Although limited in its impact, the CBI has served as a model for a sweeping Free Trade Agreement with Canada which came into effect on 1 January 1989.[62] In East Asia, Japan has built up its own economic clout, causing the United States alarm at the prospect of it forming a regional trade bloc with other East Asian manufacturing Countries. To counter such a possible development, the United States has decided to join the Japan-led co-prosperity sphere in the Pacific region.[63]

An EC analyst envisages a 'disintegration among the countries of the Group of 77, under the compulsions of economic realities'. Africa, he

[60] *Annual Report of the Secretary General*, 1990, n. 33, p. 33.

[61] *Ibid.*, p. 32.

[62] See in particular, Earl H Fry, 'Negotiations Towards a North American Free Trade Agreement', *The Journal of State Government*, October–December 1991, pp. 128–132.

[63] See, *Far Eastern Economic Review* (Hong Kong), 16 November 1989, pp. 10–14. Also see James A Baker, 'America in Asia: Emerging Architecture for a Pacific Community', *Foreign Affairs*, Winter 1991–92, pp. 7–18.

feels, will go with Europe; Southeast Asia, with the Asian-Pacific bloc dominated largely by Japan. Japan will partly share its hegemony with Canada and the United States. Brazil and the bulk of the Latin American countries will go with North America: 'These three economic poles will attract to themselves clusters of economically weaker states irrespective of political ideology.[64]

It is interesting to note that under the Lome Convention the countries of Africa have been allowed comparatively liberal access to the European Common Market (but not to India and the member countries of the ASEAN) and these concessions will continue to operate after 1992. The concession to Africa is academic in as much as there is little likelihood of African industry posing a threat to the European countries. On the question of aid also, the European priorities are clearly defined: Europe clearly favours the African, Caribbean, and Pacific countries. The argument seems to be a moral and simple one in that 'the needs of the poorest and the least developed' should have priority. Behind the facade is the inescapable reality of the mineral wealth of Africa being indispensable to European industry, while the chances of African industry turning competitive are minimal. In the course of time, the oil wealth of West Asia will run dry but not the uranium mines and other sources of nuclear minerals in Africa for the use of the industrialized countries of the North.

According to Robert B. Reich of the Kennedy School of Government at Harvard, 'the emergence of trading blocs raises the danger of a return to the colonialist relationships of the eighteenth and nineteenth centuries, when the industrial powers carved up much of what is the Third World today into spheres of their respective influence' (cited in the *Congressional Quarterly*, Washington, DC, 24 November 1989). Much depends, he notes, upon the way the industrial powers propose to include the developing countries in the trading blocs they control. He adds:

If the relationship is one of mutual dependency and gain, the result may be positive. On the other hand, if it is an exploitative relationship in which the trading bloc both protects the Third World market and also limits its development to the trajectory imposed by the most developed nations of that bloc, then the comparison with

[64] Cited in S.N. Chopra, 'India is Still Not on the World Economic Map', *Times of India* (New Delhi), 10 February 1990.

the eighteenth and nineteenth century spheres of influence becomes quite close.(47)

So far there is no indication that the major industrial Powers would allow the developing countries into a partnership with them for mutual benefit.

Paradigm of Market Economy

As noted earlier, the United States' attack on UN programmes and activities in the economic and social areas was prompted by the allegation that the programmes were encroaching on fields best left to private entrepreneurs. Time and again the US representative has argued that problems such as the development of natural resources including energy, and new and renewable sources of energy and the application of science and technology for development could best be tackled at bilateral levels through aid and that the developing countries can improve their economic condition by pursuing a market-oriented economy that would encourage foreign investment. In a world characterised by an enormously disproportionate distribution of wealth and technological advancement, where a handful of countries reap the benefit of the post-industrial era, as two-thirds of the world writhes in the misery of a feudal agricultural economy, poverty, hunger and deprivation, it is absurd to talk of the 'magic of the market place' which is a chimera.

Again, what is touted as a remedial measure for the South is not practised by the preachers themselves. Although the market economies of the North have repeatedly asserted their support for an open, multilateral trading system, they have, in fact, resorted to an increasing number and array of protectionist measures to safeguard their domestic industries from foreign competition. Closed markets and protectionism, as practised by the North, have left no scope for the South's potential export earnings or its ability to diversify its own economy. Those developing countries seeking to break out of their traditional roles as exporters of raw materials and commodities have been hit especially hard, the more processed the export commodity, the more complex become the trade restrictions affecting it.

Furthermore, even in those countries where private enterprise is treated as an article of faith, as for instance, in the United States of America, there are provisions for state intervention to protect the interests of the most vulnerable sections of society. How then can the world community ignore the plight of nearly one billion people eking out an existence below the poverty line. There is no country in the world, including the United States of America, where the free play of market forces is permitted. Rules and regulations have been laid down and parameters established within which private entrepreneurs operate. Are there any such rules and regulations operating at an international level for private entrepreneurs also known as multinationals, or more appropriately, Transnational Corporations (TNCs)?[65] Is there an international mechanism to regulate international trade, fiscal and monetary affairs and do the developing countries have any say in these matters which affect their vital interests? Should then, the Group of Seven continues to hold the monopoly on decision-making on vital international economic issues?

Is the UN Relevant ?

One serious dimension added to the exercise for reform is that some major powers have questioned, in one way or the other, the relevance of the United Nations in the context of North-South issues in general and economic development in particular. The official position taken by some of these members, particularly the United States, though couched in subtle expressions has been quite revealing. The argument advanced is that development cannot be pursued by international inter-governmental agencies which would promote statism. Only internal reforms, the free market approach and 'aid' at bilateral levels, if necessary, can promote development in the developing countries. The media and non-governmental organizations in the west have

[65] It should be noted in passing that under the growing impact of market forces at international level, there has been increasing domination of Transnational Corporations (TNCs) in international trade and services. Just to take one example: export of primary commodities accounts for about 85 per cent of the foreign exchange of developing countries. However, developing countries are not 'independent' seller or buyer. About 70 to 90 per cent of the global trade in primary commodities is controlled by a handful of TNCs. By a system of strategic alliances and acquisitions, the trade is getting controlled by fewer TNCs which dictate their terms on developing countries. This largely explains how the prices of primary commodities in 1990 are at an average 54 per cent less at 1980 prices. For details on this point, see in particular, K.P. Saksena, 'International Framework and South-South Cooperation: Constraints and Opportunities' in Steven L. Spiegel, *At Issue: Politics in the World Arena*, New York: ST Martin's Press, pp. 125–40. Also *The World Economy: A Global Challenge* (New York: United Nations Department of Public Information, 1990), pp. 39–48 and the *World Economic Survey, 1991*.

been orchestrating the same argument more explicitly. A set of studies on the subject by the UNA-USA reaches the conclusion that the existing UN machinery is not equipped to deal with developmental problems. The studies state that the United Nations should either reform itself and build up a formidable mechanism such as the one the European Community has instituted or else confine its role to those problems where the convergence of ˙common views converting into common action is possible, such as population and drug control and the environment among others.[66] A veteran western expert supporting this argument has gone a step further to contend that the existing framework of the United Nations is based on fallacious notions.[67] Another study, by two veteran UN officials, now retired, which has received wide publicity in the western media, has used, wittingly or unwittingly, a more effective 'weapon' against the United Nations' role on development issues. It has completely ignored this question in its study, financed by two prestigious institutions, the Ford Foundation and the Dag Hammarskjold Foundation.[68]

It is true that over a period of time, the objectives of the Charter as contained in Article 55 in particular, which enjoins the organization to promote a 'higher standard of living, conditions of economic and social progress and development and the solution of international economic, social and related problems' have not been attended to by concerted international action. While discussions, debates, studies and reports by experts did help identify the issues, adequate implementation measures were not taken on the recommendations that followed. Indeed, the United Nations has not acquired the authority to seek the implementation of its recommendations. In view of these limitations, it does seem plausible to discontinue the exercise and restrict its attention to less controversial problems such as population and the environment. Unfortunately the grim reality of the vicious cycle of poverty, disease and deprivation, the debt burden and the erosion of the social structure affecting two-thirds of the world's peoples cannot be wished away. If the United Nations turns a Nelson's eye to these hard realities, there is little future for the world, leave alone for the only global organization of its kind. If the United Nations

[66] Peter Fromuth, ed., *A Successor Vision: The United Nations of Tommorow* (Lanham, MD: UNA-USA, 1988), pp. xv-xxxiv.

[67] JIU Report, *Some Reflections on Reform of the United Nations*, by Maurice Bertrand, (JIU/REP/85/9), pp. 44-46.

[68] Brian Urquhart, Erskine Childers, *A World in Need of Leadership: Tommorow's United Nations*, Uppsala, Sweden: Dag Hamarskjold Foundation, 1990.

seems irrelevant, it must be realized that there is no other forum to turn to, to solve the crucial problems of our time.

The United Nations is the only international institution which has a broad mandate, compared to others which cover a very narrow specified field of activity or are primarily responsive to the interests of certain groups of countries. The United Nations provides the only framework where all interests are represented and all voices are heard, from those of representatives of the poorest to the richest of countries, debtors and creditors, non-governmental and voluntary organizations, and independent experts from business, academic and research communities. In addition to its specialized agencies which concentrate on specific areas and provide feedback to the main body, the United Nations looks to broader perspectives that take into account many and complex linkages between different economic factors. This makes it possible to see, for example, that the problems of the Third World's debt, cannot be solved without tackling trade, fiscal, monetary and other issues.

That the United Nations, constituted as it is, is an association of sovereign states, cannot alter the colossal and disproportionate distribution of economic power in the existing system, by simply passing resolutions, is evident. However, as in the field of peace and security, where the United Nations has evolved its own pragmatic approach, so in the economic field can the necessary changes towards an equitable management of the world economy be brought about through a negotiated, peaceful process. Indeed, given the willingness on the part of government representatives expressing contending views, the UN provides an array of diplomatic devices both formal and informal for reconciling an array of interests.[69] The adoption of the Law of Sea Conventions is one shining example among many in the more than four decades of UN experiences.

The Secretary-General, while submitting his first progress report on the implementation of General Assembly Resolution 41/213 referred to the serious problems afflicting the international economy and their negative impact on the prospects of the developing countries. 'In general terms', he noted, 'the challenge to the international community is how to manage the growing interdependence of states. The plight of so many developing countries, mired in debt and forced to impose

---

[69] See in particular, Maurice Williams, 'The Role of the United Nations in Meeting Global Challenges: Past Achievements—Future Potential', in *Development*, Journal of the Society for International Development, 1989/4, pp.11–16.

harsh adjustment policies that further reduce what are, in many cases, already pitifully meagre living conditions ...' drew his attention to the fact that if the necessary resources for development were not made available, social deterioration could be expected to continue and become an increasingly serious source of political unrest and instability.[70] Without responding directly to the attack on multilateralism and the demand for limiting UN activity in the economic and social fields, the Secretary-General pointed out that 'the UN is uniquely qualified to be the forum for developing a new working consensus for world economic and social development'. This is so, he noted, because:

> First the primary objectives of the United Nations as set out in the Charter coincide with the highest historical ideals of all of humanity. Second, its political base and universality makes it a natural forum in which to pursue analytical approaches that differ from those of other organizations *with* special sectoral concerns and limited membership. Third, the UN is multi-disciplinary and should take greater advantage of this asset to adopt an innovative and integrated approach to development and international economic cooperation issues. Fourth, its operational activities are neutral and have been effective, even in sensitive areas. They are, moreover, also strongly slanted towards improving the quality of life and putting a human face on development.

Stressing that these special characteristics 'must shape any restructuring proposals in the context of the review of the inter-governmental machinery',[71] he repeated the gist of his plea in all his subsequent reports on the subject. The reasoning advanced by the Secretary-General in favour of UN multilateralism carries its own weight. No extra emphasis or additional arguments can further its case.

FEASIBLE AND DESIRABLE REFORM

Given the current political climate and continued stalemate on the basic issue of what the United Nations should or should not do in the

[70] Reform and Renewal in the United Nations: Progress Report of the Secretary-General.... UN Doc.A/42/234, 23 April 1987, p. 11.
[71] *Ibid*., emphasis added.

economic and social fields, the question of reform and reorganization should be viewed, not in terms of what is best suited to improve the capacity and resources of the system, but what is desirable and, at the same time, feasible. Suggesting a blueprint for reorganizing the United Nations to make the world body more effective world amount to indulging in a purely academic exercise. Indeed, there is no dearth of such proposals, which of late have been floating around, including *A Successor Vision* or *A World in Need of Leadership* for rebuilding the *United Nations of Tommorrow*.

The primary concern should be to safeguard those UN activities and programmes under attack which, if disrupted, could lead to the weakening of the organization's role in the field of cooperation in development. The source of the attack, the reason for it and why it acquired the formidable proportions it has, have been discussed in the preceding pages, but it should be recalled that the United States alone, among the major contributors, continues to withhold a substantial part of its apportionment to the regular budget. As of February 1992, it owed $500 million. The justification of its position, that certain UN activities in the economic and social fields run counter to its interests, is not the issue to be taken up. It is its attitude, combined with the fact that it contributed 25 per cent of the UN budget, that has to be taken into account while discussing the future framework of the United Nations.

Although there has been a change in its attitude anti-UN elements have taken such root that no US administration, in the near future, can make an absolute about turn. As an objective study by two American scholars aptly noted, 'Congressmen and Senators cannot ignore the Jewish lobby and the conservative Right' and 'Right wing and pro-Israeli groups can be placated and votes garnered by disapproving gestures directed at the United Nations'. The study further stated that 'by contrast, supporting the UN no longer brings in many extra votes, and it definitely loses votes on the Right'.[72] The reality is that the US Congress is not likely to release its full dues to the United Nations. Any framework to be designed for the UN, at least for the near future, has to accept this reality.

---

[72] Donald J. Puchala and Roger A. Coate, *The State of the United Nations*, Hanover, NH: Academic Council on the United Nations System, 1988, pp. 21–23.

Revision of Scale of Assessment

As noted earlier it is not true that one member casting one vote is the process through which budgetary decisions are made. It has also been proved that the United States and other major contributors to the United Nations budget do not carry a heavy burden, as, in terms of per capita income, it is the developing countries which bear the larger burden. Furthermore, a significant proportion of the money which the major powers contribute to the system returns to them in one form or another. It is also clearly obvious that the real motive behind the US financial pressure has not been so much the questioning of the efficiency and effectiveness of the United Nations but the elimination of certain programmes in the field of economic development. Last, but not least it is evident that the United States, among the major contributors to the budget, has its own connotation of the word consensus.[73]

It is, therefore, essential that the United Nations acquires a built-in mechanism so as not to remain subject to pressure by any one member-State as it has been over the last few years. That one member, which also contributes 25 per cent of the budget, can pull strings any time or attempt to overturn the apple cart by simply withholding its contribution, is a state of affairs which has to be remedied. This withholding of dues has acquired additional muscle power in a situation where the working capital fund is kept at the low limit of $100 million and has resulted in serious cash flow problems in meeting salaries and the payment of urgent bills in certain months of the year. Members of the United Nations, especially the developing countries, should realise these facts and work out a financial arrangement where no one member-State can hold the financial trump card. Indeed, if the United Nations and its affiliated bodies are to emerge as effective and vital mechanisms of international cooperation, the vulnerability of these organizations to domestic political forces in one or two states must be substantially reduced. In large measures, this means reducing the financial obligations of any one member-state to a level that is not life-threatening, should that member-State decide to use its financial leverage against the organization.

Hence, the inevitable conclusion is that the maximum limit of any single contribution to the regular budget should be reduced, to begin with, from 25 to 15 per cent, with the objective of bringing it down further to 10 per cent. This will free the United Nations from

---

[73] See *supra*, pp. 113–18.

dependence on any one member-State. It should be noted that under the proposed revised scale of assessment, the apportionments of the major contributors will continue to be less than a hundredth fraction of one per cent of their GNP. It is also essential that the amount in the working capital fund be raised from $100 million to $500 million. Such an arrangement will provide relief to the organization from the day to day financial problems which have adversely affected its activities. It will, of course, bring about a radical change in the financing of all international UN organizations as the increase will affect US contributions to the various specialized agencies also, but the time has come for such a change. If the 15 per cent maximum for member-States, is effected the revised scale of assessment, to cover the 10 per cent reduction in the US contribution, will only marginally increase the share of some eighty member-States excluding those who are at the lowest level of the capacity to pay' and contribute the minimum scale of .01 per cent. There are reasons to believe that such a change will not be resisted by major contributors. Japan is already the largest donor of foreign aid. It has also become the second largest contributor to the regular budget of the United Nations, its assessed share having grown from 2.19 per cent in 1956 to 11.38 in 1988 and 12.45 per cent for the current triennium. If contributions to voluntary funds are taken into account, Japan is again the second largest contributor to the UN system. The reason for its munificence is that Japan, as openly acknowledged by its government, is eager to improve its status in contemporary international relations by building and nurturing a reputation for contributing to peace and development in the world. Its desire for more influence in the United Nations and the assurance of a regular (and possibly permanent) seat in the Security Council stems from entering the cancus of the ideal forum from which to acquire its reputation. Japan also wants, and is gaining, many more posts for its nationals in the UN Secretariat.[74] Neither is Germany lagging behind in its similar quest. Beginning 1992, it is likely to have become (with an apportionment of 8.93 per cent) the third largest contributor to the UN budget. In fact, there has been a marked change in the attitude of the major contributors. The erstwhile USSR, which had delayed payment of its share to the regular budget and accumulated large

[74] Sadako Ogato, 'Japan's Policy Towards United Nations', presented at the international conference on The United Nations System and its Future held in Ottawa, Canada, 3–7 January 1990. Also see, John Newhouse, 'Diplomatic Round: In a New Era and Groping', *The New Yorker*, 16 December 1991. pp. 90–105.

arrears until 1986, cleared all its dues by 1990, although, of late, because of domestic upheavals, has fallen back in its payments. Japan, Germany, Canada, France, Italy and the United Kingdom, among others, have been prompt and timely in paying their assessed contributions. In sum, the desired change in the scale of assessment is overdue and could well represent the changing international economic power structure. What is significant if that the change will give the United Nations more elbow room for independence from the budgetary strings held by the single largest contributor—the United States of America—which has also emerged the unchallenged superpower.

Inter-governmental Structure

What has been discussed in detail in the earlier parts of this study, in the context of the inter-governmental structure, is summed up here. The structure of the economic and social fields was evolved and expanded to meet the growing needs of the international community and the obligations of the Charter of the United Nations, but its growth, as discussed in Chapter 2, was characterised by ad hocism and a sectoral approach. The efficiency and efficacy of the inter-governmental structure and corresponding Secretariat support have been subjected to periodic reviews. All the exercises continued to reaffirm the validity of the issues questioned, including the relevance of the individual components of the inter-governmental structure and its units in the Secretariat. None of the periodic reviews, as the Secretary-General noted in his report (A/45/714), 'suggested that a particular structure be disbanded owing to irrelevance'. The Special Commission, instituted by the ECOSOC in 1987–88, which undertook an indepth study of the inter-governmental structure has been the latest exercise of its kind. Despite the fact that a deadlock occurred at the discussions between the developed and the developing countries over the validity of the issues, clearly indicated that each inter-governmental body reviewed was performing a useful function in its respective field. There is, however, scope for merging some of the inter-governmental bodies. For example, the Governing Council on UN Environmental Programmes could also take up the functions entrusted to the inter-governmental Commission on Human Settlements. There could be more such merging and restructuring provided that an agreement, on the contents and purposes of reform, is kept in mind.

It was also clear, however, from the study of the Special Commission that programmes and performance in the various fields had not yielded the expected results. While this was largely because of paucity of funds and lack of cooperation from the major industrialized countries, there is more to the situation. While recognizing of the fact that the sectoral approach in itself serves a useful purpose by drawing increased political attention or government awareness to certain specific fields there is at the same time need for an effective central institutional arrangement to shape the various elements into global policies. Let us take an example. The Committee on Development Planning, composed of some of the better known experts in the respective fields and drawn from twenty-four different countries, provides in its periodical reports and set of recommendations, widely acknowledged inputs to the economic and social sectors of the United Nations. Do these reports have any worthwhile impact on policies and actions that regulate world economy? Should the alternative, then be, that Committee on Development Planning be dispensed with or that efforts should be directed to seek that reports and recommendations of such an expert body should receive the consideration they deserve?

A relative and perhaps more critical issue—the built-in constraints under which the entire inter-governmental machinery has to operate—is aptly illustrated in the case of the UNCTAD. As indicated earlier the institution, inter alia, serves as a forum for negotiation between the developed and the developing countries, directed, in the main, to securing a more liberal and fair trading system for the exports of the developing countries, more stable conditions for trade in primary commodities and a more predictable and supportive international monetary and financial system. However, over the last several years, as the developed countries resorted to higher and new protectionist barriers as accommodated prices in real terms sank to the lowest level in thirty years, the debt burden escalated, leaving the debt-ridden countries finding it extremely difficult even to meet the cost of debt-servicing. The plight of the developing countries has been further compounded by fluctuating exchange rates and the increasing disorder in the international monetary system. Given the fact that the developed countries have demonstrated an increasing reluctance to discuss these issues at the forum the UNCTAD's role has been reduced to a non-entity. In such a situation, what 'reform' can be initiated to improve its efficiency and effectiveness as an inter-governmental structure of the United Nations, is a question to which there is no answer.

The situation is more or less true of the entire UN inter-governmental machinery and programmes which operate in external economic environments managed by a handful of industrialized countries operating outside the UN system and in disregard of the interests of the developing countries. The crux of the matter, therefore, is the unwillingness of the major industrialized powers in the North to match their recognition of the reality of global economic interdependence with a preparedness to share with their 'partners' in the South, the management of the global economic commons that the world's trading monetary and financial systems represent. No amount of reform and reorganization in the economic and social sectors of the United Nations can be purposeful and viable unless the major powers in the global economy agree to share, at least partially if not to the fullest extent, management of the global economic commons within the UN system. What is also necessary is a centralized global mechanism within the system to formulate policies, coordinate activities and monitor programmes in the overall fields of international economic and social cooperation for development.

An Overall Global Mechanism

As UN programmes in the economic and social fields expanded, the need for an overall global machinery increasingly manifested itself. However, as noted earlier, the major western powers had, by then, moved in the direction of building up an institutional mechanism for the management of a global economy outside the UN system. Consequently, even such modest proposals as the UNEDA and the SUNFED, initiated in the 1950s, failed to get off the ground. Similarly, the creating of a central coordinating organization as proposed by the Jackson Report in 1969[75] or a single development administration as recommended in the 1975 report of the Group of Experts on the structure of the UN system,[76] did not materialize. Of late, however, there have been a number of similar proposals. A recent UNA-USA study[77] ambitiously suggested the centralization of the UN system with the creation of a single commission on the model of the European Community. The Secretary-General, reiterating the need for

[75] Sir Robert Jackson, *A Study of the Capacity of the UN Development System*, Geneva: United Nations, 1969, vol. 1, Chapter V.

[76] *A U.N. Structure for Global Economic Cooperation* (Report of the Group of Experts... New York: United Nations, 1975, Doc. E/AC. 62/9, Chapter II).

[77] Peter Fromuth, ed., *A Successor Vision: The United Nations of Tomorrow*, pp. 53–64.

an overall inter-governmental body, suggested a 'council of ministers for economic and social affairs' with the representation of members at a ministerial level and a much smaller body than the ECOSOC itself.[78] Similar views were reiterated by the Special Advisor to the UNDP Administrator in proposing an economic security council which would be small and manageable with a veto power for some countries with financial clout in the world economy.[79]

Each of these proposals has a common element in the emphasis on an overall compact mechanism with wide-ranging authority. However, any agreement on the precise composition, powers and functions of such an inter-governmental body would require revision of the Charter. Again, most of the member-States seem to be disinclined to create yet another institution. On the other hand, if an agreement does emerge, at least in principle, on a central mechanism, it is not necessary to establish a new institution. The existing framework could easily accommodate a mechanism without revising the Charter, but some procedural changes and above all, a clear understanding of what is being sought would have to be reached among member-States both of the North and the South.

To begin with, it is necessary for the ECOSOC framework to acquire an effective management and leadership. Its fifty-four members, based on geographical representation, constitute too large a body to allow intensive discussion and evaluation of the various activities and programmes. It is therefore proposed to institute a smaller representative body within the Council, which could be achieved by expanding its Bureau. Apart from the President and Rapporteur, there could be thirteen vice-Presidents. Membership of the Bureau, instead of being on a geographical basis, could be on the representation of countries on the basis of their level of development, socio-economic approach to development, and on their population size and share in the world economy. The fifteen seats could be distributed by giving the OECD and the Group of 77 six each, the Nordic (social welfare) countries one, the erstwhile members of the CMEA one (preferably to Russia) and the socialist countries one, preferably to China. The precise number is subject to negotiation but there should be a tacit

---

[78] *Report of the Secretary-General on the Work of the Organization*, 1987, paras 48–9.

[79] On the occasion of fortieth anniversary of UN multilateral assistance, the UNDP sponsored a seminar on Development Challenges for the 1990s. One of the six panelists, Mahbub-ul-Haq of Pakistan, currently Special Advisor to the UNDP Administrator made this suggestion. For details, see, *UN Chronicle*, March 1991, p. 84.

understanding or a gentleman's agreement that that Bureau would include on a regular (or permanent) basis countries with larger populations and a larger share in the world economy.

The Bureau, thus set up, in the organizational session of the ECOSOC, would be represented by ministers of their respective countries and could meet a week in advance of the two regular sessions of the ECOSOC. The Bureau could also hold joint sessions with the ACC. The existing practice of joint CPC and ACC sessions should be done away with. The ECOSOC and ACC sessions could then decide the format of the reports to be submitted by the specialized agencies in brief. The ECOSOC should continue to hold its two regular sessions also. The organizational session should contain discussions on a thematic basis, however, while the entire programme of activity should be covered by a triennial cycle, in which one subject would be taken up for intensive discussion once in three years, leaving room for flexibility, the Bureau should consider each year, the urgency and primacy of current issues and accordingly formulate agenda items. The reports of the subsidiary bodies should be discussed in relation to the subject focused on at a given time. The Council should adopt a more 'organic' agenda for general debate reflecting the changing needs and realities of an evolving international agenda.

To make the ECOSOC's role more effective and efficient, the complete cooperation of the specialized agencies in coordinating multilateral activities towards development in the economic, social, educational, health, fiscal, monetary and other related fields is essential. It is, therefore, necessary that the specialized agencies, including the IMF and the IBRD resume their responsibilities of submitting thematic reports to the ECOSOC and be guided by the recommendations of the Council and the General Assembly.

Coordination

As discussed earlier, the withholding of funds has often been 'justified' on the grounds of the lack of coordination and inefficiency resulting in the wastage of precious resources. In this context, it is pertinent to recall Gunnar Myrdal's succinct note in that the demand for effective coordination 'stands out as an escape and substitute for action'. He also observed, 'that the Governments of the great powers have been using the demand for "coordination" in order to curtail the organization's effectiveness in substantive issues is my personal experience'.[80] Nonetheless, the importance of coordination within any organized system in the interest of efficient management of its various activities is undeniable. However, as discussed in Chapter I, not-withstanding the demand for coordination, no satisfactory mechanism for this purpose, has yet been evolved.

For various reasons, the ECOSOC has been denied this role. At the administrative level, the Advisory Committee on Coordination (ACC) performs merely a ritual and perfunctory role. The reason for its ineffective functioning is obvious; each specialized agency has built up its respective autonomy and the chief executives of these agencies and inter-governmental bodies which constitute the ACC encourage the maintainance of a status quo, i.e., each preserving its own domain. The CPC has also failed to deal with the problem of coordination effectively. In recent years joint meetings of the ACC and the CPC have been held, but the experiment has yet to yield concrete results.

In the wake of the continuing financial crisis, the report of the Group of 18 and Resolution 41/213, the Secretary-General submitted several reports regarding the renewed efforts which are underway to make coordination effective.[81] Whether the efforts will be more fruitful than what has been the experience of the past continues, however, to remain an open-ended question. In this context, this study's pragmatic approach, as suggested in the preceding pages that the ECOSOC's role be strengthened and that an enlarged bureau (of some fifteen members representing the major economic interest groups), should assume the leading role in the coordination of all operational activities within the UN system. The suggestion remains one of the most important conclusions of this study.

A realistic look at the problem of coordination shows that, in the final analysis, the United Nations and its specialized agencies are inter-governmental organizations, or, in other words, an association of sovereign states. Although the collectivity evolved and its processes have built up a momentum of their own, distinct from the will of each member-state, the collectivity can only be as effective in the discharge of its functions as each member-State wants it to be. The principle holds

[80] Foreword in Mahdi Elamandjra, *The United Nations System: An Analysis*, London: Faber and Faber, 1973, p. 12.

[81] At its Forty-sixth Session, the General Assembly decided (Decision 46/445 of 20 December 1991) to discuss anew at its Forty-seventh Session the question of administrative and budgetary coordination of the United Nations with its specialized agencies and the International Atomic Energy Agency.

true with regard to coordination which has been lacking precisely because most of the member-States, especially the developing countries, have failed to build up any mechanism for coordination at respective national levels. Delegations to various inter-governmental bodies are drawn from different ministries or departments of member governments, and there is no mechanism worth the name which coordinates, in some detail, government actions and interaction relating to what transpires at different inter-governmental bodies.

The case of India and its practice illustrates the point, which has greater significance as many of the developing countries, especially in Asia and Africa, look to India's practice as a model. Apart from the Ministry of External Affairs, there are scores of offices and functional divisions belonging to some eighteen different ministries of the Government of India, concerned with UN programmes and activities in the economic and social fields such as the ministries of agriculture, commerce, energy, environment, health and family welfare, science and technology, transport, urban development and water resources to mention a few. The Ministry of Commerce, for instance, by and large represents India in the UNCTAD and ESCAP. Representation to the ILO, and the UN Commission for Social Development and its related bodies are the concern of the Ministry of Labour and Social Welfare; the two Bretton Woods institutions and their affiliates are the concern of the Ministry of Finance; the inter-governmental Committee on Science and Technology for Development is attended by officials of the ministry concerned; the Committee on Natural Resources is represented by officials from the Ministry of Water Resources and of Energy. What is more complicated is that the UNCTAD Committee on International Trade Law is the concern of officials of the Commerce Ministry while the UN Commission on International Trade Law (UNCITRAL) receives representation from the Legal and Treaty Division of the Ministry of External Affairs.

With this complex pattern of representation, India has not yet built up any mechanism worth the name to coordinate the representation and viewpoints of its various ministries as an organic whole. There are instances galore of Indian representatives, in the UNCTAD, for instance, expressing one point of view, and a different view in the ECOSOC, leading to the assumption that the right hand does not know what the left is doing and fairly often at that. If member-States have not effected coordination at national levels, it is virtually impossible for them to consider coordination at inter-governmental levels. Hence, what is

most desirable is that serious efforts are directed at building coordination of the representational systems in the various inter-
governmental bodies at national levels. It is only then that the
representatives (duly equipped with necessary information) of those
governments concerned with the inter-governmental bodies holding
the responsibility for coordination at an international level will be able
to do their part effectively.

VITAL CHANGE NEEDED

A pertinent question that lingers at the concluding pages of this study
is whether it leads to some ready-formula for institutional reforms and
reorganization which, if implemented, would bring about the desired
results. Indeed, it suggests none. No amount of institutional reform or
restructuring can help the situation, unless the necessary political will
among those whose cooperation and support is essential to make use
of the machinery in the desired direction is forthcoming. As the
Secretary-General has clearly said:

> Attempts at renovation, revitalization, rationalization, restructuring
> will prove to be ineffective in the absence of a unifying framework
> of policies acceptable to all Governments. Restructuring and
> reform cannot be compensated for lack of political will to act.[82]

As such the vital change needed is not in regard to institutional
arrangements but attitudinal ones, on the part of member-States. This
holds good not only for the United States and other major powers but
the middle and smaller powers too. Structural changes will not make
much difference. What is needed is a convergence of views and an
evolving of a consensus on the role of the United Nations on what it
should do and what it should not do.

It is hoped that the period of uncertainty that engulfed the future of
the UN' multilateral system since the mid-1980s will prove to be a
turning point for the policies that member-States have pursued,

---

[82] Review of the Efficiency of the Administrative and Financial Functioning of the
United Nations: Report of the Secretary-General (A/45/714), 20 November 1990,
para. 33. Also see, Report of the Secretary-General (A/46/633, 12 November 1991).

especially, since the mid 1970s. It is clear that the countries of the industrialized North, particularly the United States, have not been fair in attacking the United Nations and paralysing its functioning in the economic and social fields. On the other hand, the developing countries of the South could easily be accused of misusing the UN system—the only framework which has provided each with 'sovereign equality'—irrespective of the fact that many of them do not possess even the basic attributes of a state. The South can also be accused of acting on the belief that its majority and thereby its vast voting strength is the ultimate weapon with which to mould the international system to its liking.

What is more regrettable is that a vast majority of the South did little to attempt an understanding of the UN system and its limitations. They have believed that passing a resolution is an end in itself, without realizing that membership of the UN and active participation in its work demand an appropriate pattern of national representation and policy coordination at the national level. This holds true, most unfortunately, for India, too. Almost all developing countries act on the assumption that a career diplomat who can handle an assignment, for instance, as consul at Kathmandu, London or Paris, is good enough to handle work at the United Nations. Furthermore, solidarity among the members of the Group of 77 has not yet moved beyond a voting pattern on development issues. The countries of the South constituting the Group of 77 have to do, so to speak, a lot of home work and team work before they can acquire some semblance of a bargaining position while negotiating with the North. They should not only be ready and anxious to use the diplomatic instrument which the world body provides to promote the larger interest (with which their own national interests are intertwined), but also to understand it and learn to use it with skill.

An objective analysis indicates that the framework of the United Nations is based on the hard realities of international politics and not on 'fallacious notions', as an expert-ignoramus would have us believe. It is structured as an association of independent states—no other formula for its organizational setting up was possible in 1945 nor is it today. The body cannot make member-States do better than what they are willing to do, nor can it compel them to honour their commitments under the Charter. And yet it has evolved into a world forum for discussion and negotiations on global problems. It has developed institutions and processes for harmonizing differences between member-States and for working out programmes involving a mutuality of interest and inter-dependence of welfare. And even though there have seldom been any spectacular results, step after small step continues to emerge, to lead away from the international rule of might towards the distant goal of a universal rule of law and better conditions of life. Let us keep the process moving, speed it up, if possible, but not destroy it in a frenzy of frustration or over-enthusiasm.

Indeed, except for a world government, which is not feasible in the foreseeable future, there is no alternative to the United Nations. This does not imply that there is no scope for improving its framework. In the preceding pages a number of suggestions have been made with a view to bringing about an increase in the effectiveness and efficiency of its work. But the United Nations has never stood still and, while its organization today is crisis-ridden, there is a growing readiness to make constructive changes for its better performance. 'There is nothing wrong with the United Nations except the members' may sound like a worn out cliche but it does carry a basic truth. The United Nations is and will be what member-States make of it.

The international community, as represented in the United Nations, is standing today at a critical crossroad. Having witnessed the ending of the Cold War which had, for decades, throttled progress in inter-national cooperation, it could make use of the vast arena now open in leading the United Nations into unravelling global and regional issues and towards a constructive global cooperation in meeting humanity's social and economic needs. The other course, which of late seems to be gaining ground, is of one power or group of powers imposing its own values or world view on the vast majority of nations who, at this stage, are in an extremely vulnerable state. Indeed, in the fast changing international environment characterized by what is referred to as the emergence of an 'unchallenged superpower', the United States of America, 'attended by its western allies' and with 'Soviet compliance',[83] there are serious apprehensions that the United Nations will succumb

---

[83] In certain circles in the United States there is much talk of the great opportunity now available for the establishment of a new world order based on American values. A syndicated columnist, for instance, has repeatedly harped on the advent of 'The Unipolar Moment' as seized by the unchallenged superpower, the United States of America, attended by its western allies, as the centre of world power. See Charles Krauthammer, 'Unipolar Moment', *Foreign Affairs*, vol. 70, no. 1, pp. 23–33. Also by the same author, 'Universal Dominion: Toward a Unipolar World', *The National Interest*, Winter, 1989–90, pp. 46–49. The phrase, 'Soviet compliance' is excerpted from an observation by US National Security Advisor Scowcraft. See, *supra*, p. 177.

to the mounting political and economical pressure. Such an eventuality would reveal all possibilities of the United Nations losing the very character it has evolved over four decades, of a non-partisan global organization harmonizing contending interests towards the promotion of common goals and the larger interest of mankind. The big question is whether or not the international community will rise to the occasion to make effective use of the United Nations's instrumentality in guarding against what the Secretary-General refers to as a 'countenance of dangerous unrestraints'.[84]

In this context the imposition of one set of values and world view on others should be distinguished from the exercise of greater influence on an international agenda. The United Nations' system has an inbuilt resilience and flexibility in its receptiveness to greater influence from member-States who command the resources and capability, provided that the influence stems from statesmanship and consistent conformity with international law and socio-economic justice. The one-member one-vote principle exists mainly in theory. Those who have power, political or economic, have always exercised greater influence and greater say in the U.N. system. Further, the evolution of caucusing groups have considerably circumscribed the formal voting system. A small number of members representing concerned caucusing groups can always work out consensus on critical issues which gets accepted by the larger membership.

The inevitable conclusion is that the question of reform and re-organization is merely a facade for the real issue which stems from the growing North–South conflict. It is regrettable that most of the studies on the current crisis of the UN system have failed to extend due recognition to the real question—the equitable sharing of international economic management. In the given critical situation, what means must be derived to induce the major industrial countries to raise the consensus level to the need for sharing management in the inter-national economic system, which would suit even their own long-range interests? If there are no means to generate such an inducement will the continued subservience of the South to the hegemonistic North be a politically feasible and durable proposition? The other approach available is that the United Nations continues to pursue with tenacity and advance, however marginally, which it has done since the 1970s, towards the distant goal of international cooperation. Even so, is it that

---

[84] Annual Report, 1990, p. 3.

such a course may be overwhelmed eventually by the consequence of contradictions inherent in the North–South divide? The crisis of the existing international [dis]order is clearly apparent. But the shape of the new order is still out of sight. The uncertainties are staggering and, unless removed, the world is set for greater chaos than what the two World Wars unleashed during the first half of the century.

Change in the international economic system is inevitable. The question is whether the change is brought about in an orderly transition through dialogue and a negotiated peaceful process or disorder, disruptive of peace and stability. The United Nations provides the apparatus for an orderly change and its response to the crisis posits a challenge to its relevance as a global organization.

Appendices

APPENDIX 1: CHARTER OF THE UNITED NATIONS

Preamble

We the Peoples of the United Nations Determined

to save succeeding generations from the scourge of war, which twice in our lifetime has brought untold sorrow to mankind, and
to reaffirm faith in fundamental human rights, in the dignity and worth of the human person, in the equal rights of men and women and women of nations large and small, and
to establish conditions under which justice and respect for the obligations arising from treaties and other sources of international law can be maintained, and
to promote social and better standards of life in larger freedom,

And for These Ends

to practice tolerance and live together in peace with one another as good neighbours, and
to unite our strength to maintain international peace and security, and
to ensure by the acceptance of principles and the institution of methods, that armed force shall not be used, save in the common interest, and to employ

---

* The Charter of the United Nations was adopted at San Francisco on 25 June 1945, and was signed the following day. It came into force on 24 October 1945, when a majority of the signatories had ratified it.

Amendments to Articles 23, 27 and 61 of the Charter were approved by the General Assembly on 17 December 1963, at the Assembly's eighteenth session, and came into force on 31 August 1965. A further amendment to Article 61 was adopted by the Assembly on 20 December 1971, at its twenty-sixth session, and came into force on 24 September 1973. An amendment to Article 109, adopted by the Assembly on 20 December 1965, at its twentieth session, came into force on 12 June 1968.

international machinery for the promotion of the economic and social advancement of all peoples,

Have Resolved to Combine Our Efforts to Accomplish these Aims

Accordingly, our respective Governments, through representatives assembled in the city of San Francisco, who have exhibited their full powers found to be in good and due form, have agreed to the present Charter of the United Nations and do hereby establish an international organization to be known as the United Nations.

Chapter I
Purposes and Principles

Article 1

The Purposes of the United Nations are:

1. To maintain international peace and security, and to that end: to take effective collective measures for the prevention and removal of threats to the peace, and for the suppression of acts of aggression or other breaches of the peace, and to bring about by peaceful means, and in conformity with the principles of justice and international law, adjustment or settlement of international disputes or situations which might lead to a breach of the peace;

2. To develop friendly relations among nations based on respect for the principle of equal rights and self-determination of peoples, and to take other appropriate measures to strengthen universal peace;

3. To achieve international co-operation in solving international problems of an economic, social, cultural or humanitarian character, and in promoting and encouraging respect for human rights and for fundamental freedoms for all without distinction as to race, sex, language or religion; and

4. To be a centre for harmonizing the actions of nations in the attainment of these common ends.

Article 2

The Organization and its Members, in pursuit of the Purposes stated in Article 1, shall act in accordance with the following Principles:

1. The Organization is based on the principle of the sovereign equality of all its Members.

2. All Members, in order to ensure to all of them the rights and benefits resulting from membership, shall fulfil in good faith the obligations assumed by them in accordance with the present Charter.

· 3. All Members shall settle their international disputes by peaceful means in such a manner that international peace and security, and justice, are not endangered.

4. All Members shall refrain in their international relations from the threat or use of force against the territorial integrity or political independence of any state, or in any other manner inconsistent with the Purposes of the United Nations.

5. All Members shall give the United Nations every assistance in any action it takes in accordance with the present Charter, and shall refrain from giving assistance to any state against which the United Nations is taking preventive or enforcement action.

6. The Organization shall ensure that states which are not Members of the United Nations act in accordance with these Principles so far as may be necessary for the maintenance of international peace and security.

7. Nothing contained in the present Charter shall authorize the United Nations to intervene in matters which are essentially within the domestic jurisdiction of any state or shall require the Members to submit such matters to settlement under the present Charter; but this principles shall not prejudice the application of enforcement measures under Chapter VII.

Chapter II
Membership

Article 3

The original Members of the United Nations shall be the states which, having participated in the United Nations Conference on International Organization at San Francisco or having previously signed the Declaration by United Nations of 1 January 1942, sign the present Charter and ratify it in accordance with Article 110.

Article 4

1. Membership in the United Nations is open to all other peace-loving states which accept the obligations contained in the present Charter and, in the judgment of the Organization, are able and willing to carry out these obligations.

2. The admission of any such state to membership in the United Nations will be affected by a decision of the General Assembly upon the recommendation of the Security Council.

Article 5

A Member of the United Nations against which preventive or enforcement action has been taken by the Security Council may be suspended from the exercise of the rights and privileges of membership by the General Assembly upon the recommendation of the Security Council. The exercise of these rights and privileges may be restored by the Security Council.

Article 6

A Member of the United Nations which has persistently violated the Principles contained in the present Charter may be expelled from the Organization by the General Assembly upon recommendation of the Security Council.

Chapter III
Organs

Article 7

1. There are established as the principal organs of the United Nations: a General Assembly, a Security Council, an Economic and Social Council, a Trusteeship Council, an International Court of Justice and a Secretariat.
2. Such subsidiary organs as may be found necessary may be established in accordance with the present Charter.

Article 8

The United Nations shall place no restrictions on the eligibility of men and women to participate in any capacity and under conditions of equality in its principal and subsidiary organs.

Chapter IV
The General Assembly

Composition

Article 9

1. The General Assembly shall consist of all the Members of the United Nations.
2. Each member shall have not more than five representatives in the General Assembly.

Functions and Powers

Article 10

The General Assembly may discuss any questions or any matters within the scope of the present Charter or relating to the powers and functions of any organs provided for in the present Charter, and, except as provided in Article 12, may make recommendations to the Member of the United Nations or to the Security Council or to both on any such questions or matters.

Article 11

1. The General Assembly may consider the general principles of co-operation in the maintenance of international peace and security, including the principles governing disarmament and the regulation of armaments, and may make recommendations with regard to such principles to the Members or to the Security Council or to both.

2. The General Assembly may discuss any questions relating to the maintenance of international peace and security brought before it by any Member of the United Nations, or by the Security Council, or by a state which is not a Member of the United Nations in accordance with Article 35, paragraph 2, and, except as provided in Article 12, may make recommendations with regard to any such questions to the state or states concerned or to the Security Council or to both. Any such question on which action is necessary shall be referred to the Security Council by the General Assembly either before or after discussion.

3. The General Assembly may call the attention of the Security Council to situations which are likely to endanger international peace and security.

4. The powers of the General Assembly set forth in this Article shall not limit the general scope of Article 10.

Article 12

1. While the Security Council is exercising in respect of any dispute or situation the functions assigned to it in the present Charter, the General Assembly shall not make any recommendation with regard to that dispute or situation unless the Security Council so requests.

2. The Secretary-General, with the consent of the Security Council, shall notify the General Assembly at each session of any matters relative to the maintenance of international peace and security which are being dealt with by the Security Council and shall similarly notify the General Assembly, or the Members of the United Nations if the General Assembly is not in session, immediately the Security Council ceases to deal with such matters.

Article 13

1. The General Assembly shall initiate studies and make recommendations for the purpose of:

   a. promoting international co-operation in the political field and encouraging the progressive development of international law and its codification;

   b. promoting international co-operation in the economic, social, cultural, educational and health fields, and assisting in the realization of human rights and fundamental freedoms for all without distinction as to race, sex, language or religion.

2. The further responsibilities, functions and powers. of the General Assembly with respect to matters mentioned in paragraph 1(b) above are set forth in Chapters IX and X.

Article 14

Subject to the provisions of Article 12, the General Assembly may recommend measures for the peaceful adjustment of any situation, regardless of origin, which it deems likely to impair the general welfare or friendly relations among nations, including situations resulting from a violation of the provisions of the present Charter setting forth the Purposes and Principle of the United Nations.

Article 15

1. The General Assembly shall receive and consider annual and special reports from the Security Council; these reports shall include an account of the measures that the Security Council has decided upon or taken to maintain international peace and security.
2. The General Assembly shall receive and consider reports from the other organs of the United Nations.

Article 16

The General Assembly shall perform such functions with respect to the international trusteeship system as are assigned to it under Chapters XII and XIII, including the approval of the trusteeship agreements for areas not designated as strategic.

Article 17

1. The General Assembly shall consider and approve the budget of the Organization.
2. The expenses of the Organization shall be borne by the Members as apportioned by the General Assembly.
3. The General Assembly shall consider and approve any financial and budgetary arrangements with specialized agencies referred to in Article 57 and shall examine the administrative budgets of such specialized agencies with a view to making recommendations to the agencies concerned.

Voting

Article 18

1. Each member of the General Assembly shall have one vote.

2. Decisions of the General Assembly on important questions shall be made by a two-thirds majority of the members present and voting. These questions shall include: recommendations with respect to the maintenance of international peace and security, the election of the non-permanent members of the Security Council, the election of the members of the Economic and Social Council, the election of members of the Trusteeship Council in accordance with paragraph 1(c) of Article 86, the admission of new Members to the United Nations, the suspension of the rights and privileges of membership, the expulsion of Members, questions relating to the operation of the trusteeship system, and budgetary questions.

3. Decisions on other questions, including the determination of additional categories of questions to be decided by a two-thirds majority, shall be made by a majority of the members present and voting.

Article 19

A Member of the United Nations which is in arrears in the payment of its financial contributions to the Organization shall have no vote in the General Assembly if the amount of its arrears equals or exceeds the amount of the contributions due from it for the preceding two full years. The General Assembly may, nevertheless, permit such a Member to vote if it is satisfied that the failure to pay is due to conditions beyond the control of the Member.

Procedure

Article 20

The General Assembly shall meet in regular annual sessions and in such special sessions as occasion may require. Special sessions shall be convoked by the Secretary-General at the request of the Security Council or of a majority of the Member of the United Nations.

Article 21

The General Assembly shall adopt its own rules of procedure. It shall elect its President for each session.

Article 22

The General Assembly may establish such subsidiary organs as it deems necessary for the performance of its functions.

Chapter V
The Security Council

Composition

Article 23*

1. The Security Council shall consist of fifteen Members of the United Nations. The Republic of China, France, the Union of Soviet Socialist Republics, the United Kingdom of Great Britain and Northern Ireland and the United States of America shall be permanent members of the Security Council. The General Assembly shall elect ten other Members of the United Nations to be non-permanent members of the Security Council, due regard being specially paid, in the first instance to the contribution of Members of the United Nations to the maintenance of international peace and security and to the other purposes of the Organization, and also to equitable geographical distribution.

2. The non-permanent members of the Security Council shall be elected for a term of two years. In the first election of the non-permanent members after the increase of the membership of the Security Council from eleven to fifteen, two of the four additional members shall be chosen for a term of one year. A retiring member shall not be eligible for immediate re-election.

3. Each member of the Security Council shall have one representative.

Functions and Powers

Article 24

1. In order to ensure prompt and effective action by the United Nations, its Members confer on the Security Council primary responsibility for the maintenance of international peace and security, and agree that in carrying out its duties under this responsibility the Security Council acts on their behalf.

---

* As amended. The original text of Article 23 reads as follows:

[1] The Security Council shall consist of eleven Members of the United Nations. The Republic of China, France, the Union of Soviet Socialist Republics, the United Kingdom of Great Britain and Northern Ireland and the United States of America shall be permanent members of the Security Council. The General Assembly shall elect six other Members of the United Nations to be non-permanent members of the Security Council, due regard being specially paid in the first instance to the contributions of Members of the United Nations to the maintenance of international peace and security and to the other purposes of the Organization, and also to equitable geographical distribution.

[2] The non-permanent members of the Security Council shall be elected for a term of two years. In the first election of the non-permanent members, however, three shall be chosen for a term of one year. A retiring member shall not be eligible for immediate re-election.

[3] Each member of the Security Council shall have one representative.

2. In discharging these duties the Security Council shall act in accordance with the Purposes and Principles of the United Nations. The specific powers granted to the Security Council for the discharge of these duties are laid down in Chapters VI, VII, VIII and XII.

3. The Security Council shall submit annual and, when necessary, special reports to the General Assembly for its considerations.

Article 25

The Members of the United Nations agree to accept and carry out the decisions of the Security Council in accordance with the present Charter.

Article 26

In order to promote the establishment and maintenance of international peace and security with the least diversion for armaments of the world's human and economic resources, the Security Council shall be responsible for formulating, with the assistance of the Military Staff Committee referred to in Article 47, plans to be submitted to the Members of the United Nations for the establishment of a system for the regulation of armaments.

Voting

Article 27*

1. Each member of the Security Council shall have one vote.

2. Decisions of the Security Council on procedural matters shall be made by an affirmative vote of nine members.

3. Decisions of the Security Council on all other matters shall be made by an affirmative vote of nine members including the concurring votes of the permanent members; provided that, in decisions under Chapter VI, and under paragraph 3 of Article 52, a party to a dispute shall abstain from voting.

---

* As amended. The original text of Article 27 reads as follows:

[1] Each member of the Security Council shall have one vote.

[2] Decisions of the Security Council on procedural matters shall be made by an affirmative vote of seven members.

[3] Decisions of the Security Council on all other matters shall be made by an affirmative vote of seven members including the concurring votes of the permanent members; provided that, in decisions under Chapter VI, and under paragraph 3 of Article 52, a party to a dispute shall abstain from voting.

Procedure

Article 28

1. The Security Council shall be so organized as to be able to function continuously. Each member of the Security Council shall for this purpose be represented at all times at the seat of the Organization.

2. The Security Council shall hold periodic meetings at which each of its members may, if it so desires, be represented by a member of the government or by some other specially designated representative.

3. The Security Council may hold meetings at such places other than the seat of the Organization as in its judgment will best facilitate its work.

Article 29

The Security Council may establish such subsidiary organs as it deems necessary for the performance of its functions.

Article 30

The Security Council shall adopt its own rules of procedure, including the method of selecting its President.

Article 31

Any Member of the United Nations which is not a member of the Security Council may participate, without vote, in the discussion of any question brought before the Security Council whenever the latter considers that the interests of that Member are specially affected.

Article 32

Any Member of the United Nations which is not a member of the Security Council or any state which is not a Member of the United Nations, if it is a party to a dispute under consideration by the Security Council, shall be invited to participate, without vote, in the discussion relating to the dispute. The Security Council shall lay down such conditions as it deems just for the participation of a state which is not a Member of the United Nations.

Chapter VI
Pacific Settlement of Disputes

Article 33

1. The parties to any dispute, the continuance of which is likely to endanger the maintenance of international peace and security, shall, first of all, seek a solution by negotiation, enquiry, mediation, conciliation, arbitration, judicial settlement, resort to regional agencies or arrangements, or other peaceful means of their own choice.

2. The Security Council shall, when it deems necessary, call upon the parties to settle their dispute by such means.

Article 34

The Security Council may investigate any dispute, or any situation which might lead to international friction or give rise to a dispute, in order to determine whether the continuance of the dispute or situation is likely to endanger the maintenance of international peace and security.

Article 35

1. Any Member of the United Nations may bring any dispute, or any situation of the nature referred to in Article 34, to the attention of the Security Council or of the General Assembly.

2. A state which is not a Member of the United Nations may bring to the attention of the Security Council or of the General Assembly any dispute to which it is a party if it accepts in advance, for the purposes of the dispute, the obligations of pacific settlement provided in the present Charter.

3. The proceedings of the General Assembly in respect of matters brought to its attention under this Article will be subject to the provisions of Articles 11 and 12.

Article 36

1. The Security Council may, at any stage of a dispute of the nature referred to in Article 33 or of a situation of like nature, recommend appropriate procedures or methods of adjustment.

2. The Security Council should take into consideration any procedures for the settlement of the dispute which have already been adopted by the parties.

3. In making recommendations under this Article the Security Council should also take into consideration that legal disputes should as a general rule be referred by the parties to the International Court of Justice in accordance with the provisions of the Statute of the Court.

Article 37

1. Should the parties to a dispute of the nature referred to in Article 33 fail to settle it by the means indicated in that Article, they shall refer it to the Security Council.

2. If the Security Council deems that the continuance of the dispute is in fact likely to endanger the maintenance of international peace and security, it shall decide whether to take action under Article 36 or to recommend such terms of settlement as it may consider appropriate.

Article 38

Without prejudice to the provisions of Articles 33 to 37, the Security Council may, if all the parties to any dispute so request, make recommendations to the parties with a view to a pacific settlement of the dispute.

Chapter VII
Action With Respect to Threats to the Peace, Breaches of the Peace and Acts of Aggression

Article 39

The Security Council shall determine the existence of any threat to the peace, breach of the peace, or act of aggression and shall make recommendations, or decide what measures shall be taken in accordance with Articles 41 and 42, to maintain or restore international peace and security.

Article 40

In order to prevent an aggravation of the situation, the Security Council may, before making the recommendations or deciding upon the measures provided for in Article 39, call upon the parties concerned to comply with such provisional measures as it deems necessary or desirable. Such provisional measures shall be without prejudice to the rights, claims or position of the parties concerned. The Security Council shall duly take account of failure to comply with such provisional measures.

Article 41

The Security Council may decide what measures not involving the use of armed force are to be employed to give effect to its decisions, and it may call upon the Members of the United Nations to apply such measures. These may include complete or partial interruption of economic relations and of rail, sea, air, postal, telegraphic, radio and other means of communication, and the severance of diplomatic relations.

Article 42

Should the Security Council consider that measures provided for in Article 41 would be inadequate or have proved to be inadequate, it may take such action by air, sea or land forces as many be necessary to maintain or restore international peace and security. Such action may include demonstrations, blockade, and other operations by air, sea, or land forces of Members of the United Nations.

Article 43

1. All Members of the United Nations, in order to contribute to the maintenance of international peace and security, undertake to make available to the Security Council, on its call and in accordance with a special agreement or agreements, armed forces, assistance and facilities, including rights of passage, necessary for the purpose of maintaining international peace and security.

2. Such agreement or agreements shall govern the numbers and types of forces, their degree of readiness and general location, and the nature of the facilities and assistance to be provided.

3. The agreement or agreements shall be negotiated as soon as possible on the initiative of the Security Council. They shall be concluded between the Security Council and Members or between the Security Council and groups of Members and shall be subject to ratification by the signatory states in accordance with their respective constitutional processes.

Article 44

When the Security Council has decided to use force it shall, before calling upon a Member not represented on it to provide armed forces in fulfilment of the obligations assumed under Article 43, invite that Member, if the Member so desires, to participate in the decisions of the Security Council concerning the employment of contingents of that Member's armed forces.

Article 45

In order to enable the United Nations to take urgent military measures, Members shall hold immediately available national air-force contingents for combined international enforcement action. The strength and degree of readiness of these contingents and plans for their combined action shall be determined, within the limits laid down in the special agreement or agreements referred to in Article 43, by the Security Council with the assistance of the Military Staff Committee.

Article 46

Plans for the application of armed force shall be made by the Security Council with the assistance of the Military Staff Committee.

Article 47

1. There shall be established a Military Staff Committee to advise and assist the Security Council on all questions relating to the Security Council's military requirements for the maintenance of international peace and security, the employment and command of forces placed at its disposal, the regulation of armaments, and possible disarmament.

2. The Military Staff Committee shall consist of the Chiefs of Staff of the permanent members of the Security Council or their representatives. Any Member of the United Nations not permanently represented on the Committee shall be invited by the Committee to be associated with it when the efficient discharge of the Committee's responsibilities requires the participation of that Member in its work.

3. The Military Staff Committee shall be responsible under the Security Council for the strategic direction of any armed forced placed at the disposal of the Security Council. Questions relating to the command of such forces shall be worked out subsequently.

4. The Military Staff Committee, with the authorization of the Security Council and after consultation with appropriate regional agencies, may establish regional sub-committees.

Article 48

1. The action required to carry out the decisions of the Security Council for the maintenance of international peace and security shall be taken by all the Members of the United Nations or by some of them, as the Security Council may determine.

2. Such decisions shall be carried out by the Members of the United Nations directly and through their action in the appropriate international agencies of which they are members.

Article 49

The Members of the United Nations shall join in affording mutual assistance in carrying out the measures decided upon by the Security Council.

Article 50

If preventive or enforcement measures against any state are taken by the

Security Council, any other state, whether a Member of the United Nations or not, which finds itself confronted with special economic problems arising from the carrying out of those measures shall have the right to consult the Security Council with regard to a solution of those problems.

Article 51

Nothing in the present Charter shall impair the inherent right of individual or collective self-defence if an armed attack occurs against a Member of the United Nations, until the Security Council has taken measures necessary to maintain international peace and security. Measures taken by Members in the exercise of this right of self-defence shall be immediately reported to the Security Council and shall not in any way affect the authority and responsibility of the Security Council under the present Charter to take at any time such action as it deems necessary in order to maintain or restore international peace and security.

Chapter VIII
Regional Arrangements

Article 52

1. Nothing in the present Charter precludes the existence of regional arrangements or agencies for dealing with such matters relating to the maintenance of international peace and security as are appropriate for regional action, provided that such arrangements or agencies and their activities are consistent with the Purposes and Principles of the United Nations.

2. The Members of the United Nations entering into such arrangements or constituting such agencies shall make every effort to achieve pacific settlement of local disputes through such regional arrangements or by such regional agencies before referring them to the Security Council.

3. The Security Council shall encourage the development of pacific settlement of local disputes through such regional arrangements or by such regional agencies either on the initiative of the states concerned or by reference from the Security Council.

4. This Article in no way impairs the application of Article 34 and 35.

Article 53

1. The Security Council shall, where appropriate, utilize such regional arrangements or agencies for enforcement action under its authority. But no enforcement action shall be taken under regional arrangements without the authorization of the Security Council, with the exception of measures against any enemy state, as defined in paragraph 2 of this Article, provided for

pursuant to Article 107 or in regional arrangements directed against renewal
of aggressive policy on the part of any such state, until such time as the
Organization may, on request of the Governments concerned, be charged
with the responsibility for preventing further aggression by such a state.

2. The term enemy state as used in paragraph 1 of this Article applies to any
state which during the Second World War has been an enemy of any signatory
of the present Charter.

Article 54

The Security Council shall at all times be kept fully informed of activities
undertaken or in contemplation under regional arrangements or by regional
agencies for the maintenance of international peace and security.

Chapter IX
International Economic and Social Co-operation

Article 55

With a view to the creation of conditions of stability and well-being which
are necessary for peaceful and friendly relations among nations based on
respect for the principle of equal rights and self-determination of peoples, the
United Nations shall promote:

a. higher standards of living, full employment, and conditions of
economic and social progress and development;

b. solutions of international economic, social, health, and related
problems; and international cultural and educational co-operation; and

c. universal respect for, and observance of, human rights and fundamental freedoms for all without distinction as to race, sex, language, or
religion.

Article 56

All Members pledge themselves to take joint and separate action in cooperation with the Organization for the achievement of the purposes set forth
in Article 55.

Article 57

1. The various specialized agencies, established by intergovernmental
agreement and having wide international responsibilities, as defined in their
basic instruments, in economic, social, cultural, educational, health, and related
fields, shall be brought into relationship with the United Nations in accordance
with the provisions of Article 63.

2. Such agencies thus brought into relationship with the United Nations are hereinafter referred to as specialized agencies.

Article 58

The Organization shall make recommendations for the co-ordination of the policies and activities of the specialized agencies.

Article 59

The Organization shall, where appropriate, initiate negotiations among the states concerned for the creation of any new specialized agencies required for the accomplishment of the purposes set forth in Article 55.

Article 60

Responsibility for the discharge of the functions of the Organization set forth in this Chapter shall be vested in the General Assembly and, under the authority of the General Assembly, in the Economic and Social Council, which shall have for this purpose the powers set forth in Chapter X.

Chapter X
The Economic and Social Council

Composition

Article 61*

1. The Economic and Social Council shall consist of fifty-four Members of the United Nations elected by the General Assembly.

2. Subject to the provisions of paragraph 3, eighteen members of the Economic and Social Council shall be elected each year for a term of three years. A retiring member shall be eligible for immediate re-election.

3. At the first election after the increase in the membership of the Economic and Social Council from twenty-seven to fifty-four members, in addition to the

---

* As amended. The original text of Article 61 reads as follows:

[1] The Economic and Social Council shall consist of eighteen Members of the United Nations elected by the General Assembly.

[2] Subject to the provisions of paragraph 3, six members of the Economic and Social Council shall be elected each year for a term of three years. A retiring member shall be eligible for immediate re-election.

[3] At the first election, eighteen members of the Economic and Social shall be chosen. The term office of six members so chosen shall expire at the end of one year, and of six other members at the end of two years, in accordance with arrangements made by the General Assembly.

[4] Each member of the Economic and Social Council shall have one representative.

members elected in place of the nine members whose term of office expires at the end of that year, twenty-seven additional members shall be elected. Of these twenty-seven additional members, the term of office of nine members so elected shall expire at the end of one year, and of nine other members at the end of two years, in accordance with arrangements made by the General Assembly.

4. Each member of the Economic and Social Council shall have one representative.

Functions and Powers

Article 62

1. The Economic and Social Council may make or initiate studies and reports with respect to international economic, social, cultural, educational, health, and related matters and may make recommendations with respect to any such matters to the General Assembly, to the Members of the United Nations, and to the specialized agencies concerned.

2. It may make recommendations for the purpose of promoting respect for, and observance of, human rights and fundamental freedoms for all.

3. It may prepare draft conventions for submission to the General Assembly, with respect to matters falling within its competence.

4. It may call, in accordance with the rules prescribed by the United Nations, international conferences on matters falling within its competence.

Article 63

1. The Economic and Social Council may enter into agreements with any of the agencies referred to in Article 57, defining the terms on which the agency concerned shall be brought into relationship with the United Nations. Such agreements shall be subject to approval by the General Assembly.

2. It may co-ordinate the activities of the specialized agencies through consultation with and recommendations to such agencies and through recommendations to the General Assembly and to the Members of the United Nations.

Article 64

1. The Economic and Social Council may take appropriate steps to obtain regular reports from the specialized agencies. It may make arrangements with the Members of the United Nations and with the specialized agencies to obtain reports on the steps taken to give effect to its own recommendations and to recommendations on matters falling within its competence made by the General Assembly.

2. It may communicate its observations on these reports to the General Assembly.

Article 65

The Economic and Social Council may furnish information to the Security Council and shall assist the Security Council upon its request.

Article 66

1. The Economic and Social Council shall perform such functions as fall within its competence in connexion with the carrying out of the recommendations of the General Assembly.

2. It may, with the approval of the General Assembly, perform services at the request of Members of the United Nations and at the request of specialized agencies.

3. It shall perform such other functions as are specified elsewhere in the present Charter or as may be assigned to it by the General Assembly.

Voting

Article 67

1. Each member of the Economic and Social Council shall have one vote.

2. Decisions of the Economic and Social Council shall be made by a majority of the members present and voting.

Procedure

Article 68

The Economic and Social Council shall set up commissions in economic and social fields and for the promotion of human rights, and such other commissions as may be required for the performance of its functions.

Article 69

The Economic and Social Council shall invite any Members of the United Nations to participate, without vote, in its deliberations on any matter of particular concern to that Member.

Article 70

The Economic and Social Council may make arrangements for representatives of the specialized agencies to participate, without vote, in its deliberations and in those of the commissions established by it, and for its representatives to participate in the deliberations of the specialized agencies.

Article 71

The Economic and Social Council may make suitable arrangements for consultation with non-governmental organizations which are concerned with matters within its competence. Such arrangements may be made with international organizations and, where appropriate, with national organizations after consultation with the Member of the United Nations concerned.

Article 72

1. The Economic and Social Council shall adopt its own rules of procedure, including the method of selecting its President.
2. The Economic and Social Council shall meet as required in accordance with its rules, which shall include provision for the convening of meetings on the request of a majority of its members.

Chapter XI
Declaration Regarding Non-self-governing Territories

Article 73

Members of the United Nations which have or assume responsibilities for the administration of territories whose peoples have not yet attained a full measure of self-government recognize the principle that the interests of the inhabitants of these territories are paramount, and accept as a sacred trust the obligation to promote to the utmost, within the system of international peace and security established by the present Charter, the well-being of the inhabitants of these territories and, to this end:

a. to ensure, with due respect for the culture of the peoples concerned, their political, economic, social, and educational advancement, their just treatment, and their protection against abuses;

b. to develop self-government, to take due account to the political aspirations of the peoples, and to assist them in the progressive development of their free political institutions, according to the particular circumstances of each territory and its peoples and their varying stages of advancement;

c. to further international peace and security;

d. to promote constructive measures of development, to encourage research, and to co-operate with one another and, when and where appropriate, with specialized international bodies with a view to the practical achievement of the social, economic, and scientific purposes set forth in this Article; and

e. to transmit regularly to the Secretary-General for information purposes, subject to such limitation as security and constitutional considerations
may require, statistical and other information of a technical nature relating
to economic, social, and educational conditions in the territories for which
they are respectively responsible other than those territories to which
Chapters XII and XIII apply.

Article 74

Members of the United Nations also agree that their policy in respect of the
territories to which this Chapter applies, no less than in respect of their
metropolitan areas, must be based on the general principle of good-
neighbourliness, due account being taken of the interests and well-being of the
rest of the world, in social, economic, and commercial matters.

Chapter XII
International Trusteeship System

Article 75

The United Nations shall establish under its authority an international
trusteeship system for the administration and supervision of such territories as
may be placed thereunder by subsequent individual agreements. These territories are hereinafter referred to as trust territories.

Article 76

The basic objectives of the trusteeship system, in accordance with the
Purposes of the United Nations laid down in Article 1 of the present Charter,
shall be:
a. to further international peace and security;
b. to promote the political, economic, social, and educational advancement of the inhabitants of the trust territories, and their progressive
development towards self-government or independence as may be appropriate to the particular circumstances of each territory and its peoples and
the freely expressed wishes of the peoples concerned, and as may be
provided by the terms of each trusteeship agreement;
c. to encourage respect for human rights and for fundamental freedoms
for all without distinction as to race, sex, language, or religion, and to
encourage recognition of the interdependence of the peoples of the world;
and
d. to ensure equal treatment in social, economic, and commercial matters
for all Members of the United Nations and their nationals, and also equal
treatment for the latter in the administration of justice, without prejudice

to the attainment of the foregoing objectives and subject to the provisions of Article 80.

Article 77

1. The trusteeship system shall apply to such territories in the following categories as may be placed thereunder by means of trusteeship agreements:
  a. territories now held under mandate;
  b. territories which may be detached from enemy states as a result of the Second World War; and
  c. territories voluntarily placed under the system by states responsible for their administration.
2. It will be a matter for subsequent agreement as to which territories in the foregoing categories will be brought under the trusteeship system and upon what terms.

Article 78

The trusteeship system shall not apply to territories which have become Members of the United Nations, relationship among which shall be based on respect for the principle of sovereign equality.

Article 79

The terms of trusteeship for each territory to be placed under the trusteeship system, including any alteration or amendment, shall be agreed upon by the states directly concerned, including the mandatory power in the case of territories held under mandate by a Member of the United Nations and shall be approved as provided for in the Articles 83 and 85.

Article 80

1. Except as may be agreed upon in individual trusteeship agreements, made under Articles 77, 79 and 81, placing each territory under the trusteeship system, and until such agreements have been concluded, nothing in this Chapter shall be construed in or of itself to alter in any manner the rights whatsoever of any states or any peoples or the terms of existing international instruments to which Members of the United Nations may respectively be parties.
2. Paragraph 1 of this Article shall not be interpreted as giving grounds for delay or postponement of the negotiation and conclusion of agreements for placing mandated and other territories under the trusteeship system as provided for in Article 77.

Article 81

The trusteeship agreement shall in each case include the terms under which the trust territory will be administered and designate the authority which will exercise the administration of the trust territory. Such authority, hereinafter called the administering authority, may be one or more states or the Organization itself.

Article 82

There may be designated, in any trusteeship agreement, a strategic area or areas which may include part or all of the trust territory to which the agreement applies, without prejudice to any special agreement or agreements made under Article 43.

Article 83

1. All functions of the United Nations relating to strategic areas, including the approval of the terms of the trusteeship agreements and of their alteration or amendment, shall be exercised by the Security Council.
2. The basic objectives set forth in Article 76 shall be applicable to the people of each strategic area.
3. The Security Council shall, subject to the provisions of the trusteeship agreements and without prejudice to security considerations, avail itself of the assistance of the Trusteeship Council to perform those functions of the United Nations under the trusteeship system relating to political, economic, social, and educational matters in the strategic areas.

Article 84

It shall be the duty of the administering authority to ensure that the trust territory shall play its part in the maintenance of international peace and security. To this end the administering authority may make use of volunteer forces, facilities, and assistance from the trust territory in carrying out the obligations towards the Security Council undertaken in this regard by the administering authority, as well as for local defence and the maintenance of law and order within the trust territory.

Article 85

1. The functions of the United Nations with regard to trusteeship agreements for all areas not designated as strategic, including the approval of the terms of the trusteeship agreements and of their alteration or amendment, shall be exercised by the General Assembly.

2. The Trusteeship Council, operating under the authority of the General Assembly, shall assist the General Assembly in carrying out these functions.

Chapter XIII
The Trusteeship Council

Composition

Article 86

1. The Trusteeship Council shall consist of the following Members of the United Nations:
 a. those Members administering trust territories;
 b. such of those Members mentioned by name in Article 23 as are not administering trust territories; and
 c. as many other Members elected for three-year terms by the General Assembly as may be necessary to ensure that the total number of members of the Trusteeship Council is equally divided between those Members of the United Nations which administer trust territories and those which do not.
2. Each member of the Trusteeship Council shall designate one specially qualified person to represent it therein.

Function and Powers

Article 87

The General Assembly and, under its authority, the Trusteeship Council, in carrying out their functions, may:
 a. consider reports submitted by the administering authority;
 b. accept petitions and examine them in consultation with the administering authority;
 c. provide for periodic visits to the respective trust territories at times agreed upon with the administering authority; and;
 d. take these and other actions in conformity with the terms of the trusteeship agreements.

Article 88

The Trusteeship Council shall formulate a questionnaire on the political, economic, social, and educational advancement of the inhabitants of each trust territory, and the administering authority for each trust territory within the competence of the General Assembly shall make an annual report to the General Assembly upon the basis of such questionnaire.

Voting

Article 89

1. Each member of the Trusteeship Council shall have one vote.

2. Decisions of the Trusteeship Council shall be made by a majority of the members present and voting.

Procedure

Article 90

1. The Trusteeship Council shall adopt its own rules of procedure, including the method of selecting its President.

2. The Trusteeship Council shall meet as required in accordance with its rules, which shall include provision for the convening of meetings of the request of a majority of its members.

Article 91

The Trusteeship Council shall, when appropriate, avail itself of the assistance of the Economic and Social Council and of the specialized agencies in regard to matters with which they are respectively concerned.

Chapter XIV
The International Court of Justice

Article 92

The International Court of Justice shall be the principal judicial organ of the United Nations. It shall function in accordance with the annexed Statute, which is based upon the Statute of the Permanent Court of International Justice and forms an integral part of the present Charter.

Article 93

1. All Members of the United Nations are *ipso facto* parties to the Statute of the International Court of Justice.

2. A state which is not a Member of the United Nations may become a party to the Statute of the International Court of Justice on conditions to be determined in each case by the General Assembly upon the recommendation of the Security Council.

Article 94

1. Each Member of the United Nations undertakes to comply with the decision of the International Court of Justice in any case to which it is a party.

2. If any party to a case fails to perform the obligations incumbent upon it under a judgement rendered by the Court, the other party may have recourse to the Security Council, which may, if it deems necessary, make recommendations or decide upon measures to be taken to give effect to the judgment.

Article 95

Nothing in the present Charter shall prevent Members of the United Nations from entrusting the solution of their differences to other tribunals by virtue of agreements already in existence or which may be concluded in the future.

Article 96

1. The General Assembly or the Security Council may request the International Court of Justice to give an advisory opinion on any legal question.

2. Other organs of the United Nations and specialized agencies, which may at any time be so authorized by the General Assembly, may also request advisory opinions of the Court on legal questions arising within the scope of their activities.

Chapter XV
The Secretariat

Article 97

The Secretariat shall comprise a Secretary-General and such staff as the Organization may require. The Secretary-General shall be appointed by the General Assembly upon the recommendation of the Security Council. He shall be the chief administrative officer of the Organization.

Article 98

The Secretary-General shall act in that capacity in all meetings of the General Assembly, of the Security Council, of the Economic and Social Council, and of the Trusteeship Council, and shall perform such other functions as are entrusted to him by these organs. The Secretary-General shall make an annual report to the General Assembly on the work of the Organization.

Article 99

The Secretary-General may bring to the attention of the Security Council any matter which in his opinion may threaten the maintenance of international peace and security.

Article 100

1. In the performance of their duties the Secretary-General and the staff shall not seek or receive instructions from any government or from any other authority external to the Organization. They shall refrain from any action which might reflect on their position as international officials responsible only to the Organization.

2. Each Member of the United Nations undertakes to respect the exclusively international character of the responsibilities of the Secretary-General and the staff and not to seek to influence them in the discharge of their responsibilities.

Article 101

1. The staff shall be appointed by the Secretary-General under regulations established by the General Assembly.

2. Appropriate staffs shall be permanently assigned to the Economic and Social Council, the Trusteeship Council, and, as required, to other organs of the United Nations. These staffs shall form a part of the Secretariat.

3. The paramount consideration in the employment of the staff and in the determination of the conditions of service shall be the necessity of securing the highest standards of efficiency, competence, and integrity. Due regard shall be paid to the importance of recruiting the staff on as wide a geographical basis as possible.

Chapter XVI
Miscellaneous Provisions

Article 102

1. Every treaty and every international agreement entered into by any Member of the United Nations after the present Charter comes into force shall as soon as possible be registered with the Secretariat and published by it.

2. No party to any such treaty or international agreement which has not been registered in accordance with the provisions of paragraph 1 of this Article may invoke that treaty of agreement before any organ of the United Nations.

Article 103

In the event of conflict between the obligations of the Members of the United Nations under the present Charter and their obligations under any other international agreement, their obligations under the present Charter shall prevail.

Article 104

1. The Organization shall enjoy in the territory of each of its Members such legal capacity as may be necessary for the exercise of its functions and the fulfilment of its purpose.

Article 105

1. The Organization shall enjoy in the territory of each of its Members such privileges and immunities as are necessary for the fulfilment of its purposes.

2. Representatives of the Members of the United Nations and officials of the Organization shall similarly enjoy such privileges and immunities as are necessary for the independent exercise of their functions in connexion with the Organization.

3. The General Assembly may make recommendations with a view to determining the details of the application of paragraphs 1 and 2 of this Article or may propose conventions to the Members of the United Nations for this purpose.

Chapter XVII
Transitional Security Arrangements

Article 106

Pending the coming into force of such special agreements referred to in Article 43 as in the opinion of the Security Council enable it to begin the exercise of its responsibilities under Article 42, the parties to the Four-Nation Declaration, signed at Moscow, 30 October 1943, and France, shall, in accordance with the provisions of paragraph 5 of that Declaration, consult with one another and as occasion requires with other Members of the United Nations with a view to such joint action on behalf of the Organization as may be necessary for the purpose of maintaining international peace and security.

Article 107

Nothing in the present Charter shall invalidate or preclude action, in relation to any state which during the Second World War has been an enemy

of any signatory to the present Charter, taken or authorized as a result of that
war by the Governments having responsibility for such action.

Chapter XVIII
Amendments

Article 108

Amendments to the present Charter shall come into force for all Members
of the United Nations when they have been adopted by a vote of two thirds of
the members of the General Assembly and ratified in accordance with their
respective constitutional processes by two thirds of the Members of the
United Nations including all the permanent members of the Security Council.

Article 109*

1. A General Conference of the Members of the United Nations for the
purpose of reviewing the present Charter may be held at a date and place to be
fixed by a two-thirds vote of the members of the General Assembly and by a
vote of any nine members of the Security. Each Member of the United Nations
shall have one vote in the conference.

2. Any alteration of the present Charter recommended by a two-thirds vote
of the conference shall take effect when ratified in accordance with their
respective constitutional processes by two thirds of the Members of the
United Nations including all the permanent members of the Security Council.

3. If such a conference has not been held before the tenth annual session of
the General Assembly following the coming into force of the present Charter,
the proposal to call such a conference shall be placed on the agenda of that
session of the General Assembly, and the conference shall be held if so
decided by a majority vote of the members of the General Assembly and by a
vote of any seven members of the Security Council.

---

* As amended. The original text of Article 109 reads as follows:

[1] A General Conference of the Members of the United Nations for the purpose of reviewing the
present Charter may be held at a date and place to be fixed by a two-thirds vote of the members of
the General Assembly and by a vote of any seven members of the Security Council. Each Member of
the United Nations shall have one vote in the conference.

[2] Any alteration of the present Charter recommended by a two-thirds vote of the conference shall
take effect when ratified in accordance with their respective constitutional processes by two thirds of
the Members of the United Nations including all the permanent members of the Security Council.

[3] If such a conference has not been held before the tenth annual session of the General Assembly
following the coming into force of the present Charter, the proposal to call such a conference shall be
placed on the agenda of that session of the General Assembly, and the conference shall be held if so
decided by a majority vote of the members of the General Assembly and by a vote of any seven
members of the Security Council.

[4] The states signatory to the present Charter which ratify it after it has come into force will become
original Members of the United Nations on the date of the deposit of their respective ratifications.

Chapter XIX
Ratification and Signature

Article 110

1. The present Charter shall be ratified by the signatory states in accordance with their respective constitutional processes.

2. The ratifications shall be deposited with the Government of the United States of America, which shall notify all the signatory states of each deposit as well as the Secretary-General of the Organization when he has been appointed.

3. The present Charter shall come into force upon the deposit of ratifications by the Republic of China, France, the Union of Soviet Socialist Republics, the United Kingdom of Great Britain and Northern Ireland and the United States of America, and by a majority of the other signatory states. A protocol of the ratifications deposited shall thereupon be drawn up by the Government of the United States of America which shall communicate copies thereof to all the signatory states.

4. The states signatory to the present Charter which ratify it after it has come into force will become original Members of the United Nations on the date of the deposit of their respective ratifications.

Article 111

The present Charter, of which the Chinese, French, Russian, English, and Spanish texts are equally authentic, shall remain deposited in the archives of the Government to the United States of America. Duly certified copies thereof shall be transmitted by that Government to the Governments of the other signatory states.

IN FAITH WHEREOF the representatives of the Governments of the United Nations have signed the present Charter.

DONE at the city of San Francisco the twenty-sixth day of June, one thousand nine hundred and forty-five.

APPENDIX II: UNITED NATIONS MEMBER-STATES

The 175 States-Members of the United Nations are listed below with dates on which they became Members

Member	Date of Admission
Afghanistan	19 November 1946
Albania	14 December 1955

Algeria	8 October 1962
Angola	1 December 1976
Antigua and Barbuda	11 November 1981
Argentina	24 October 1945
Armenia	2 March 1992
Australia	1 November 1945
Austria	14 December 1955
Azerbaijan	2 March 1992
Bahamas	18 September 1973
Bahrain	21 September 1971
Bangladesh	17 September 1974
Barbados	9 December 1966
Belarus*	24 October 1945
Belgium	27 December 1945
Belize	25 September 1981
Benin	20 September 1960
Bhutan	21 September 1971
Bolivia	14 November 1945
Botswana	17 October 1966
Brazil	24 October 1945
Brunei Darussalam	21 September 1984
Bulgaria	14 December 1955
Burkina Faso	20 September 1960
Burundi	18 September 1962
Cambodia	14 December 1955
Cameroon	20 September 1960
Canada	9 November 1945
Cape Verde	16 September 1975
Central African Republic	20 September 1960
Chad	20 September 1960
Chile	24 October 1945
China	24 October 1945
Colombia	5 November 1945
Comoros	12 November 1975
Congo	20 September 1960
Costa Rica	2 November 1945
Côte d'Ivoire	20 September 1960
Cuba	24 October 1945
Cyprus	20 September 1960
Czechoslovakia	24 October 1945
Democratic People's Republic of Korea	17 September 1991

* On 19 September 1991, Byelorussia informed the United Nations that it had changed its name to Belarus.

Denmark	24 October 1945
Djibouti	20 September 1977
Dominica	18 December 1978
Dominican Republic	24 October 1945
Ecuador	21 December 1945
Egypt*	24 October 1945
El Salvador	24 October 1945
Equatorial Guinea	12 November 1968
Estonia†	17 September 1991
Ethiopia	13 November 1945
Federated States of Micronesia	17 September 1991
Fiji	13 October 1970
Finland	14 December 1955
France	24 October 1945
Gabon	20 September 1960
Gambia	21 September 1965
Germany‡	18 September 1973
Ghana	8 March 1957
Greece	25 October 1945
Grenada	17 September 1974
Guatemala	21 November 1945
Guinea	12 December 1958
Guinea-Bissau	17 September 1974
Guyana	20 September 1966
Haiti	24 October 1945
Honduras	17 December 1945
Hungary	14 December 1955
Iceland	19 November 1946
India	30 October 1945

* Egypt and Syria were original Members of the United Nations from 24 October 1945. Following a plebiscite on 21 February 1958, the United Arab Republic was established by a union of Egypt and Syria and continued as a single Member. On 13 October 1961, Syria, having resumed its status as an independent State, resumed its separate membership in the United Nations. On 2 September 1971, the United Arab Republic changed its name to the Arab Republic of Egypt.

† On 17 September 1991, Estonia was admitted to United Nations membership as an independent State.

‡ The Federal Republic of Germany and the German Democratic Republic were admitted to membership in the United Nations on 18 September 1973. Through the accession of the German Democratic Republic to the Federal Republic of Germany, effective from 3 October 1990, the two German States have united to form one sovereign State.

Indonesia*	28 September 1950
Iran	24 October 1945
Iraq	21 December 1945
Ireland	14 December 1955
Israel	11 May 1949
Italy	14 December 1955
Jamaica	18 September 1962
Japan	18 December 1956
Jordan	14 December 1955
Kazakhstan	2 March 1992
Kenya	16 December 1963
Kuwait	14 May 1963
Kyrgyzstan	2 March 1992
Lao People's Democratic Republic	14 December 1955
Latvia†	17 September 1991
Lebanon	24 October 1945
Lesotho	17 October 1966
Liberia	2 November 1945
Libya	14 December 1955
Liechtenstein	18 September 1990
Lithuania+	17 September 1991
Luxembourg	24 October 1945
Madagascar	20 September 1960
Malawi	1 December 1964
Malaysia‡	17 September 1957
Maldives	21 September 1965
Mali	28 September 1960
Malta	1 December 1964
Marshall Islands	17 September 1991
Mauritania	27 October 1961
Mauritius	24 April 1968
Mexico	7 November 1945

* By letter of 20 January 1965, Indonesia announced its decision to withdrew from the United Nations "at this stage and under the present circumstances". By telegram of 19 September 1966, it announced its decision "to resume full cooperation with the United Nations and to resume participation in its activities". On 28 September 1966, the General Assembly took note of this decision and the President invited representatives of Indonesia to take seats in the Assembly.

† On 17 September 1991, Latvia and Lithuania were admitted to United Nations membership as independent States.

‡ The Federation of Malaya joined the United Nations on 17 September 1957. On 16 September 1963, its name was changed to Malaysia, following the admission to the new federation of Singapore, Sabah (North Borneo) and Sarawak. Singapore became an independent State on 9 August 1965 and a Member of the United Nations on 21 September 1965.

Moldova	2 March 1992
Mongolia	27 October 1961
Morocco	12 November 1956
Mozambique	16 September 1975
Myanmar	19 April 1948
Namibia	23 April 1990
Nepal	14 December 1955
Netherlands	10 December 1945
New Zealands	24 October 1945
Nicaragua	24 October 1945
Niger	20 September 1960
Nigeria	7 October 1960
Norway	27 November 1945
Oman	7 October 1971
Pakistan	30 September 1947
Panama	13 November 1945
Papua New Guinea	10 October 1975
Paraguay	24 October 1945
Peru	31 October 1945
Philippines	24 October 1945
Poland	24 October 1945
Portugal	14 December 1955
Qatar	21 September 1971
Republic of Korea	17 September 1991
Romania	14 December 1955
Russian Federation*	24 October 1945
Rwanda	18 September 1962
Saint Kitts and Nevis	23 September 1983
Saint Lucia	18 September 1979
Saint Vincent and the Grenadines	16 September 1980
Samoa	15 December 1976
San Marino	2 March 1992
Sao Tome and Principe	16 September 1975
Saudi Arabia	24 October 1945
Senegel	28 September 1960
Seychelles	21 September 1976
Sierra Leone	27 September 1961
Singapore	21 September 1965
Solomon Islands	19 September 1978

* The Union of Soviet Socialist Republics was an original Member of the United Nations from 24 October 1945. In a letter dated 24 December 1991, Boris Yeltsin, the President of the Russian Federation, informed the Secretary-General that the membership of the Soviet Union in the Security Council and all other United Nations organs was being continued by the Russian Federation with the support of the 11 member countries of the Commonwealth of Independent States.

Somalia	20 September 1960
South Africa	7 November 1945
Spain	14 December 1955
Sri Lanka	14 December 1955
Sudan	12 November 1956
Suriname	4 December 1975
Swaziland	24 September 1968
Sweden	19 November 1946
Syria*	24 October 1945
Tajikistan	2 March 1992
Thailand	16 December 1946
Togo	20 September 1960
Trinidad and Tobago	18 September 1962
Tunisia	12 November 1956
Turkey	24 October 1945
Turkmenistan	2 March 1992
Uganda	25 October 1962
Ukraine	24 October 1945
United Arab Emirates	9 December 1971
United Kingdom	24 October 1945
United Republic of Tanzania†	14 December 1961
United States	24 October 1945
Uruguay	18 December 1945
Uzbekistan	2 March 1992
Vanuatu	15 September 1981
Venezuela	15 November 1945
Viet Nam	20 September 1977
Yemen‡	30 September 1947
Yugoslavia	24 October 1945
Zaire	20 September 1960
Zambia	1 December 1964
Zimbabwe	25 August 1980

* Egypt and Syria were original Members of the United Nations from 24 October 1945. Following a plebiscite on 21 February 1958, the United Arab Republic was established by a union of Egypt and Syria and continued as a single Member. On 13 October 1961, Syria, having resumed its status as an independent State, resumed its separate membership in the United Nations.

† Tanganyika was a Member of the United Nations from 14 December 1961 and Zanzibar was a Member from 16 December 1963. Following the ratification on 26 April 1964 of Articles of Union between Tanganyika and Zanzibar, the United Republic of Tanganyika and Zanzibar continued as a single Member, changing its name to the United Republic of Tanzania on 1 November 1964.

‡ Yemen was admitted to membership in the United Nations on 30 September 1947 and Democratic Yemen on 14 December 1967. On 22 May 1990, the two countries merged and have since been represented as one Member with the name "Yemen".

APPENDIX III: BUDGET APPROPRIATIONS FOR THE BIENNIUM 1992–1993

The General Assembly Resolves that for the biennium 1992–1993:

1. Appropriations totalling 2 389 234 900 United States dollars are hereby voted for the following purposes:

Section	(Thousands of US dollars)
PART I Overall policy-making, direction and coordination	
1. Overall policy-making, direction and corodination	35,545.5
Total, Part I	35,545.5
PART II Political affairs	
2. Good offices and peacemaking; peace-keeping; research and the collection of information	97,580.6
3. Political and Security Council affairs	15,822.8
4. Political and General Assembly affairs and Secretariat services	12,486.3
5. Disarmament	13,264.4
6. Special political questions, regional cooperation, trusteeship and decolonization	9,499.1
7. Elimination of apartheid	8,300.3
Total, Part II	156,953.5
PART III International justice and law	
8. International Court of Justice	17,606.5
9. Legal activities	21,821.8
10. Law of the sea and ocean affairs	9,088.3
Total Part III	48,516.6
PART IV International cooperation for development	
11. Development and international economic cooperation	19,047.0
12. Regular programme of technical cooperation	42,285.9
13. Department of International Economic and Social Affairs	54,828.1
14. Department of Technical Cooperation for Development	27,482.7
15. United Nations Conference on Trade and Development	90,477.1
16. International Trade Centre	17,916.2
17. United Nations Environment Programme	12,927.4
18. Centre for Science and Technology for Development	4,851.0
19. United Nations Centre for Human Settlements (Habitat)	11,500.5
20. United Nations Centre on Transnational Corporations	12,839.5
21. Social development and humanitarian affairs	13,898.8
22. International drug control	13,651.4
Total, Part IV	321,705.6

Section	(Thousands of US dollars)
PART V Regional cooperation for development	
23. Economic Commission for Africa	74,959.3
24. Economic and Social Commission for Asia and the Pacific	51,887.5
25. Economic Commission for Europe	41,242.9
26. Economic Commission for Latin America and the Caribbean	67,753.7
27. Economic and Social Commission for Western Asia	50,660.6
Total, Part V	286,504.0
PART VI Human rights and humanitarian affairs	
28. Human rights	23,391.2
29. Protection of and assistance to refugees	60,823.0
30. Disaster relief operations	7,824.6
Total, Part VI	92,038.8
PART VII Public information	
31. Public information	100,977.0
Total, Part VII	100,977.0
PART VIII Common support services	
32. Conference services	422,414.6
33. Administration and management	421,935.4
Total Part VIII	844,350.0
PART IX Special expenses	
34. Special expenses	45,035.0
Total, Part IX	45,035.0
PART X Capital expenditures	
35. Construction, alteration, improvement and major maintenance	96,815.6
Total, Part X	96,815.6
PART XI Staff assessment	
36. Staff assessment	374,137.2
Total, Part XI	374,137.2
GRAND TOTAL	2,402,578.8
Reduction from underutilized balances	13,343.9

2.   The Secretary-General shall be authorized to transfer credits between sections of the budget with the concurrence of the Advisory Committee on Administrative and Budgetary Questions;

3. The total net provision made under the various sections of the budget for contractual printing shall be administered as a unit under the direction of the United Nations, except that the definition of obligations and the period of validity of obligations shall be subject to the following procedures:

(a) Obligations for personal services established in the current shall be valid by the succeeding biennium, provided that appointments of the experts concerned are effected by the end of the current biennium, and that the total period to be covered by obligations established for these purposes against the resources of the current biennium shall not exceed twenty-four months;

(b) Obligations established in the current biennium for fellowships shall remain valid until liquidated, provided that the fellow has been nominated by the requesting Government and accepted by the Organization, and that a formal letter of award has been issued to the requesting Government.

Abbreviations

ACABQ	Advisory Committee on Administrative and Budgetary Questions
ACC	Administrative Committee on Coordination
ACASTD	Advisory Committee on the Application of Science & Technology for Development
APCTT	Asian and Pacific Centre for Transfer of Technology
CCAQ	Consultative Committee on Administrative Questions
CDP	Committee for Development Planning
CIAV	International Commission for Support and Verification
CPC	Committee for Programme and Coordination
CSDHA	Centre for Social Development and Humanitarian Affairs
CSTD	Centre for Science and Technology for Development
DIESA	Department of International Economic and Social Affairs
DTCD	Department of Technical Cooperation for Development
ECA	Economic Commission for Africa
ECE	Economic Commission for Europe
ECLAC	Economic Commission for Latin America and the Caribbean
ECOSOC	Economic and Social Council
ESCAP	Economic and Social Commission for Asia
ESCWA	Economic and Social Commission for Western Asia
FAO	Food and Agriculture Organization of the United Nations
GATT	General Agreement on Tariffs and Trade
IAEA	International Atomic Energy Agency
ICAO	International Civil Aviation Organization
ICSC	International Civil Service Commission
IFAD	International Fund for Agricultural Development
ILO	International Labour Organization
IMO	International Maritime Organization
ITC	International Trade Centre
ITU	International Telecommunication Union

JIU	Joint Inspection Unit
MINURSO	United Nations Observer Mission in Western Sahara
ONUCA	United Nations Observer Group in Central America
ONUSAL	United Nations Observer Mission in El Salvador
ONUVEN	**United Nations Observer Mission in Nicaragua**
OSSECS	Office of Secretariat Services for Economic and Social Matters
TCDC	Technical Cooperation among Developing Countries
UNAMIC	United Nations Advance Mission in Cambodia
UNAVEM	United Nations Angola Verification Mission
UNCHS	United Nations Centre for Human Settlements (HABITAT)
UNCITRAL	United Nations Commission on International Trade Law
UNCTAD	United Nations Conference on Trade and Development
UNCTC	United Nations Centre for Transnational Corporations
UNDOF	United Nations Disengagement Observer Force
UNDP	United Nations Development Programme
UNDRO	Office of the United Nations Disaster Relief Coordinator
UNEF	United Nations Emergency Force
UNEP	United Nations Environment Programme
UNFDAC	United Nations Fund for Drug Abuse Control
UNFICYP	United Nations Peace-Keeping Force in Cyprus
UNFSSTD	UN Financing System for Science and Technology for Development
UNFPA	United Nations Fund for Population Activities
UNHCR	Office of the United Nations High Commissioner for Refugees
UNICER	United Nations Children's Fund
UNIDO	United Nations Industrial Development Organisation
UNIFIL	United Nations Interim Force in Lebanon
UNIIMOG	United Nations Iran-Iraq Military Observer Group
UNIKOM	United Nations Iraq-Kuwait Observation Mission
UNITAR	United Nations Institute for Training and Research
UNPROFOR	United Nations Protection Force
UNRWA	United Nations Relief and Works Agency for Palestine Refugees in the Near East
UNTAC	United Nations Transition Authority in Cambodia
UNTAG	United Nations Transition Assistance Group
UNU	United Nations University
UPU	Universal Postal Union
WFP	World Food Programme
WHO	World Health Organization
WMO	World Meterological Organization

Select Bibliography

Adiseshiah, Malcolm S., *Forty years of Economic Development: UN Agencies and India,* Delhi: Lancer International, 1987.

Administrative and Budgetary Reforms of the United Nations New York: The Stanley Foundation, 1987.

A New United Nations Structure for Global Economic Cooperation Report of the Group of Experts on the Structure of the United Nations System, Doc. E/AC. 62/9, New York, United Nations, 1975.

Baehr, Peter, and **Gordenker, Leon,** *The United Nations: Reality and Ideal,* Praeger, New York, 1984.

Bardonnet, Daniel, ed., *The Adaptation of Structures and Methods at the United Nations,* Hague Academy of International Law Workshop, Lancaster, Martinus Nijhoff, 1986.

Beigbeder, Yves, *Management Problems in United Nations Organizations: Reform or Decline,* London, Frances Pinter, 1987.

Berridge, G.R., and **Jennings, A.,** eds., *Diplomacy at the UN,* London, Macmillan, 1985.

Blejer, Mario I. and **Chu, Ke-Young,** *Fiscal Policy, Stabilization and Growth in Developing Countries,* Washington DC: IMF, 1989.

Brandt, Willy, *The World: Ten Years After the Brandt Commission,* Vienna: Institute for Development and Cooperation, 1988.

Cordier, Andrew *et al.* eds., *Public Papers of the Secretaries-General of the United Nations,* 8 vols., New York, Columbia University Press, 1969–77.

Dubey, Muchkund, "Threat to UN Multilateral System", *Mainstream,* New Delhi, 20 October, 1984.

Elmandjra, Mahdi, *The United Nations System: An Analysis,* London Faber and Faber 1973.

Finger, Seymour Maxwell, "Reagon-Kirkpatrick Policies and the United Nations", *Foreign Affairs,* Winter, 1983–84.

"Focus on Multilateralism", *Development,* Journal of the Society for International Development, 1989/4.

Forsythe, David P., ed. *The United Nations in the World Political Economy,* London: Macmillan, 1989.

Franck, Thomas., *Nation Against Nation: What happened to the UN Dream and What the US can do about it.* New York, Oxford University Press, 1985.

Franck, Thomas M., "Soviet Initiative: US Responses—New Opportunities for Reviving the United Nations System", *American Journal of International Law,* vol. 83 no: 3, 1989.

Fromuth, Peter, ed. *A Successor Vision: The United Nations of Tomorrow,* Lanham M.D. UNA-USA, 1988.

Gati, Tobi Trister, ed., *The US, the UN, and the Management of Global Change,* London, New York University Press, 1983.

Global Outlook 2000: *An Economic Social and Environmental Perspective,* New York: United Nations, 1990, (Sales no: E.90 II c.3)

Griffin, Keith and **Knight, John** eds., *Human Development in the 1980s and Beyond,* New York: UN Publications, 1989 (Sales no: E.89 II A.2)

Harrod Jeffrey & Shrijver, Nico, eds., *The UN under Attack,* Aldershot: Grover, 1988.

Head, Ivan L., "North-South Interdependence" Steven L. Spiegel ed. *At Issue: Politics in the World Arena,* New York: Martin's Press, 1988.

Jackson, Richard, *Non-Aligned, the United Nations and the Super Powers,* New York: Praeger, 1983.

Jackson, Sir Robert, *A Study of the Capacity of the United Nations Development System,* 2 vols. Geneva: United Nations, 1969.

Jha, L.K. *North-South Debate,* Delhi: Chanakya Publications, 1982.

Kaufmann, Johan, *United Nations Decision-Making,* Rockville, Sijthoff & Noordhoff, MI, 1981.

Krauthammer, Charles, "The Unipolar Moment", *Foreign Affairs,* vol. 70 no: 1, 1991.

Lall K.B., *Struggle for Change,* New Delhi: Allied Publishers, 1983.

Moynihan, Daniel Patrick, *A Dangerous Place,* London, Secker & Warburg, 1979.

Murphy, John F., *The United Nations and the Control of International Violence: A Legal and Political Analysis,* Manchester, Manchester University Press, 1983.

Nicholas, B.G., *The United Nations as a Political Institution,* 5th edn., Oxford: Oxford University Press, 1975.

ORR, Robert M., *The Emergence of Japan's Foreign Aid and Power,* New York: Colombia University Press, 1990.

Peterson, M.J., *The General Assembly in World Politics,* Boston, Allen & Unwin, 1986.

Pines, Burton Yol. *A World Without a UN,* Washington DC. The Heritage Foundation, 1984.

Puchala, Donald J. and **Coate, Roger A.,** *The Challenge of Relevance: the United Nations in a changing World Environment,* Hanover NH: ACUNS, 1989.

—— *The State of the United Nations, 1988,* Hanover, NH: ACUNS, 1988.

Rajan, M.S. *et al., The Non-Aligned and the United Nations,* New Delhi, South Asian Publishers, 1987.

Ramcharan B.G., *Keeping Faith with the United Nations,* Dordrecht: Martinus Nijhoff, 1987.

Report on the US and the UN: A Balance Sheet: Washington DC: The Heritage Foundation, 1984.

Report of the Special Commission of the Economic and Social Council on Indepth study of the United Nations Intergovernmental Structure and Functions in the Economic and social Fields, (E/1988/75) 1 June 1988.

Report of the Group of High Level Intergovernmental Experts to Review the efficiency of the Administrative and Financial Functioning of the United Nations, *General Assembly Official Record,* Forty-First Session, supplement no: 49 (A/41/49)

Rikhye, Indar Jit, *The Theory and Practice of Peacekeeping,* London, Hurst, 1984.

Roberts, Adam and Kingsbury Benedict, *United Nations, Divided World The Role of the United Nations in International Relations* London: Oxford Clarendon Press, 1989.

Russell, Ruth, *The United Nations and United States Security Policy,* Washington DC, Brookings Institution, 1968.

Saksena K.P., "Forty Years of the United Nations: A Perspective", *International Studies,* Delhi, vol. 22, no. 4, 1985.

——— "International Framework and South-South Cooperations: Constraints and Opportunities", Steven L. Spiegel, ed. *At Issue: Politics in the World Arena,* New York, Martin Press 1988.

——— *The United Nations and Collective Security, A Historical Analysis,* Delhi, D.K. Publishing House, 1974.

——— "North South Conflict and the United Nations", in M.S. Rajan and S. Ganguly, eds. *Great Power Relations, World Order and the Third World,* Delhi Vikas, 1979.

——— "Not by Design: Evolution of UN Peace Keeping Operations", *International Studies,* New Delhi, April 1977.

Steele, David, *Reform of the United Nations,* London: Croomhelm, 1987.

Study on the Economic and Social Consequences of the Arms Race and Military Expenditure, New York: UN Publications, 1989 (Sales no: E. 89. IX. 2)

The Blue Helmets: A Review of United Nations Peace keeping New York: UN Publications, 1990.

The Challenge to the South: Report of the South Commission New York: Oxford University Press, 1990.

The State of International Economic Co-operation and Effective ways Means of Revitalizing the Economic Growth and Development of Developing Countries, Report of the UN Secretary General, DOC. A/AC/ 233/5, 30 January, 1990.

The World Economy: A Global Challenge, New York: UN Dept of Public Information (DPI), 1991.

Urquhart, Brian, *A Life in Peace and War,* New York: Harper and Row, 1987.

——— *Hammarskjold,* New York, Alfred A. Knopf, 1972.

——— *A Life in Peace and War,* Weidenfeld & Nicolson, London 1987.

——— *The Challenge of Peace,* London, Weidenfeld & Nicolson, 1980.

Urquhart, Brian, and **Childers, Erskine,** *A World in Need of Leadership: Tomorrow's United Nations,* Uppsala: Dag Hammarsjold Foundation, 1990.

Waldheim, Kurt, *In the Eye of the Storm:* The Memories of Kurt Waldheim, London, Weidenfeld & Nicolson, 1985.

Weiss, Thomas, *Multilateral Development Diplomacy in UNCTAD: the Lessons of Group Negotiations 1964–84,* London, Macmillan, 1986.

Williams, Douglas, *The Specialized Agencies and the United Nations: The System in Crisis,* David Davis Memorial Institute, London: HURST, 1987.

Yeselson, Abraham, and **Gaglione, Anthony,** *A Dangerous Place: The United Nations as a Weapon in World Politics,* New York, Grossman, 1974.

Index